Economic Incentives in Sub-Saharan African Urban Planning

This book explores incentives capable of enhancing the effectiveness of urban planning systems in Sub-Saharan Africa using economic theory as a framework. It argues that urban planning is fundamental to the achievement of sustainable and resilient cities, but against the backdrop of rising levels of urbanisation and growth, poverty, informal development, and climate change, such systems are failing to be promoted and successfully maintained in the region.

Across ten chapters, it analyses the connection between urban planning and socio-economic development, indicators of effective urban planning systems, and the role and influence of incentives with real-world evidence. It develops quantitative models to estimate the costs and benefits of urban planning systems, focussing on the developing world where organised data is less accessible. Using Ghana as a case study, it demonstrates a step-by-step approach on how to implement the quantitative models discussed.

Economic Incentives in Sub-Saharan African Urban Planning will be useful reading for researchers, policy-makers, development agencies, and students in urban planning, sustainable development, and economics.

Kwasi Gyau Baffour Awuah (BSc (Hons), MA, PGCAP, PhD, MGhIS, MGHACMA, MRICS, FHEA) is an interdisciplinary academic and practitioner with over 22 years of experience in international real estate/urban development projects and sustainability/sustainable development issues. Kwasi is currently an academic and the lead for the real estate research and consultancy cluster at the University of Salford, Manchester. He has occupied several positions, both in academia and in practice, and was a founding member of the International Land Measurement Standard Coalition and part of its Standard Setting Committee. Kwasi has published widely. He has been an Engineering and Physical Sciences Research Council (EPSRC) panel member and some of his works have benefitted from funding from institutions, such as the Royal Institution of Chartered Surveyors (RICS), the Department for International Development (DFID) in the UK, the European Union (EU), the Art and Humanities Research Council (AHRC), the Academy of Medical Sciences, and the Royal Academy of Engineering.

Routledge Research in Planning and Urban Design

Routledge Research in Planning and Urban Design is a series of academic monographs for scholars working in these disciplines and the overlaps between them. Building on Routledge's history of academic rigour and cutting-edge research, the series contributes to the rapidly expanding literature in all areas of planning and urban design.

The City in Transgression
Human Mobility and Resistance in the 21st Century
Benedict Anderson

The City Makers of Nairobi
An African Urban History
Anders Ese and Kristin Ese

Race, Faith and Planning in Britain
Richard Gale and Huw Thomas

Planning within Complex Urban Systems
Shih-Kung Lai

The Narrative Turn in Urban Planning
Plotting the Helsinki Waterfront
Lieven Ameel

Economic Incentives in Sub-Saharan African Urban Planning
A Ghanaian Case Study
Kwasi Gyau Baffour Awuah

For more information about this series, please visit: https://www.routledge.com/Routledge-Research-in-Planning-and-Urban-Design/book-series/RRPUD

Economic Incentives in Sub-Saharan African Urban Planning

A Ghanaian Case Study

Kwasi Gyau Baffour Awuah

Routledge
Taylor & Francis Group
LONDON AND NEW YORK

First published 2021
by Routledge
2 Park Square, Milton Park, Abingdon, Oxon OX14 4RN

and by Routledge
605 Third Avenue, New York, NY 10017

Routledge is an imprint of the Taylor & Francis Group, an informa business

British Library Cataloguing-in-Publication Data
A catalogue record for this book is available from the British Library

Library of Congress Cataloging-in-Publication Data
Names: Baffour Awuah, Kwasi Gyau, author.
Title: Economic incentives in Sub-Saharan African urban planning : a Ghanaian case study / Kwasi Gyau Baffour Awuah.
Other titles: Routledge research in planning and urban design.
Description: Abingdon, Oxon ; New York, NY : Routledge, 2021. | Series: Routledge research in planning and urban design | Includes bibliographical references and index.
Identifiers: LCCN 2020048090 (print) | LCCN 2020048091 (ebook) | ISBN 9780367558864 (hardback) | ISBN 9781003098515 (ebook)
Subjects: LCSH: City planning—Economic aspects—Ghana. | Economic development projects—Ghana. | Ghana—Economic conditions.
Classification: LCC GT169.G4 B34 2021 (print) | LCC GT169.G4 (ebook) | DDC 307.1/1609667—dc23
LC record available at https://lccn.loc.gov/2020048090
LC ebook record available at https://lccn.loc.gov/2020048091

ISBN 13: 978-0-367-55886-4 (hbk)
ISBN 13: 978-0-367-56588-6 (pbk)
ISBN 13: 978-1-003-09851-5 (ebk)

Typeset in Sabon
by codeMantra

This book is dedicated to my children – Nana Ama, Maame Ama, and Ewura Akosua.

Contents

Tables

Figures

Box

Preface

Urban planning is fundamental to the solution of sustainable development challenges and occupies a central position in the United Nations (UN)'s proposed actions to address the sustainable development goals. However, urban planning systems in Sub-Saharan Africa (SSA) and indeed the developing world are deficient and weak, implying their inability to facilitate sustainable development in these regions. Yet application of insights from economics to SSA planning systems demonstrating their impact on the economic well-being of individuals and society to enhance understanding and inform sustainable solutions is limited. This situation is exacerbated by the lack of simplified and bespoke methodologies for calibrating the economic impacts of planning policies, even in the developed world, where there are relatively huge volumes of organised data. This book contributes to addressing the above knowledge lacuna by applying economic theory to the SSA urban planning conundrum and devises an analytical framework to demonstrate how incentives can improve planning systems in the region. It further prescribes a simplified quantitative methodology, which is subsequently deployed on a case study in Ghana to demonstrate how to gauge the economic impacts of SSA planning regimes and evidence of the impacts based on insights from the analytical framework.

In addition to addressing the above-mentioned knowledge lacuna, the book discusses the relevant literature and relies greatly on the author's research evidence as well as his extensive knowledge and experience as an academic and practitioner in urban development and management in SSA. Accordingly, the narrative in this book initially outlines the SSA urban environment challenge in the context of sustainable development and the expected role of urban planning to redress the challenge. This is followed by discussions on justification of urban planning and the conceptual basis, evaluation of the role of urban planning in socio economic development, indicators of a good urban planning system, and the analytical framework on the role of incentives in effective urban planning. Thereafter, the book opens discussions on urban planning systems in SSA; the influence of incentives on urban planning practice based on experiences of the UK, Japan, and SSA; the economic evaluation framework for appraising the impact of planning policies with a prescription of a simplified methodology for the calibration of a planning system in SSA; and the findings from the application of the methodology to a case study in Ghana. Finally, the book summarises all the discussions and draws conclusions with proposals for improvement in SSA urban planning systems before prescribing areas for further research and discussions.

This book, therefore, is useful to national, urban, and local governments; civil society; and practitioners and stakeholders in urban development and management, especially in the developing world and international development agencies in terms of provision of insights, reference, and policy formulation and practice. It is also useful to academics, researchers, and students for their teaching and learning as well as for identifying areas for further research and developing the right knowledge and insights for the implementation of their research projects.

Acknowledgements

My foremost thanks go to God Almighty for the gift of life and his grace upon me. I offer thanks to my wife, Alice Kwabi, and to all those who provided me with data as well as reviewers, proofreaders, and publishers of this manuscript.

Abbreviations

AfDB	African Development Bank
CBD	Central Business District
CVM	Contingent Valuation Method
GAMA	Greater Accra Metropolitan Area
GAR	Greater Accra Region
GDP	Gross Domestic Product
GEMA	Ga East Municipal Assembly
GSS	Ghana Statistical Service
LC	Ghana's Lands Commission
LED	Local Economic Development
MDGs	Millennium Development Goals
NGOs	Non-Governmental Organisations
SDGs	Sustainable Development Goals
SSA	Sub-Saharan Africa
UK	United Kingdom
UN	United Nations
UN-Habitat	United Nations Human Settlements Programme
US	United States of America

1 Sub-Saharan Africa urban centres and urban planning

1.1 Background

This book investigates compliance with urban planning and development regulations in Sub-Saharan Africa (SSA) using Austrian economics theory of human action (Chapter 5) as the main analytical lens to demonstrate how incentives can improve planning systems in the region and the determination of incentives. Current wisdom professes that headway for human development and socio-economic progress is predicated on the adoption of sustainability principles, particularly in relation to the three main sustainability pillars: environmental, economic, and social. This followed the sustainability revolution, which emerged about five decades ago. The revolution was a global action that challenged the then existing thinking relating to 'progress', 'growth', and 'development'. Prior to that, there was a belief that development problems especially those of the developing world could be addressed through world-wide economic growth. However, that belief was later seen as unreliable (Du Pisani, 2006). Development and conservation were also misconstrued to be conflicting issues. This was because development was perceived as exploitation of natural resources whilst conservation was regarded as protection of natural resources, but both are now seen as interdependent issues. These imperatives, among other things, necessitated a paradigm shift to a new notion of development, which later emerged as sustainable development (Du Pisani, 2006). Sustainable development professes a compromise between development and conservation, and it is defined as:

> .... development that meets the needs of the present without compromising the ability of future generations to meet their own needs.
> (Brundtland Report, WCED, 1987, p. 43)

The sustainability revolution made a clarion call for the pursuit of sustainable development as a global goal. Accordingly, sustainability principles have since seen application in several disciplines and fields. These include commerce and business, education, agriculture, engineering to mention but a few. In the built environment, there are increasing calls for the implementation of sustainable urban development and management, especially in developing countries, such as those in SSA. Fundamental to these calls is the need for cities and urban centres to be sustainable. More recently, the United Nations (UN) reinforced the above call by launching the 17 Sustainable Development Goals (SDGs) in 2015, which were developed from the 2030 UN Agenda for Sustainable Development. Goal 11 of the SDGs subscribes to the promotion of safe, inclusive, resilient, productive, and liveable cities and human settlements. A New Urban Agenda (NUA) has since been also formulated and adopted. According to the UN (2017), the NUA, which was adopted at the UN Conference on Housing and Sustainable Urban Development (Habitat III) (global summit held every 20 years) in October 2016 in Quito, was produced from the effort of several stakeholders. These included member states of the UN, intergovernmental organisations; the UN-Habitat, over 40 UN agencies, funds, and programmes; 200 Policy Unit experts with 20 co-leading organisations; 16 partner constituent groups of the General Assembly of Partners; thousands of subnational and local governments and all major networks of local and regional governments coordinated by the Global Taskforce of Local and Regional Governments; 197 participating states; over 1,100 organisations; and over 58,000 networks.

The NUA is a framework for urban development and excepting the UN's 2030 Agenda for Sustainable Development, including the SDGs, the framework takes on board several other existing initiatives such as the Addis Ababa Action Agenda of the Third International Conference on Financing for Development, the Paris Agreement adopted under the UN Framework Convention on Climate Change, the Sendai Framework for Disaster Risk Reduction 2015-20304, the Vienna Programme of Action for Landlocked Developing Countries for the Decade 2014-20245, the Small Island Developing States (SIDS) Accelerated Modalities of Action (SAMOA) Pathway, and the Istanbul Programme of Action for the Least Developed Countries for the Decade 2011–2020 (UN, 2017). Essentially, the NUA is therefore a further confirmation of the global assurance towards the pursuit of sustainable urban development as a necessary action for the realisation of sustainable development in an integrated and coordinated way at the global, regional, national, subnational, and local levels, with the participation of all relevant actors ensuring the implementation and localisation of the above initiatives, particularly the 2030 Agenda for Sustainable Development with the SDGs and its target of Goal 11. The UN (2017, pp. 5–7) notes that, through the NUA, eight distinct end states of cities and human settlements are envisaged as follows:

- Honour their social functions extending to the social and environmental functions of land to ensure adequate housing as a component of adequate standard of living, access to safe and affordable drinking water and sanitation, and equal access for all to public goods and quality services, among others;

- Ensure the meeting of needs of all inhabitants and recognise the particular needs of people in vulnerable situations through participatory administration and management, and the promotion of civic engagement to achieve we-feeling and belonging, among other things, as well as foster cohesion, inclusion, and safety in peaceful and pluralistic societies;
- Achieve gender equality and empowerment of all women and girls through complete and effective participation and equal rights in all fields and in leadership at all levels of decision-making;
- Ensure the meeting of challenges and opportunities of both the present and the future as well as sustain inclusive and sustainable economic growth and leverage urbanisation for structural transformation, high productivity, value-added activities and resource efficiency, and harnessing local economies among others;
- Promote integrated and sustainable urban and territorial development at all levels as well as ensure the fulfilment of territorial functions across administrative boundaries including serving as hubs and drivers for balanced, integrated, and sustainable urban and territorial development;
- Foster age- and gender-responsive planning and investment for sustainable, safe, accessible, and resource-efficient mobility systems for humans and goods and services;
- Undertake disaster risk reduction and management, reducing vulnerability, building resilience and responsiveness to natural and human-made hazards, and fostering mitigation of and adaptation to climate change; and
- Protect, conserve, restore, and promote cities and human settlements, ecosystems, water, natural habitats, and biodiversity, as well as minimise their environmental impact and change to sustainable consumption and production patterns.

The call for sustainable urban development and management in SSA and other developing regions stems partly from rapid urban growth and urbanisation, rising levels of urban informality, poverty, and social exclusion, among others. Despite European colonial authorities' deliberate policy to hold down the populations of Africa's urban centres through imposition of restrictions on migration of indigenous African population to towns prior to the 1960s (Satterthwaite, 1996; Njoh, 2009), urban growth in Africa accelerated in the 1950s (Rakodi, 1998). Rakodi (1998) reports that the African continent, except for South Africa, recorded urban growth of between 4% and 6% in the 1950s and accelerated after 1960s when most African states attained independence. According to a 1998 UN report, Africa's urban population grew from 14.6% in 1950 to 20.7% in 1965 and then to 27.3% and 34.9% by 1980 and 1995, respectively, compared with the Asian urban population, which stood at 17.4%, 22.4%, 26.7%, and 34.7% in the same years. Presently, more than 50% of the world's population lives in urban areas and this is expected to increase to 75% by 2050, at a growth rate of 65 million urban dwellers per annum (UN, 2017). However, SSA with a current estimated urban population of 472 million people is considered the fastest urbanising region in the world and its urban population is expected to double over the next 25 years (CSIS, 2018). In fact, the urban population of the continent of Africa is projected to increase from 11.3% in 2010 to 20.20% by 2050 (UN, 2017).

Cities and urban areas in Africa, like their counterparts across the globe, play a vital role in socio-economic development. Cities in Africa account for 80% of the continent's gross domestic product (GDP) (African Development Bank (AfDB), 2013). Earlier, the World Bank (2009, p. 48) noted that no country in the world has developed without growth of its cities. The Bank (p. 57) buttressed this observation with evidence that the top 30 cities in the world ranked by GDP in 2005 accounted for 16% of the world's output, whilst the top 100 cities generated almost 25% of the global output. The Bank pointed out that cities in SSA, such as Luanda, Nairobi, and Lagos in 2005, contributed around 20% of each of their countries' (Angola, Kenya, and Nigeria, respectively) GDP, whilst Mexico City, another city in a developing region, generated 30% of Mexico's GDP.

Experts opine that the current spate of urbanisation and urban growth taking place in Africa, if properly managed and harnessed, could significantly strengthen the role of cities and urban areas on the continent as engines of sustainable economic growth and development. For example, the scenario-based approach, one of the popular policy prescriptions for Africa's sustainable development, which is based on the global economy and methodology model, acknowledges the significant influence of urbanisation in Africa's development discourse. The approach uses three scenarios, namely, convergence, business-as-usual, and downside. Based on long-term projection of the evolution of 186 countries as a function of labour force, capital stock and total factor productivity, it recommended the convergence scenario (JICA, 2013). According to the convergence scenario, Africa's per capita income is expected to grow by around 4.6% per annum over the next 40 years, converging with those of the world moving from 27% of the world's average in recent times to 52%. The per capita growth will also introduce several changes and transform the lives of people on the continent and its role in the world. The size of the middle class will grow more than tenfold, an increase from 12% to 68%, whilst poverty levels are projected to decline from 380 million to 53 million (37% to under 3%). Further, Africa's contribution of under 3% to global GDP will increase to 9%. However, these expected development outcomes are dependent on factors, such as macroeconomic performance, poverty and inequality demography, urbanisation, and access to natural resources (JICA, 2013).

Apart from the above conditions, it is argued that cities' and urban areas' continuous performance as an engine of sustainable growth and development depends on the institution of appropriate regulations for their configuration and intervention, to ensure efficient land use and management of diseconomies of agglomeration. This implies that for SSA cities and urban areas to promote growth and development, there is a need for their effective and efficient management (UN-Habitat, 2008; World Bank, 2009). Thus, the idea of urbanisation being a tool to spur Africa's economic growth and development fundamentally hinges on the multiplier agglomeration of people and economic activities and institution of regulation for configuration of urban areas, and efficient land use and management of diseconomies of agglomeration. Africa's urbanisation is, however, occurring under weak and fragile economies, and has outrun the capacities of constituent states to provide developable land, affordable housing, and adequate infrastructure and services (Baffour Awuah, 2018). African cities and urban areas are characterised by several deformities. They are typically crowded especially within the central areas and offer poor housing conditions (UN-Habitat, 2014; Lall et al., 2017). Most of the urban population in Africa does not have access to formal housing. This population lives in informal settlements and slums, which are sometimes co-located with first-class settlements (Figures 1.1 and 1.2) with no or less adequate infrastructure and service provision. For instance, 60% out of the over 1 billion global urban slum dwellers live in SSA (Gilbert, 2014). Lall et al. (2017) note that 28% of urban residents in Dar es salaam, Tanzania, live at least three to a room and that percentage is higher (50%) in cities like Abidjan, Cote D'Ivoire. Further, around 60% of the urban population in Africa lives in slums. This is far higher than the average (34%) for other developing regions of the world.

In addition to the above is the recent outbreak of the Novel Coronavirus Disease (COVID-19), which has already started posing several socio-economic and environmental impacts on urban environments in Africa and indeed the entire continent, threatening efforts towards sustainable development. COVID-19 originated from the Chinese city of Wuhan in the Hubei province in the latter part of 2019 and has since spread across the world (Huang et al., 2020; Zhu, et al., 2020), resulting in the World Health Organisation (WHO) declaring it a global health pandemic (WHO, 2020). Apart from the rapid spread of the disease and its associated deaths, particularly in Europe, the US, and Brazil, among others, it has generated and continues to generate several socio-economic and environmental impacts (see Chapter 3), predominantly through the several measures instituted to contain it, such as imposition of partial or total lockdowns, social distancing and stay-at-home policies, wearing of face masks, and the use of gloves and hand sanitisers. Environmentally, the outbreak of the disease has resulted in increase in domestic energy consumption and generation of waste pollution in the form of used ordinary and surgical face masks, plastic sanitiser bottles, solid tissue papers, and other clinical trash, which end up in the environment; cities, towns, communities, neighbourhoods, etc.; water bodies; and the ecosystem in general (Zhu et al., 2020). Conversely, the socio-economic impacts include contraction in production; loss of income and jobs, among other things; increased domestic violence; as well as disruption in market activities and depreciation in asset prices and values across several sectors of the global economy, such as financial markets; the aviation, hospitality, entertainment, grocery, and pharmaceutical industries; the real estate and tourism sectors; the events, sports, banking, and education sectors; and oil-dependent countries (Zhu et al., 2020).

The rate of the spread and magnitude of COVID-19 in Africa have not been that swift and intense compared with that in the Western developed nations, but there are projections that the continent could be hard hit with dire consequences. Africa had its first case of COVID-19 in Egypt on 14 February 2020, and the disease has been reported in all the countries on the continent since then (OECD, 2020). According to the OECD (2020) as of 4 May 2020, there were 44,873 COVID-19 cases reported on the continent, with 1,807 deaths. That said, the WHO (2020) estimates that between 83,000 and 190,000 people in Africa could die of COVID-19, and 29 million to 44 million could become infected in the first year of the pandemic if containment measures fail. Obviously, the infection and death rates could exacerbate in the long term if effective measures are not put in place to decisively address it. In terms of impact, it is anticipated that the disease could have disastrous impacts on the continent's already strained health systems and could quickly turn into a social and economic emergency (OECD, 2020). Apart from the health impact, the OECD (2020) reports that COVID-19 will adversely affect African countries' economies in three main ways as follows: (i) lower trade and investment from China in the immediate term; (ii) a demand slump associated with the lockdowns in the European Union and OECD countries; and (iii) a continental supply shock affecting domestic and intra-African trade. The above imperatives are said to affect Africa's economic growth with a significant impact on the well-being and number of people living in poverty, and the forecasts suggest that there will be a GDP contraction in most countries in 2020, the first in 25 years, and nearly 30 million more people could fall into poverty (OECD, 2020).

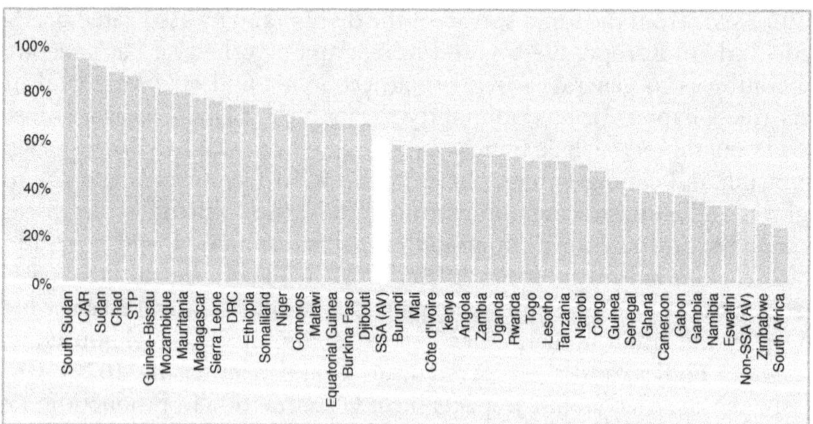

Figure 1.1 Percentage of urban population living in slums in Africa.
Source: Adapted from Lall et al. (2017).

Figure 1.2 Extract of co-located urban areas in Accra.
Source: Author's field survey – Airport Residential Area and Nima, co-located first-class residential area and shanty settlement.

Urban planning is the central tool for promoting effective and efficient functioning of cities and development of sustainable cities and urban areas (Roy, 2009; Bart, 2010). Yet the urban planning systems in SSA countries, which are supposed to help manage the current urban growth and urbanisation, provide developable land, housing, and the associated necessary infrastructure and services, have proven weak and ineffective (Watson, 2009a; Baffour Awuah, 2018). This means that existing planning systems are incapable of promoting sustainable urban development and management as well as growth and development.

1.2 Purpose of the book

Several studies have been undertaken on urban planning systems in constituent countries of SSA (Larbi, 1996; Njoh, 1997, 2004, 2009; UN-Habitat, 1999, 2009; Arimah and Adeagbo, 2000; Mwimba, 2002; Payne and Majale, 2004; Kombe, 2005; Kironde, 2006; Oyugi and K'Akumu, 2007; Watson, 2009a, 2009b; Bolay, 2015; Cobbinah et al., 2015; Braimah et al., 2016; Lall et al., 2017; Keeton and Nijhuis, 2019; Mutuku et al., 2019; Splinter and Leynseele, 2019). Consistent with discussions in the previous section, the studies established that planning systems in the region are inadequate and weak. One of the weakest links of the planning systems is low compliance with urban planning and development regulations (Larbi, 1996; UN-Habitat, 1999, 2009; Arimah and Adeagbo, 2000; Friedmann, 2005; Lall et al., 2017). Economic principle illustrates that people respond to incentives (Glaeser, 2004; O'Sullivan and Sheffrin, 2007; Mankiw, 2011). This means the incentives that the current SSA planning systems are offering are inadequate to promote compliance and effective urban planning. However, there is a dearth of in-depth studies that apply insights from economics to

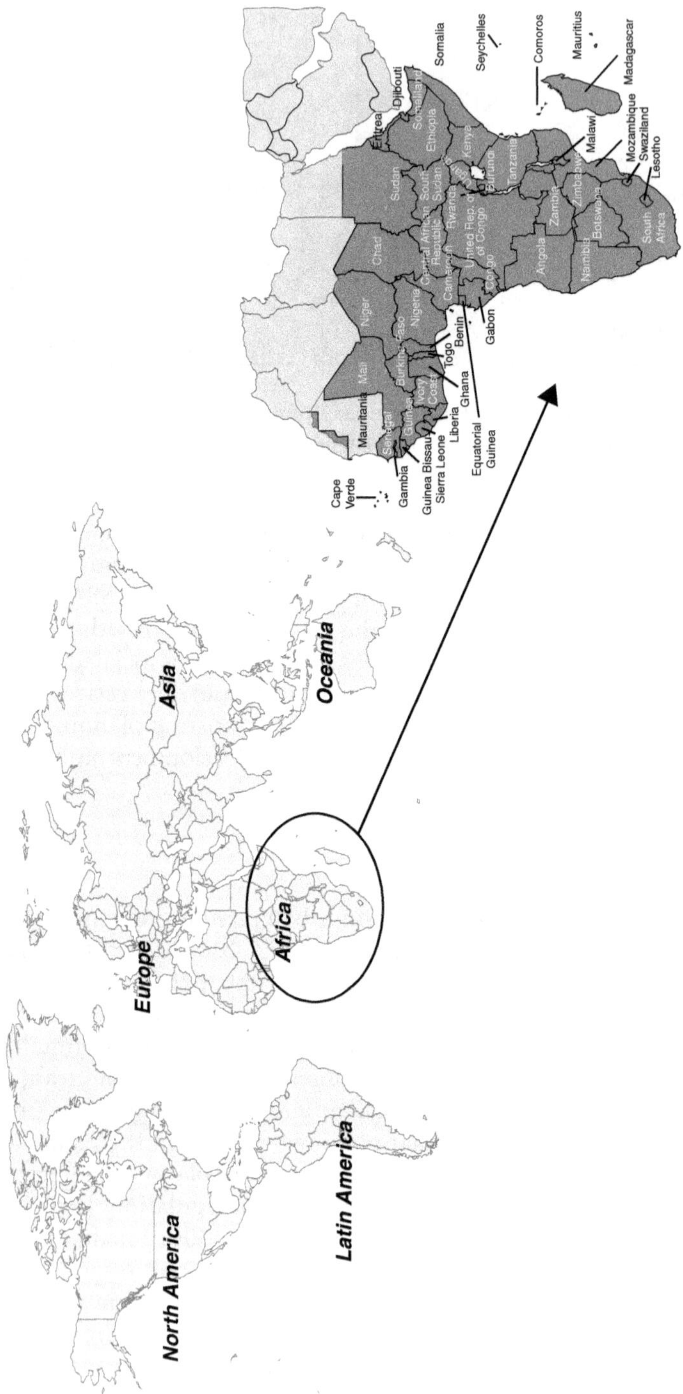

Figure 1.3 Geographical context of Africa & SSA.
Adapted from http://www.luventicus.org/maps/world/africa.html.

urban planning systems in SSA to conceptually explain this weakness and lay bare the extent of the economic impact of these planning regimes (Egbu et al., 2008; Baffour Awuah et al., 2010) for a far-reaching policy solution.

The purpose of this book is to provide an understanding of the weakness of urban planning systems in SSA using the Austrian economics theory of human action (Chapter 5) and devise an analytical framework to demonstrate how incentives can improve the planning systems and the determination of incentives. The book argues that SSA urban planning systems are weak and dysfunctional in part, with low compliance with planning regulations, because they do not provide incentives to property owners/developers/land users. Figure 1.3 provides the geographical location of Africa and SSA relative to other continents around the globe. The definition of SSA is also given at the glossary. This introductory chapter now turns its attention to the definition and meaning of urban planning.

1.3 Definition and meaning of urban planning

Urban planning is as old as human settlements and has existed in many forms in various communities across the world (UN-Habitat, 2009). However, formal urban planning emerged in Western Europe and North America at the turn of the nineteenth century and spread across the globe. This followed the adverse effects of industrialisation and urbanisation that occurred during the first industrial revolution (Dale and McLaughlin, 1999; UN-Habitat, 2009; Watson, 2009b). The spread of planning was fundamentally achieved through importation of planning ideas and colonialism (Nadin and Stead, 2008; UN-Habitat, 2009).

Urban planning is an intricate and constantly evolving concept. It is a manifestation of planning's historical response to the prevailing environmental, economic, and socio-cultural challenges that existed at the time of its emergence (Thompson, 2007; Baffour Awuah et al., 2010). Several terminologies depending on the jurisdiction are often ascribed to planning (Gleeson and Low, 2000; Thompson, 2007). Terms such as town and country planning, physical planning, regional and urban planning, and spatial planning are usually used in the literature to describe it. For example, planning was referred to as town and country planning in the UK, but it has been renamed as spatial planning (Shaw and Lord, 2009). In Continental Europe and North America, it is referred to as spatial planning, and regional and urban planning, respectively (Thompson, 2007).

Several definitions, as well as meanings of planning, are encountered in the literature. One of the earliest and commonest definitions given by Keeble (1959, p. 9) states that urban planning is:

> The art and science of ordering the use of land and the character and siting of buildings and communication routes so as to secure the maximum practicable degree of economy, convenience and beauty.

Keeble (1959) underscored the difficulty of having a comprehensive definition for the term 'planning'. Brown and Sherrard (1951) had also intimated the dangers involved in attempts to give a comprehensive definition of planning. Gleeson and Low (2000) define urban planning as a governance activity with the responsibility of ensuring that all services people need in a city are provided when and where the need occurs. Conversely, Healey (2004) argues that planning is a self-conscious collective effort of imagining or reimagining a town, an urban region, or a wider territory, which conveys the result into priorities for area investment, conservation measures, new and upgraded areas of settlement, strategic infrastructure investments, and principles of land use regulations. Healey (2004) further states that planning is also a mode of governance driven by the articulation of policies through some form of deliberative process and judgement of collective action in relation to these policies. Urban planning is now considered as an exercise that goes beyond traditional land use planning, perhaps as defined by Keeble (1959), with the purpose of bringing together and integrating policies and programmes which influence the nature of places and how they can function (Nadin, 2007). This planning exercise is categorised into two different parts, namely, urban planning and planning and land use regulations (Watson, 2009b).

According to Hopkins (2001), planning provides information with respect to expected outcomes devoid of influencing the scope of permissible actions directly. Regulation, conversely, connotes enforceable assignment and re-assignment of rights, which influences the scope of permissible actions (Kim, 2009a). Thus, urban planning entails the process by which decisions in respect of global configuration of a city and its projection for expansion are taken. These decisions are usually presented in a plan, which serves as a reference framework for the application and the use of regulations (Farvacque and McAuslan, 1992), while regulations are the vehicle by which planning is governed and implemented. The decision-making process can be conceived in various forms, such as the traditional rational comprehensive or master planning, and recent planning models, such as collaborative/communicative, Just City, and multi-culturalist planning models.

Urban planning and land use regulation occur in various forms (Mayer and Somerville, 2000) and may be defined in several ways (Farvacque and McAuslan, 1992; Tiesdell and Allmendinger, 2005). However, it is clear from relevant studies that planning and land use regulations are sets of interconnected legal and semi-legal instruments and techniques prescribed by an authority that specifies or prohibits certain behaviours to safeguard, regulate, conserve, and disburse land in the interest of an entire community, health, safety, convenience, and good environmental condition. This implies that planning and land use regulations encompass policy documents; laws and legislations; orders-in-councils; proclamations; notices; guidelines; ministerial directives, which specify what development is permitted on urban land; standards that outline the official level of quality that land and housing development should conform to; administrative processes and procedures that set out official steps that all urban developments must follow for them to be acceptable; and financial auditing of urban planning (Farvacque and McAuslan, 1992; Payne and Majale, 2004).

It is evident from the discussions so far that there appears to be a lack of consensus on the definition of urban planning. This book adopts the definition given by UN-Habitat (2009) for a planning system. This definition states, among others, that "urban planning is a collection of agencies, procedures, instruments and protocols that are often sanctioned by the formal state, backed by formal law and linked particularly to rights to develop and use housing, land and property". The adoption of the above definition stems from its comprehensive nature and direct relevance to the subject of this book.

1.4 Chapter summary

Sub-Saharan African cities and urban areas like urban centres across the globe play a vital role in the region's socio-economic growth and development. However, for cities and urban centres to continue to play such a vital role, there is a need for them to be sustainable particularly against the backdrop of rising levels of urban growth. This chapter highlighted the above imperative and noted that current urban growth and urbanisation levels have outrun the capacities of constituent states to manage and leverage them for socio-economic progress. Urban planning systems of constituent countries, which are supposed to help manage current urban growth and provide available land for development and associated housing and infrastructure services, have proven weak and ineffective, culminating in urban challenges, such as informality, social exclusion, poor housing conditions, and inadequate infrastructure. Yet there is a dearth of studies that apply insights from economics to the planning question in SSA and lay bare its economic impact for policy formulation and practice. The chapter then outlined the purpose of the book based on the preceding narrative and concluded with a discussion on the definition and meaning of urban planning to set the tone for the discussion on the justification of urban planning and the conceptual basis in the next chapter.

2 Justification of urban planning and conceptual basis

2.1 Introduction

An essential part of urban planning practice is the lens through which it is conceptualised and practised. This is particularly so at a time when the world is putting in several efforts to promote and achieve sustainable cities and by extension sustainable development (Godschalk, 2004; Baffour Awuah et al., 2014). Bolay (2015) construes urban planning as both a technique and a method for the observation and analysis of spatial, material, and human reality, and provides a vision of the end state in terms of what a city or settlement will be in the future. However, for urban planning to accomplish its functions, it requires theoretical foundations, which is a body of knowledge and ideas that enable the understanding of a reality, and that give it direction, in the present, in its historical foundations, and in projections made in the future, and it is dangerous to separate the two dimensions of planning: the reflective and the more applied aspects. Earlier, Campbell and Fainstein (2003) had argued that a robust and appropriate underpinning theory is critical to the success of urban planning practice as it always provides a basis for reference.

The above expressions mean planning theory is very important to planning practice. Indeed, planning theory enables the development of a framework to improve the living standards of human settlements (El-Khole, 2018) as well as provides a basis for reference (Abukhater, 2009). It is a system of knowledge organisation for the creation of a knowledge base for the development of future research and contribution to the discipline (Abukhater, 2009), and thus encompasses scientific ideas, behavioural interactions, and norms which detail urban planning's epistemology (El-Khole, 2018). Planning theory is also very important because of the difficulty often associated with the definition of planning, which has the tendency to create an overlap between the subject and other fields of study. An extension to this is the discipline's constant borrowing of ideas and principles from other disciplines such as psychology, social sciences, economics, political science, and management (Abukhater, 2009; El-Khole, 2018). This has often resulted in the lack of clarity in the role, purpose, and tasks of planning as a profession (Allmendinger, 2002; Allmendinger and Haughton, 2012). Furthermore, planning theories may mean different things to different people, and while planning theory is generally perceived as useless by practitioners, academics see it as a very important component of the profession (Abukhater, 2009). Consequently, a robust planning theory is needed more than ever in this twenty-first century to improve the capabilities of planners to comprehensively address important practical issues based on a holistic appreciation of the larger picture within which issues are often generated and evolved (Baffour Awuah et al., 2014). The primary focus of planning theory, however, is to address the goals, form, procedure, and justification of urban planning. This chapter discusses some of the justifications and forms of urban planning and the conceptual basis.

2.2 Conventional justification of urban planning

Urban planning has long been described as a socialist resource allocation doctrine (Hayek, 1944, 1976; Pasour, 1983). This doctrine has survived all forms of capitalists' attacks and continues to be used even in market economies. The justification for the introduction of planning and its continuous usage may differ depending on the actors and the jurisdictions involved. However, one of the conventional justifications of urban planning, particularly in market economics, is found in economics. Economic theory postulates that the efficient allocation of resources, including land resources, underpins economic growth and development (Harrison, 1977; Corkindale, 2004). Although the meaning and achievement of efficient allocation of resources are open to debate, one of the often-cited definitions of efficient allocation of resources was given by the Italian economist Vilfredo Pareto (1843–1923). His definition considers resources to be efficiently allocated if they at least improve the welfare of one person in a society without rendering another person worse off.

Neo-classical economics is premised on a pure price-operated market, as espoused by Smith (1776) who suggested that market as an institution is the most appropriate mechanism to ensure efficient allocation of scarce societal resources, including land (Harrison, 1977; Hayek, 1983; Adams, 2008; Qian, 2010). This economic framework functions on the rational choice principle. It professes that parties to a transaction in a market setting driven by their self-interest will make rational decisions to promote the efficient allocation of resources. That is, driven by the incentive of profit revealed through price signals in a market, economic agents will allocate their scarce resources in a rational manner to ensure overall efficient resource allocation towards the growth and development of society.

Assumptions underlying pure price-operated markets may not be reflected in real markets (Harrison, 1977; Adams, 2008; Qian, 2010). Apart from economic agents making rational decisions, pure price operated market theory assumes identical commodities and the availability of enough information based on which rational choices are made. Other assumptions include the existence of perfect mobility of production, labour, and consumption, and that the choice of buyers is unaffected by the preferences of others (Harrison, 1977; Klosterman, 2003). Conversely, real-world economic agents hardly act solely on rational models because they often patronise shirking and opportunism (Williamson, 1994; Lai, 2005). This creates a problem of risk and uncertainty in human exchange (North, 1995). Further, there is lack of perfect information in real markets based on which rational choices can be made (Stigler, 1971; Harrison, 1977; Klosterman, 2003). It is argued, for example, that in the real world, institutions such as property rights are not clearly defined (Alchian and Demsetz, 1973). Consequently, the market fails in efficient allocation of societal resources (Pigou, 1932; Harrison, 1977; Klosterman, 2003; Adams, 2008).

Market failure in the property sector is often associated with negative externalities, including incompatible land uses, environmental degradation, and the lack of provision of public goods such as public parks and roads requiring intervention of planning regulation (Harrison, 1977; Klosterman, 2003; Lai, 2005; Adams, 2008). Ratcliff (1949), for example, notes that, under a pure price-operated urban property market, natural land use zoning emerges with maximum benefit to urban property owners. This results in an unpleasant arrangement of land use and haphazard development due to the poor judgement of land and real estate owners, individuals acting on self-interest, the existence of relative indifference use locations, and the existence of short-term advantages in certain locations. Since the market is not perfect, the city planner should determine the most advantageous groupings of land use and enforce them through a zoning ordinance.

In practice, pure price-operated urban property markets by themselves have proved incapable of promoting the efficient allocation and economic use of society's land resources and require planning regulation intervention. Even avowed capitalists, like Hayek (1944), Popper (1945), Friedman (1962), Mundell (1968), and Nozick (1974), accept the need for some form of planning in land resources allocation, though they continue to vehemently warn against outright supplanting of the market with central planning. Hayek (1944, p. 40), for example, observes:

> Thus, neither the provision of signposts on the roads, nor, in most circumstances, that of the roads themselves, can be paid for by every individual user. Nor can certain harmful effects of deforestation, or of some methods of farming, or of smoke and noise of factories, be confined to the owner of the property in question or to those who are willing to submit to the damage for an agreed compensation. In such instance we must find some substitute for the regulation by the price mechanism.

Based on the above argument, the fundamental economic justification of urban planning as an intervention in the property market is constructed on Pigou's (1932) welfare market failure orthodoxy (Lai, 2005; Mulherin, 2007). This market failure orthodoxy has since been expanded and popularised by commentators such as Klosterman (2003), Cheshire and Shepherd (2002, 2004), Fainstein (2003), Evans (2003), Lichfield et al. (2003), Adams et al. (2005), and Adams (2008). From the welfare economics stance, the overall logic of planning intervention in the property market is premised on the idea that every public action should maximise collective interest or efficiency (Campbell and Marshall, 2002; Pinkerton et al., 2002). Several arguments have been professed in relation to the idea of maximisation of societal interest or efficiency. However, the main factor points to utilitarian considerations (Garber et al., 1996; Pinkerton et al., 2002; Khakee, 2003). The genesis of utilitarian considerations is often traced to the Greek philosopher Epiricus (342–270 BCE). Yet it took the explanations of classical utilitarianists like Jeremy Bentham (1748–1832) and John Stuart Mills (1806–1873) to popularise these utilitarian thoughts (Ryan, 1987; Pinkerton et al., 2002). The utilitarian calculus primarily confers that action is assessed on its production of happiness and, otherwise, action's production of utility and disutility. However, the concepts of utility and disutility were conceived measurable in discrete units. Thus, they were subject to mathematical analysis. Therefore, the judgement of an action is carried out intuitively by comparing its accumulation of utility known as welfare and disutility, also known as cost. Consequently, an action is judged right when it produces greater utility compared to its disutility or promotes welfare more than cost (Garber et al., 1996; Pinkerton et al., 2002).

Based on the above discussion, the economic analysis for justification of planning as a public interventionist action examines the extent to which it promotes social welfare against social cost. That is, the extent to which planning in the urban property market ensures allocative efficiency (Buitelaar, 2004; Adams et al., 2005; Adams, 2008). This traditional basis for planning intervention in the urban property market has come under serious criticism for its public interest claims (Campbell and Marshall, 2002; Lai, 2005). Public regulation of urban property markets through planning is based on the presumption that the public authority charged with the responsibility for regulation will act in the best interest of society (Bertaud and Malpelzzi, 2001; Khakee, 2003). However, advocates of public choice economics argue that the rationale for intervention is to facilitate private interest rather than to address failure of the market to allocate societal scarce resources efficiently (Stigler, 1974; Posner, 1975; Niskanen, 1994). It is argued that most people do not consistently follow political processes and may not even have the resources to influence decisions. The few interest groups who are interested in political processes and have the resources determine the direction of regulation. Thus, because politicians are driven by their quest to be in power and interest groups hold the key to their success, politicians respond to their requests through regulation in return for their support (Tullock, 1967; Posner, 1975; Niskanen, 1994; Carnis, 2009).

Planning intervention from a public choice economics standpoint can be seen to satisfy the interest of minority groups, but this could potentially further exacerbate the market failure problem (Evans, 2003; Quigley, 2007). Evans (2003) argues that, though insights from public choice economics are imperative, analysis of planning justifications based on insights from public choice economics lacks predictive power. Further, such analyses of planning intervention in urban property market from a public choice economics standpoint have remained theoretical due to empirical data difficulties. Other methods used to analyse planning intervention have emphasised the argument that planning is used to promote group interest. For example, Baffour Awuah et al. (2014) note that land markets in SSA at the time planning was introduced were not developed. There was no 'industrial revolution', suggesting that there was no market failure requiring planning intervention. However, Western Europe's colonisation of Africa was carried out with the purpose of exploiting the resources of the continent (Nkrumah, 1970; Amin, 1972; Njoh, 2004) and planning was used as a tool to facilitate that agenda through opening the continent, ensuring that colonial officials live in healthy conditions and preventing nationalistic reprisals from natives. Njoh (2009), using the power theoretical framework, also demonstrates how planning was used as a suppressive tool in SSA to ensure the achievement of colonisation objectives. History demonstrates further how planning was used as a tool of suppression and oppression, as well as segregation in certain parts of the Middle East.

2.3 Emerging case for urban planning

Following insights from Coase (1960) though earlier misconstrued to mean the demise of market intervention, and others, such as Demsetz (1967) and Alchian and Demsetz (1973), it is now emerging that market failure itself is caused by the existence or magnitude of transaction cost (Lai, 2005; Qian, 2010). Applying insights from transaction cost and property rights economics, Coase (1960) demonstrates that neo-classical economics had earlier assumed zero transaction cost, signifying a simple production function. However, the transaction cost in real markets is not zero. For example, there is information asymmetry in real markets. This means that economic agents incur costs to obtain information for decision-making purposes. This can potentially result in market failure. Therefore, planning is now being justified from a property rights and transaction cost economics perspective. This justification is based on the creation of institutions, such as clearly defined property rights, to aid efficient functioning of the urban property market to reduce transaction costs (Alexander, 1992;

Webster and Lai, 2003; Buitelaar, 2004; Lai, 2005; Musole, 2009). For example, this could be outlining the permitted size and use of land through zoning regulations.

Economic analysis of planning from the above justification is premised on the idea that planning fails if the cost of creating and managing such institutions is greater than the benefits. While the welfare economics justification for planning is based on allocative efficiency, this emerging economic justification for planning intervention in urban property market concentrates on process efficiency (Buitelaar, 2004; Lai, 2005). That notwithstanding, the justification of planning intervention for the provision of information to aid efficient functioning of the urban property market has long been and continues to be questioned. It is argued that regulators (planners) themselves have no adequate knowledge about societal land use requirements (Hayek, 1945, 1976, 1983; Pennington, 2000; Staley, 2004).

Emphasising the lack of knowledge problem, Lavoie (1985) demonstrates there are two types of knowledge: articulate and inarticulate knowledge. Articulate knowledge is information that can be objectively measured and accessed from market surveys, interview guides, and questionnaires. In the urban property market such information may include, for example, size, topography, and location of a land (Staley, 2004). Inarticulate knowledge, otherwise known as implicit knowledge, reflects the complexities of consumer behaviour (Staley, 2004). It is thus very difficult if not impossible to objectively measure. This makes planners' knowledge of society's land resource needs inadequate. Besides, the concept of transaction cost though conceived as all cost outside physical production (Webster and Lai, 2003; Buitelaar, 2004), is very elusive. To date, there is no consensus on the definition or measurement of transaction costs (Buitelaar, 2004; Musole, 2009). For example, questions such as can the clothes worn by a managing director of a firm to the office and the pen used by him or her to sign a contract be classified as part of transaction costs? Indeed, it has been described as a misnomer since there are two main types of costs in economics: cost and opportunity cost (Hülsmann, 2004). Given these discussions, it appears unclear what appropriate framework should be used to examine planning. This has culminated in the constant adoption of insights from other disciplines to analyse planning.

2.4 Forms of urban planning

Following its inception, formal land use planning was based on the modernist rational comprehensive model (Naess, 2001; Rakodi, 2001; Campbell and Fainstein, 2003; Thompson, 2007). The rational comprehensive planning model fundamentally operates from the standpoint that planning is essentially a technocratic activity and the professional planner is presumed to be an objective expert (Heikkila, 2000; Rakodi, 2001). It proceeds with a situation analysis based on which a problem is identified and planning goals are set. This is then followed by the determination and evaluation of alternative courses of action for addressing the identified problem. Next is the selection and implementation of an appropriate course of action. The final stage is monitoring the implementation of the course of action to ascertain whether the planning goals set at the outset are being achieved; if not, the whole process repeats itself. The operation of the rational comprehensive planning model is therefore cast in a cyclical mode (Ratcliffe, 1983; Egbu, 2007). This planning model is also based on the land use segregation concept, which is underpinned by unifunctional land use, discrete zoning, regulation and consensus, and the use of master plans (Afrane, 1993; Njoh, 2009). Further, governments often fund such planning projects, and it is assumed that their decisions are always in the best interest of society (Rakodi, 2001).

The rational comprehensive planning model is often criticised as being too technocratic and fails to consider the socio-economic, cultural, and political context within which planning is conceived and practised (Naess, 2001; Campbell and Fainstein, 2003; Thompson, 2007). Over the years, especially since the 1980s, there has been a proliferation of works on planning theory. These works have sought to examine planning from several disciplines such as economics, political economy, and sociology (Allmendinger, 2002). Emerging out of these works have been several planning theories and models like multi-culturalist, the just city, new urbanism, and collaborative planning models (Allmendinger, 2002; Watson, 2002; Campbell and Fainstein, 2003; Harrison, 2006). These planning theories and models predominantly attempt to introduce democracy into planning practice through larger stakeholder participation in the planning process. However, the one which has comparatively gained acceptance and seems to be driving planning practice across the globe is the collaborative planning model (Naess, 2001; Agger and Lofgren, 2008; Allmendinger and Haughton, 2012).

2.4.1 The collaborative planning model

The collaborative planning model, also known as the communicative planning model, hinges on American pragmatism developed by John Dewey and Richard Rorty and on Jurgen Habermas's communication rationality idea (Watson, 2002; Campbell and Fainstein, 2003). This planning paradigm posits the adoption of democracy in planning through citizens, interest groups, and other stakeholders' participation in the planning process. It subscribes to creating a medium for these players to form arguments, debate differences, exchange ideas towards understanding and negotiating proposals to arrive at a consensus on goal(s) and course of action(s). The planner's role in this process is more of a facilitator, negotiator, and experiential learner to contribute to building consensus instead of determining goals and framing blueprint(s) or plan(s) (Harley, 1996, 2003; Agger and Lofgren, 2008). Although this planning model attempts to bring on board diverse interests as well as place an emphasis on the value of local experience, it has not gone without criticism (Huxley and Yiftachel, 2000; Naess, 2001; Agger and Lofgren, 2008; Lovering, 2009; Purcell, 2009). For example, Agger and Lofgren (2008) point out that this planning model does not provide a basis for the determination of how deliberative a planning process is. Further, it increases the likelihood that sub-standard planning projects will be delivered without express decisions from experts in certain cases (Naess, 2001) as was the case with several community projects in India (Friedmann, 2005). Most importantly, in a world full of unbalanced power relationships, it is debatable whether this planning model will not rather advance the interest of the powerful in society to the detriment of marginalised groups. In developing regions like SSA Home (2012, p. 42) observes that the marginalised and poor communities are generally pre-occupied with day-to-day existence, rather than engaged with time-consuming non-essential activities, such as a deliberative planning process, while outside elites may manipulate the process to their own advantage. Nonetheless, unlike the rational comprehensive planning model, where a government and its agents set planning goals and prescribe the form and procedure for planning practice, these issues are supposed to be determined by wider stakeholder interests in society through deliberation and negotiations under a collaborative planning model.

2.5 Chapter summary

An important aspect of planning practice is the lens through which it is conceptualised and practised. This hinges on planning theory, which fundamentally addresses the justification and form of urban planning. The justification and form of urban planning have been examined from several theoretical standpoints relying on insights from different disciplines. This chapter discussed some of the justifications and forms of urban planning. The chapter notes that due to numerous justifications and forms of urban planning, which are based on insights from several disciplines, it remains unclear what the standard justifications and forms of urban planning are. However, collaborative or communicative planning as a form or model of urban planning is increasingly gaining popularity as a required planning model for the twenty-first century. Having discussed some of the theoretical justifications and forms of urban planning, the next chapter examines the role of urban planning.

3 Evaluation of the role of urban planning in socio-economic development

3.1 Introduction

The fundamental function of urban planning is to allocate land resources efficiently across various desired uses of land to ensure adequate provision for the range of needs a society has. Although not often thought of as such, planning promotes more than allocation of land resources to a variety of uses. It also promotes certain allocation of financial and human resources. Consequently, the contribution of urban planning to socio-economic development cannot be adequately understood merely by evaluating the adequacy of its land use provisions but also by its incidental financial and human resource allocation. This chapter evaluates the role of urban planning in socio-economic development based on existing literature. In doing so, the chapter first discusses some of the practical roles or functions of planning in society and thereafter examines their implementation.

3.2 The role of urban planning

Urban planning is a resource allocation tool. As a resource allocation tool, planning plays ecological, economic, and social roles in society. Keeble (1951), one of the renowned experts on the subject, notes that the outcome of planning should promote health and safety; convenience; economy; aesthetics; and, above all, liveability. It is therefore within the context of the foregoing that the role of planning is discussed.

3.2.1 Planning as a tool for promoting good urban environment

A fundamental position under the welfare economics justification for planning intervention in the operations of the urban property market is that the market fails as a resource allocation mechanism. As noted in the preceding chapter, one of the impacts of market failure is the destruction of the environment due to unbridled market operations. History shows that although planning practice might have started at different times and for different purpose, modern formal urban planning emerged at the turn of the nineteenth century. This was largely in response to the rapid rate of urbanisation and chaotic urban growth with their associated pollution and insanitary conditions that existed in Western European societies, particularly in the UK, because of the industrial and agricultural revolutions (Simpson et al., 1989). The market, at the time, could not provide an adequate and decisive response to these chaotic urbanisation and urban growth. The urban environment was therefore characterised by unfit housing conditions and several other social and environmental ills, such as pollution of residential areas, emergence of slums and houses with poor water and sewerage services, small houses with damp and poor ventilation, and over-crowding.

Although the UK Government did not initially want to intervene, due to the high cost of intervention and the Government's unwillingness to distort market operations, it eventually decided to do so (refer to Chapter 7 for full discussions). The intervention was by means of legislation, such as the 1830 Public Health Act; the 1848 Public Health Act; the 1851 Labouring Classes' Lodging Houses Act and the 1866 Labouring Classes' Dwelling Houses Act; the Health Acts of 1872, 1875, and 1890; and the 1890 Housing of the Working Classes Act. These interventions were supported by voluntary efforts and working-class self-help through new initiatives in urban control, civic design, and rural rehabilitation, such as the Ebenezer Howard' Garden City concept around the latter part of the nineteenth century. Further legislation, such as the 1909 and 1919 (Addison Act) Housing and Town Planning Acts and the 1932 Town and Country Planning Act, were passed to partly ensure good urban environmental conditions (see Chapter 7).

Similar interventionist activities occurred in the US. The US is known for the protection and preservation of private property rights based on its market-oriented philosophy. Excepting the right of eminent domain clause in the US Constitution, which ordinarily allowed for acquisition of private property, intervention of the Federal Government in the urban property market was limited (Pena, 2002; Schmidt and Buehler, 2007). However, with unbridled market activities, which resulted in adverse externalities, zoning was introduced in the 1920s. When a suit was brought before the supreme court in *Village of Euclid, Ohio v. Ambler Realty Co.*, 272 U.S. 365 (1926) challenging the constitutionality of zoning as an infringement on private property rights, it was ruled that zoning was constitutional (Dale and McLaughlin, 1999). Planning activities were parachuted into SSA at the turn of the nineteenth century by the British and the French; initiatives such as passage of legislation, slum clearance, preparation of development schemes and road improvements were partly to provide good spatial environment, especially for the areas occupied by the colonial officials.

The role of urban planning in promoting good urban environment is ultimately to ensure good health for urban residents. This is in terms of not only direct physical impacts, such as preventing contaminated air or water, but indirect impacts including social and behavioural effects, on the exercise we take, the people we meet, and the degree of inequality in access to housing, employment opportunities, health services and other facilities (Barton, 2009). Barton (2009) notes the environment is one of the key determinants of health, in addition to inherited characteristics, lifestyles, social and economic variables and underscores the fact that the environment is umbilically linked to human health. He further stated four reasons why planning health into environment is essential as follows:

1 Reduction in the inequalities that exist in access to housing, facilities and transport for different socio-economic groups and vulnerable groups in the population, such as the elderly or children;
2 Increment in the amount of incidental physical activity necessary to reduce the burden of disease, disability and mortality, due to sedentary lifestyles, by improving access to services and providing walkable, mixed-use communities;
3 Contribution to the improved health of the population by reducing air and water pollution and greenhouse emissions, combating the threat of climate change; and
4 Contribution to a changed social environment by improving the security of streets, making them safer, improving communication between people and therefore ensuring a good living environment.

One of the ultimate goals of improving people's access to good living spaces through legislation and other planning activities at the time of its inception in the UK, the US, and colonial Sub-Saharan Africa (SSA) was the preservation of human health (Simpson et al., 1989; Pena, 2002; Njoh, 2009). Studies over the years including more recent ones have also demonstrated the link between urban planning and good environment and by extension good health. Baffour Awuah (2018) highlights that urban morphology or design and human action or activities are fundamental to the activities that lead to pollution (Panagopoulos et al., 2016; Perera and Emmanuel, 2016) and that the extent to which urban planning can configure good urban design to prevent or mitigate urban pollution and unhealthy human action will determine the level of diseases borne out of pollution. Viegas et al. (2013) demonstrate how planning is used to manage issues related to climate variation in urban environments. The study developed a framework with ten categories for assessment of climate variation with each category displaying indicators that describe a complex relationship that influences temperature variations. These were applied to the Master Plan of Porto Alegre in Brazil and the evidence shows the plan is climate sensitive and is helping to address the effects of climate variation in the city. Rosalía et al. (2017) cited in Baffour Awuah (2018) also modelled six distinct types of urban designs to determine their impact on waste management and carbon emissions, and established that urban morphology has a substantial impact on the use of public services and appliances, and it represents up to 2.6% of the total carbon emission per capita. More so, the study found that the most contaminating urban designs are those based on single-family buildings as during their use stage they emit up to 155% more carbon emissions per inhabitant and this was because their designs comparatively call for longer waste collection service routes, as well as more collection points given that the dwellings were more dispersed.

Beyond the above discourse, and as noted in Chapter 1, it is important to stress the point that the United Nations (UN) in 2015 formulated 17 Sustainable Development Goals (SDGs) for the realisation of its 2030 sustainable development agenda. Given that sustainability and sustainable development have three dimensions, namely, environmental, economic, and social (Salas-Zapata and Ortiz-Muñoz, 2019), these SDGs set out principles of good development that are expected to guide government policy; regulatory authorities; and other stakeholders, such as funding bodies and developers in the foreseeable future to protect people's rights to a decent quality life and the protection of the planet's environment. Further to the SDGs, the UN adopted the New Urban Agenda (NUA), which is a framework for urban development, enshrining the principles of the SDGs also in 2016 in Quito, Ecuador, at UN-Habitat III (UN, 2017). A core acknowledgement of both the SDGs and NUA is the role urban planning could play in the achievement of the environmental goals of sustainable development (UN, 2017).

As can be gleaned from the foregoing discussions, urban planning improves urban environments and could lead to the achievement of the environmental goals of sustainable development (UN, 2017) because it is the main tool for the design of cities and urban areas (Baffour Awuah, 2018). This is often undertaken through its instruments: typically, the regulatory frameworks and their enforcement to achieve development control, which were discussed in Chapter 1. These regulatory frameworks, like the legislation mentioned in the earlier paragraphs in the UK, US, and colonial SSA, set standards and principles of developments, among others. Other legislation, such as the zoning ordinance or regulation, also separate incompatible land uses and bring together compatible land uses (Baffour Awuah, 2018). Indeed, the master planning philosophy, which is still in force in many countries across the globe (UN-Habitat, 2009), is based on the land use segregation concept, which is underpinned by unifunctional land use, discrete zoning, regulation and consensus, and the use of master plans (Njoh, 2009). The regulatory frameworks further require the provision of infrastructure, amenities, and services and until recently these were provided solely by governments in many countries. Apart from regulations, Baffour Awuah (2018) identifies urban planning system's ability to provide information, for example, by way of capacity development of stakeholders as well as the provision of incentives, to help the reduction or mitigation of pollution. The study emphasised that such capacity development could enlighten urban sector stakeholders on urban pollution, its sources and effects or impact, as well as interventions such as land use decisions and practices, and development materials that can prevent air, water, noise, and visual pollution. The study also noted that incentives could impel behaviours, which are environmentally friendly.

3.2.2 Urban planning as an economic tool

Urban planning as an economic tool promotes more than allocation of land resources to various uses. It also promotes certain allocation of financial and human resources (Lichfield et al., 2003; Cheshire, 2008). Indeed, urban planning as a tool for economic progress has long been acknowledged in the literature (Faludi, 1994; Fainstein, 2003). This recognition has once again received a massive boost following the resurgence of spatial economics' postulation of cities and urban areas as engines of growth and development. It is argued that cities and urban areas hold the key to the world's prosperity, as cities account for over 80% of global GDP (McKinsey Institute, 2012). The World Bank (2009, p. 48) notes that no country in the world has developed without the growth of its cities. The Bank (p. 57) buttresses this observation with evidence that the top 30 cities in the world ranked by their GDP in 2005 accounted for 16% of the world's output, whilst the top 100 cities generated almost 25% of the global output. However, cities and urban areas' continuous performance as engines of growth is dependent, among other things, on the institution of appropriate regulation for their configuration and intervention, to ensure efficient land use and management of diseconomies of agglomeration. This is where urban planning becomes vital as a tool for configuration of cities through zoning and other development regulations.

Indeed, planning systems' ability to configure effective and efficient settlements particularly urban areas is to manage urbanisation sustainably to partly bring about economic gains (Lall et al., 2017; UN, 2017). This is expected to be done through growth in economic density to benefit people and businesses, ensuring that people can easily commute and have access to a wide variety of goods and services as well as businesses in cities having access to wider markets and enjoying economies of scale. This will, in turn, reduce their production cost, making the prices of goods and services comparatively cheaper for consumers (Lall et al., 2017). Thus, urban planning's ability to sustainably manage urbanisation makes it a huge tool to turn the development fortunes of regions such as Africa around. For example, if such transformation occurs through urban planning, JICA (2013) based on the global economy and methodology model prepared by the Centennial Group International, which informs development of the scenarios, notes progress in Africa. The model projects long-term evolution of 186 countries as a function of labour force, capital stock, and total factor productivity. The Convergence scenario is the most preferred among the three scenarios. According to JICA (2013), the Convergence scenario professes per capita income growth of around 4.6% per annum over the next 40 years, exceeding US$17,000 in 2050, which will be higher than recent figures for Russia, Malaysia, Mexico, or Turkey. This per capita income will converge with those of the world, moving from 27% of the world's average recently to 52%. Further, the per capita growth will introduce several changes and transform the lives of people on the continent and its role in the world. In particular, the size of the middle class will grow more than tenfold, an increase from 12% to 68%, whilst poverty levels will decline from 380 million to 53 million: 37% to under 3%. In addition, Africa's contribution of under 3% to global GDP will increase to 9%.

Apart from its role in the production of good spatial environments, the idea of urban planning as an economic tool, especially in a typical capitalist society, traditionally is to address market inefficiencies often described as market failure and promote allocative efficiency. For example, until the emergence of public-private participation (PPP) in infrastructure provision, infrastructure provision was traditionally considered the responsibility of government in most societies and planning systems of such societies were mandated to supply infrastructure. This is because investments in infrastructure often require huge capital outlay, which the private sector is often unable to raise. Furthermore, the investments often have a long gestation period and therefore do not create incentives to impel the private sector to undertake such investments.

Since planning systems have provided and continue to provide infrastructure, they promote economic growth, development, and poverty reduction. This is because infrastructure creates incentives for investment and makes cities more productive and liveable (Gutman et al., 2015; Baffour Awuah, 2016). AfDB (2013), for instance, notes that an adequate provision of transportation networks between cities and rural areas, reliable and less costly sources of electricity and water provision, and expansive coverage of ITC in African cities could improve rural-urban links on the continent. In fact, it has been acknowledged by authors such as Baffour Awuah et al. (2014) that properly constructed roads with drains are essential for community growth and development. This is because in addition to property value appreciation, roads ensure the smooth traffic flow of people and materials in society, good drainage and sanitation, reduction in pollution and associated health problems. Further, coupled with other infrastructure, roads create incentives for investment in commercial developments (such as shops, offices, banks, and schools).

Urban planning can be used to bring about urban redevelopment and regeneration. In the UK, for instance, through planning and other enabling legislation, disused sites could be acquired through compulsory purchase and re-planned for development projects. The idea is to improve relevant communities from economic, social, and environmental standpoints. Premised on the same principle, redevelopments are undertaken through planning legislation. A typical example of this is the inner-city redevelopment in Birmingham, the UK's second largest city, which has become the largest inner-city example of mixed-use developments ensuring appreciation in property values and offering job opportunities, efficient use of space, attracting investments, and transforming the entire city centre. As can be gleaned from the above discussions, these planning interventions lead to not only allocation of land usage but investments and creation of jobs, among other things, signifying that capital and labour resources are also being reallocated.

Planning can also be used to support real estate market activities through clear definition of property rights, such as use rights of individual parcels of land and the design and implementation of a property address system. This has the tendency to improve market transparency and reduce transaction cost. The address system can help boost city and municipal governments' revenue mobilisation drive through, for example, property taxation. This may be particularly useful in developing countries where the incidence of informal developments is high, and it is being compounded by rapid urbanisation. The significance of urban planning as an economical tool nowadays can be seen in the conceptualisation and implementation of Local Economic Development (LED). This is a recent concept that hinges on a result-oriented participatory process, which ensures the coming together of local people to stimulate commercial activities, culminating in a resilient and sustainable economy (UN-Habitat, 2005). The argument is that the outcome of LED in terms of stimulating commercial or economic activities and the processes, such as bringing local people together, as demonstrated in Figure 3.1, may be prompted by urban planning. The point is that urban planning policies and practices often emerge from socio-economic, political, and cultural, among others, dynamics in a society; and these same planning policies and practices, and their resultant opportunities and constraints, shape further socio-economic dynamics in society. Therefore, as seen in Figure 3.1, the ultimate goals of a LED may be employment promotion and a higher standard of living, and these can be instigated and achieved through the last row of urban or spatial planning interventions and activities.

3.2.3 Urban planning as a social tool

Urban planning can be used to address social issues in society (Figure 3.1). Fundamentally, the idea of urban planning as a social tool is to promote good social ideals of society's development on the one hand and correct or address the social ills associated with society's development on the other hand. Planning is expected to ensure the adequate provision of housing and other social amenities and employment; promote integration and social cohesion; prevent social exclusion; address the negative externalities of economic growth, such as poverty; and promote equity in terms of investment and access to society's resources.

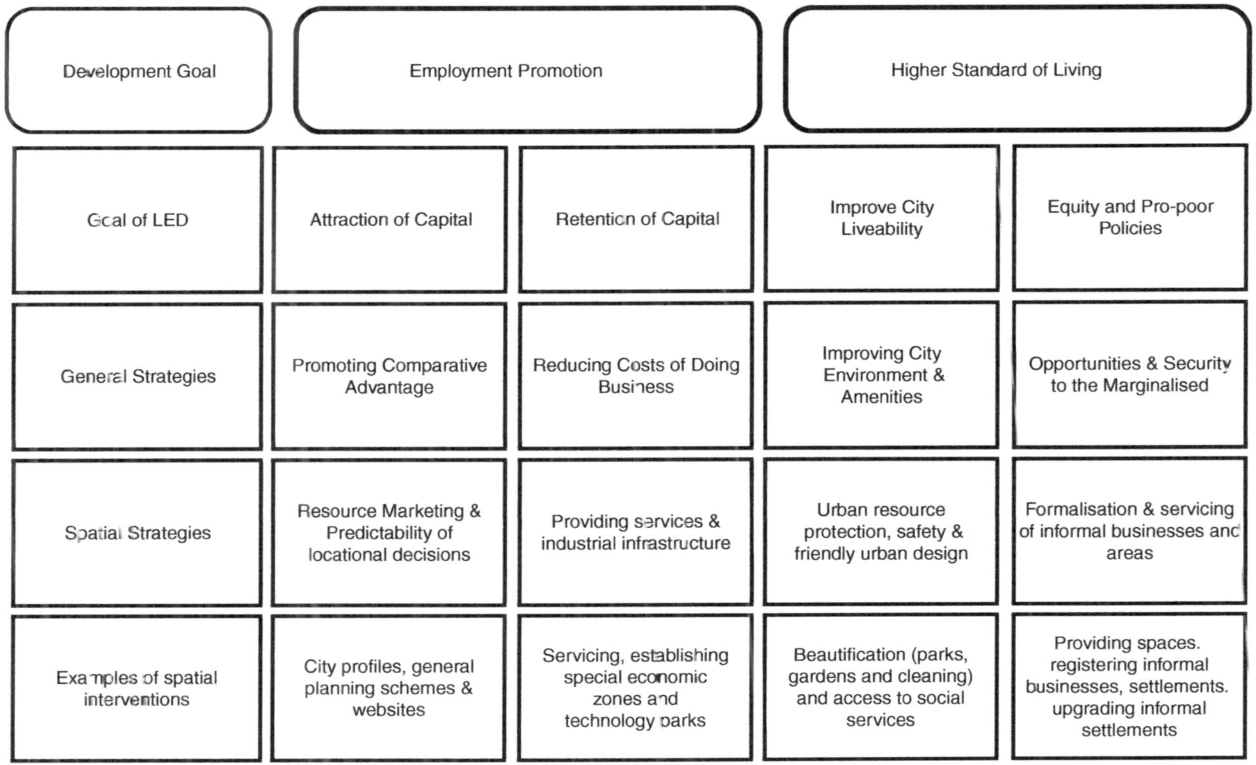

Figure 3.1 Linkage between LED and urban planning.
Source: Adapted from Namangaya (2014).

Cities and urban areas are an accretion of people and economic activities. This increase of people in cities and urban areas continues to grow very fast, especially in Africa and Asia. As can be seen from Figure 3.2, in 1950 70% (two-thirds) of the world's population lived in rural areas. However, by 2018 it was estimated that 55% of the world's population constituting 4.2 billion people lived in urban areas compared to 3.4 billion people who lived in rural areas (UN-DESA, 2018). Further, the UN-DESA (2018) projects that by 2030 and 2050, the share of the world's population living in urban areas is expected to rise to 60% and 68%, respectively, roughly a reverse of the situation that existed in 1950. The urbanisation rates are also estimated to increase across all regions of the world. For example, according to UN-DESA (2018) the urbanisation rate in Latin America and the Caribbean, and Northern America estimated at over 80% will increase almost to 90% in 2050 and Europe, with about 75% of its population living in urban areas in 2018, is expected to have an 80% urbanisation rate in 2040 and almost 85% by 2050. Africa and Asia with urbanisation rates of a little over 40% and 50% are projected to increase to 59% and 66%, respectively, by 2050.

Apart from the ecological and economic implications from the rising levels of urbanisation, there are also socio-cultural implications. These include the need to increase housing opportunities; infrastructure; and amenities such as transportation, schools, worship and recreation centres, theatres, and employment for the growing numbers of urban population as well as putting in place arrangements to ensure fair and equitable access to resources within the urban space to make urban centres liveable. There is also a need for the preservation of society's heritage (both tangible and intangible) from the effects of the current spate of urbanisation such as the coming together of people with different cultural and religious backgrounds, who have varying interests and social statuses in particular urban centres,

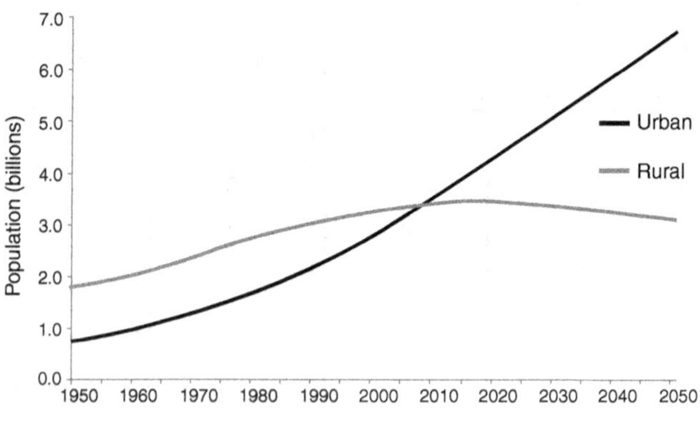

Figure 3.2 Urban and rural populations of the world, 1950–2050.
Source: Adapted from UN-DESA (2018).

which hitherto have their own culture and set of practices, which may stand the risk of being adulterated by foreign cultures. Urban planning is expected to put in place the necessary institutions and policies, and create the required incentives to ensure that all these social issues are addressed (UN-Habitat, 2009; Watson, 2009a).

3.3 Evaluation of the role of urban planning

The discussions so far show that urban planning is useful and crucial in any development discourse and over the years planning has performed significant development roles in many countries around the globe. For example, planning played a central role in the development of the nation-state of Japan (Shibata, 2008a). Planning was part of Western technology, which the Iwakura mission (the ruling elite), bureaucrats, and students of Japan imported from Western Europe (between 1871 and 1873) as part of the Meiji leadership strategy to pursue enlightenment – civilisation as the West did through a massive programme of building infrastructure and industrialisation (Sorensen, 2002; Friedmann, 2005; Shibata, 2008a; see also Chapter 7). As mentioned earlier, urban planning was very instrumental in addressing social and environmental ills – pollution in residential areas, the emergence of slums and houses with poor water and sewerage services, small houses with damp and poor ventilation, and the over crowding that characterised the industrial and agricultural development that took place in the UK during the nineteenth century (Hall, 2002; Boelens, 2006; Mullins and Murie, 2006; see also Chapter 7).

Beyond past performance, urban planning is also considered to be the central tool for the effective and efficient management of the two main challenges that confront the world in the twenty-first century, which are urbanisation and climate change – environmental challenges (Hammond et al., 2012). Indeed, as noted earlier, following the expiration of the UN Millennium Development Goals (MDGs) in 2015, the UN launched the SDGs. The SDGs is the UN's 2030 agenda for sustainable development, which provides a shared blueprint for peace and prosperity for people and the planet, now and in the future. The SDGs is made up of 17 goals and central to these goals is the clarion call for action by both developed and developing countries to end poverty and deprivations whilst devising strategies that improve health and education, reduce inequality and spur economic growth, tackle climate change, and work to preserve oceans and forests (UN, 2019). Urban planning is recognised as one of the fundamental proposed actions by the UN for the achievement of the targets for the SDGs (Baffour Awuah, 2018).

However, the twenty-first century has witnessed several imperatives, the impacts of which have called into question the effectiveness of urban planning as has been practised over the years. As reported elsewhere in this chapter, the world is currently experiencing rising levels of urbanisation and re-urbanisation, which have never been seen before, with its greatest incidence in Africa and Asia. These rising levels of urbanisation continue to pose significant socio-economic challenges across the world. To this urbanisation challenge is added the growing environmental concern of the impact of climate change, which is affecting access to water and rendering hundreds of millions of people vulnerable to coastal flooding and related natural disasters as global warming increases (UN-Habitat, 2009; Booth et al., 2012). Another environmental concern is the impact of fossil fuel use, particularly in urban areas, and its direct connection to climate change predominantly through vehicular emissions as well as its significant contribution to greenhouse gas emissions and hence global warming, as has been well documented (Booth et al., 2012). Additionally, the processes of globalisation and ongoing economic restructuring across the world continue to pose significant challenges especially to urban labour markets. In fact, commentators such as UN-Habitat (2009) and Watson (2009a) had long noted that these phenomena are causing an increasing polarisation of occupational and income structures in industries such as the service industry, which is experiencing growth, and the manufacturing sector, which is on the decline. These commentators also noted that the consequences of the phenomena have dimensions of gender, with more women taking up paid jobs and rising levels of "casualisation" of labour through part-time contract and home-based work, making the relevant labour force highly vulnerable to the ongoing economic challenges.

What is worthy of note is that all the above imperatives are taking place at a time where most urban planning systems across the world are being criticised as inadequate, weak, and ineffective. For example, most planning systems are said to be a formal government activity practised in a more technocratic manner devoid of wider citizenry and stakeholder participation contrary to the paradigm shift from government to governance as a new urban political system in response to the need to address the challenges posed by imperatives such as globalisation and the global economic restructuring. Further, it is noted that instead of the re-orientation of planning systems to practise on a much larger scale, such as urban/city-regions, and introduce multilevel and collaborative governance to address the afore-mentioned challenges, most planning systems operate on a smaller scale.

Consequently, the twenty-first century challenges discussed earlier coupled with weak planning regimes have culminated in growing informality especially in the developing world and several other urban ills such as rising urban poverty, social exclusion and inequality, inadequate infrastructure and services, poor housing and insanitary conditions, traffic jams, and urban pollution, among other things. For example, estimates suggest that the informal sector accounts for about 80% of employment in the developing world (Brown, 2012), and this is translated into landforms and uses, which are increasingly being characterised by informal developments on the one hand and gentrification on the other hand (Keeton and Nijhuis, 2019).

Research evidence shows that most of the over 1 billion urban slum dwellers without proper water, electricity, and sanitation facilities live in the developing world (Gilbert, 2014). For Africa, the situation is far worse and accounts for 60% of the aforesaid population. This is compounded by the fact that African cities are challenged by many natural and man-made hazards such as surface and coastal flooding, drought, extreme temperatures, vector-borne diseases, as well as seismic hazards from local fault lines, air or water pollution, depletion of natural resources and related health impacts including respiratory illness and waterborne pathogens like cholera (ARUP and Cities Alliance, 2016).

The above situation is expected to be exacerbated by the recent emergence of the novel coronavirus disease (COVID-19), which originated from Wuhan in the Chinese province of Hubei and has since spread across the world (Huang et al., 2020; Zhu et al., 2020). According to the European Centre for Disease Prevention and Control (ECDPC, 2020), the global deaths from the disease since 31 December 2019 and as of 19 May 2020 was **318,201**, whilst **4,766,468 cases** of infections were reported. The UN-Habitat (2020) also reported that, as of February 2020, **1,430** cities out of **210** countries around the globe were infected with COVID-19. Significantly, the impacts of the disease, which cut across environmental, economic, and social lines, have been dire. These are mainly borne out of the measures instituted to contain the disease across the world, such as the imposition of partial or total lockdowns; banning of large gatherings/public meetings; social distancing and stay-at-home policies; closure of schools; imposition of restrictions on travellers from particularly hard-hit countries; closure of countries' borders; closing or limiting internal transport systems; encouraging of the citizenry to wear face masks; and the use of gloves and hand sanitisers. Environmentally, the measures have led to a rise in domestic energy consumption and generation of waste pollution by way of used ordinary and surgical face masks, plastic sanitiser bottles, solid tissue papers, and other clinical trash, which end up in the environment – cities, towns, communities, neighbourhoods, water bodies, etc. – and the ecosystem in general (Saadat et al., 2020). In terms of economic impact, there has been contraction of the world's economy and virtually every country in the world has been affected, with various sectors of countries' economies suffering. For example, the US' GDP dropped by 4.8% in the first quarter of 2020, which is the sharpest contraction since the global financial crisis of 2007–2009, ending the longest economic expansion in the country's history (Mutikani, 2020). The European Union (EU)'s GDP is forecast to contract by 7.4% during 2020, the worst economic shock since the 1930s (Amaro, 2020). The Chinese economy (the world's second-largest economy) contracted in the first quarter of 2020 for the first time since quarterly records began in 1992 where its GDP fell by 6.8% in January–March year-on year, which is more than the 6.5% forecast by analysts and reverses a 6% expansion in the fourth quarter of 2019. Furthermore, the country's economic growth is expected to fall to 2.5% for 2020, the slowest in almost 50 years (Zhang et al., 2020). Due to COVID-19, the IMF (2020), in April 2020, predicted that growth in SSA in 2020 is projected at –1.6%, the lowest level on record, a downward revision of 5.2 percentage points compared with six months ago whilst the World Bank (2020) observed that GDP growth in the region could fall sharply from 2.4% in 2019 to between -2.1% and –5.1% in 2020. The Africa Union Commission also forecasts a negative growth from 3.4% to between –0.8% and –1.1% for the region. The social impacts relate to a rise in cases of domestic violence, like physical, emotional, and sexual abuses, among others (Refuge, 2020). Overall, the world's most vulnerable people are the very ones the pandemic is impacting the hardest (UN-Habitat, 2020).

It is, however, refreshing to note that in the last couple of years several initiatives are being implemented by national governments and international development agencies to address the imperatives and their effects discussed in this section. These initiatives include, for example, the UN-Habitat's sustainable cities programmes and the introduction of new national urban policies. It remains to be seen how current initiatives can address the imperatives. Nevertheless, what is significant is that urban planning practices need to be responsive to twenty-first-century urban challenges if planning is supposed to be the central tool for the promotion of sustainable urban development and management.

3.4 Chapter summary

This chapter set out to discuss the role of urban planning in socio-economic development. In so doing, the chapter acknowledged and discussed the role of planning as an ecological, economic, and social tool to motivate transformation and promote sustainable development. However, urban planning as a practice over the years has proven incapable of addressing the twenty-first-century urban challenges fully, notably rapid urbanisation and the effects of climate change, and therefore requires some changes in approach. Although some initiatives by national governments and international development agencies are under way, it is paramount that any such initiative should be effective enough to make planning responsive to the challenges.

4 Indicators of a good urban planning system

4.1 Introduction

Sustainable urban development and management are vital to sustainable development. This is because they promote productive, resilient, and inclusive urban areas as well as attractive, high-quality, and sustainable places where people work and live, which are essential to sustainable development. A good urban planning system is central to the achievement of the above-mentioned ideals. This chapter discusses indicators of a good urban planning systems. Although the discussion may not be exhaustive as there is no "one size fit all" set of indicators for every part of the world, it gives a useful guide for putting in place an effective and efficient planning system.

4.2 Definition of goals

Every good planning system should clearly define its goals in terms of the aim the planning system intends to achieve. For individual countries or economies, this will, in turn, give national direction on issues such as the role of rural areas or country sides and urban areas, as well as the different regions or the geographical partitions of a country. This is very useful in the formulation of national planning policies, for example, regarding such geographical areas of a country. UN-Habitat (2009) notes that the definition of an urban planning system's goal is a pre-requisite for its success and that such exercise, for instance, can help formulate a national perspective on the role of urban areas and challenges of urbanisation and subsequently national urban policy to leverage urbanisation for sustainable development. Furthermore, Splinter and Leynseele (2019) demonstrate how satellite cities' developments, which are driven by the belief that economic growth is spurred by an emerging middle class and investors in Kenya, are connected with the visionary policy objects that help to inform national economic policies and spatial planning strategies such as Vision 2030 under the country's planning system, thereby showing that planning systems should be able to clearly state its goals.

4.3 Promotion of optimal urban design

A good urban planning system is expected to promote optimal urban design. One of the manifestations in an urban area where effective urban planning is practised and implemented is the sight of the physical environment, its functioning, and how urban activities take place. This manifestation starts with urban design, which is defined as the art of creating places for people. This encompasses the way places work, as well as issues relating to community safety, its appearance, the connections between people and places, movement and urban form, nature and the built fabric, and the processes for ensuring successful villages, towns, and cities (Department of the Environment, Transport and the Regions (DETR), 2000). According to DETR (2000), optimal urban design is fundamental to the production of attractive, high-quality, sustainable places where people live, work, and relax, and prevents shoddy, unimaginative, and second-rate buildings and urban areas. Furthermore, it is responsible for promoting sustainable developments and an enabling environment for the economic, effective, and efficient use of natural resources and social progress, as optimal design contributes to the development of lively places with unique characters, streets, and public spaces that are safe, accessible, pleasant to use and human in scale, and places that inspire because of the imagination and sensitivity of their designers. For example, an exercise to ensure that urban areas function as living organisms with buildings that return nutrients to the environment and promote a material flow management to make buildings like trees and cities like forests, as espoused by the cradle-to-cradle concept to achieve a positive environmental footprint, needs to be informed by optimal urban design.

The starting point to optimal urban design is a clear and suitable framework within which the design should take place. The framework is provided by an urban planning system, which can be in the form of a development, strategic, or any other relevant plan with supplementary guidance (Mutuku et al., 2019; Splinter and Leynseele, 2019). However, a good planning system should be able to set out laws, which may include policies, orders-in-councils, proclamations, notices, guidelines, directives, standards, and administrative processes and procedures for crafting and implementing the framework. A typical example of this is the UK's National Planning Policy Framework (CP48), which was presented to Parliament by the Secretary of State for Housing, Communities and Local Government in February 2019. Another such example is the crafting of the Spatial Development Framework (SDF) by Rwanda to ensure that the country's developed National Urbanisation Policy (NUP) identifies six secondary cities where efforts to promote urbanisation and economic growth should focus (Mutuku et al., 2019). In the same way, the framework or plan needs to have policies, standards, processes, and procedures to guide the production and implementation of optimal urban designs. These serve as part of the tools for the creation of optimal urban design. A critical point here is the need for the laws and policies setting forth the framework for urban design and those that the framework stipulates to be simple, clear, unambiguous, and not outmoded. The processes and procedures the laws and policies prescribe by the framework should not also be complex or too technocratic and must be devoid of bureaucratic tendencies. Furthermore, there may be a need for such laws and policies to consider local norms and practices. The rationale is to ensure understanding of the laws and policies and their requirements, as well as make them relevant to the socio-economic needs of society and promote such relevance.

As highlighted by UN-Habitat (2009), and noted in Chapter 7, urban planning was transported to many parts of the world, especially in areas which are today referred to as the developing world, following its emergence at the turn of the nineteenth century through colonialism. Although regarded as outmoded, the colonial laws and policies which set up the planning systems for most of these areas continue to dictate urban planning practice, and this has been identified as partly responsible for the inadequacies of these planning systems. This is because these laws and policies are couched in very technical language, which are difficult to understand by even planning officers who work with them and have become irrelevant to the socio-economic needs of most people in the above-mentioned societies (Payne and Majale, 2004; UN-Habitat, 2009).

Another important consideration is the need for the framework that drives optimal urban design to be locally responsive. This means that the framework should incorporate local content or socio-economic needs as much as possible (DETR, 2000; UN-Habitat, 2009). The previous chapter laid bare some of the challenges that confront the world today, particularly in urban areas, such as the rapid rate of urbanisation and its implications and the effects of climate change. However, these issues are not even across the world, meaning that the kind of attention given to these issues in one region or country may not necessarily require the same sort of attention elsewhere. UN-Habitat (2009) notes that whilst interrelated issues, such as rapid urbanisation, urban poverty, informality, slums and infrastructure provision, and access to basic services, are germane to Asia and Africa, the causes and impacts of climate change and ensuring sustainable urbanisation are more pressing in developed, transitional, and several developing countries, all of which require good planning systems to redress. The study further notes that in several parts of both developed and developing regions, there is a need to enhance urban safety by ensuring disaster preparedness, post-disaster and post-conflict reconstruction and rehabilitation, and redressing issues such as crime and violence. Beyond the differences in the socio-economic needs at the region or country level, there are further major differences or nuances in these needs at the city and local community levels within specific countries, which need to be identified and addressed.

The need for the passage of relevant laws to drive the crafting of optimal urban design and the incorporation of local content into the design are essential. This is because they can help to legitimise urban designs in terms of owning the designs and ensuring their goals are achieved. As discussed later in this chapter, these considerations require a good planning system to institute planning laws and policies, as well as processes and procedures, which ensure the creation of awareness of the planning system, its requirements and participation in the planning process.

4.4 Ensuring development control

A key component of a good urban planning system is its ability to promote and ensure development control. The core rationale for development control is to ensure that the implementation of planning proposals is on 'track' and that the ultimate goals of planning proposals are achieved. Clear and unambiguous planning and urban development regulations, as well as good planning proposals in the form of strategic, regional, or development plans, are requirements for development control. However, compliance with planning and urban development regulations is fundamental to the achievement of development control (Mckay, 2003). Compliance is not only about property developers obeying planning and urban development regulations, but it is also about full implementation of planning proposals. This may encompass adhering to regulations requiring:

- the need for zoning and preparation of various plans including strategic, regional, and development plans;
- acquisition of planning permission and building permit and obeying their conditions;
- the development of right and appropriate levels of infrastructure, amenities, and services; and
- equal and equitable access to infrastructure, amenities, and services as well as other resources and opportunities.

The above requirements will need a huge financial investment from government at all levels – national, urban, and local governments – to pass the necessary legislation and directly participate in the implementation of plans as, for example, the building of infrastructure and amenities. Private individual developers and land users may also need financial capacity to comply with planning and urban development regulations whether in the form of undertaking actual developments or how the development should take place and its usage. Furthermore, there is a need for an institutional framework, particularly the establishment of the right kind of planning institution to oversee urban planning practice. This may be an elaborate bureaucracy well-resourced in terms of material resources, such as finance, office space, vehicles, and state-of-the-art technology, among others, and human resources who are well trained and motivated to put in place an effective and efficient urban planning practice. This bureaucracy will be responsible for issues such as:

- developing standards, guidelines, administrative processes, and procedures for planning practice;
- identifying investment and livelihood opportunities that can be built on, as well as factors that could motivate planning officials to perform well or pressures that could corrupt them; and
- undertaking surveillance and identifying non-compliance with regulations, as well as applying the appropriate sanction to ensure compliance.

Closely aligned to the above point is the need for a very effective and efficient court system that will be able to trial cases of non-compliance with planning and urban development regulations at the right time and in an expeditious manner to determine appropriate sanctions. What is also important is for planning institutions to incentivise property owners, developers, and land users to comply with regulations. The starting point may be for planning institutions to determine the sort of things that could motivate compliance with regulation and the corresponding quantum of them that could lead to desired levels of compliance. This, for example, could be the nature and implications of legislation, which may promote investment and development rather than restrict developments.

4.5 Effective and efficient urban planning practice

Evidence from urban planning literature shows that planning practice in several parts of the world is considered the sole preserve of the government. Although government is or should be a major player in planning practice, a good urban planning system should regard urban planning practice as a collective exercise and promote such ideals. A good urban planning system should ensure the collaboration and inclusion of all stakeholders, such as government planning institutions and officials; private sector, land and property owners; communities; professional bodies; academia; civil society, including non-governmental organisations (NGOs); and community-based organisations (CBOs) in planning practice. This means that the formulation of planning proposals in terms of deciding planning goals, strategies for achieving the goals, consideration of the resources for the achievement of the goals and their mobilisation, the implementation of the proposals, and the assessment of the implementation to determine whether the goals are being achieved, among others, should all be pursued as collective exercises involving all stakeholders.

To achieve the above ideal of effective and efficient urban planning practice, there must be a continuous planning education. First, there must be a continuous programme to educate planning institutions and their officials, including professional planners on planning and urban development laws and regulations, as well as their roles and responsibilities under planning systems. Further, professional planners must be equipped to imbibe and put into practice innovative planning ideas, especially regarding possessing skills in participatory planning, communication, and negotiation, as well as being aware of current and emerging issues that impinge on planning, such as urbanisation, climate change, and infrastructure provision (UN-Habitat, 2009).

There is also a need for planners to be abreast with planning conditions in different parts of the world, as well as issues on ethics and social values such as justice and social equity and social and economic rights. Planners can receive education or training on the above-mentioned issues through short course capacity development training and continuous professional development workshops and seminars. However, it is important that planning educational institutions introduce such issues in their training curricula and that a good planning system should ensure that all the issues raised in the paragraph are addressed.

Second, there is a need for a continuous programme to be put in place by planning institutions and their officials as part of a good planning system to educate other stakeholders, particularly the public on planning and urban development laws and regulations, their roles and responsibilities, and other planning activities. Apart from creating awareness of planning processes, laws, and regulations, which is essential for compliance with regulations, such education is also important to equip other stakeholders and members of the public to make a meaningful contribution to the planning process. This public education, particularly in developing countries, can be carried out by using national and local media platforms, like radio and television stations; YouTube broadcasts; and periodic interactions between planning institutions and stakeholders, such as professional bodies, local communities, land and property owners, and civil society groups.

Indeed, it is partly because of the above needs that the Rwandan SDFs are making use of Planning Support Systems (PSSs) to communicate the goals of the SDFs to the local level and present opportunities for stakeholders to understand and translate national policies to their local planning contexts (Mutuku et al., 2019). According to Geertmann and Stillwell (2009), cited in Mutuku et al. (2019), the support systems are a set of computer-based geo-information tools, which are made of special characteristics that stakeholders within a planning process can rely on to undertake assignments, such as analysis, communication, and handling information. The authors further intimate that the PSS could be used to perform four distinct functions in terms of supporting planning and decision-making. These are assisting and boosting stakeholders' participation in planning processes; addressing a planning problem and promoting standard solutions; informing stakeholders about key policies being implemented or targeted to their local area or at the country level; and helping professionals in specific planning tasks such as transport, policy planning, land use planning, and environmental planning to mention but a few.

Beyond the above uses, other authors such as Klosterman (1997) suggest that PSS may be construed as information infrastructure – organised system of tools, a set of organised tools for planning that enhance interaction, and idea sharing among stakeholders, which should aim at supporting a continuous and interactive process of designing, analysing, and evaluating outcomes, and making meaningful use of the outcomes while adapting to any changes in the information demands. Thus, PSS functions to improve planning by creating a platform to promote interaction and participation in the planning process as it focusses on outcomes, which are reflective of plans, policies, and strategies (Te Brömmelstroet, 2013). Despite these benefits of PSS, they are very difficult to produce (Mutuku et al., 2019).

4.6 Monitoring and evaluation

A good planning system should undertake periodic introspection. In other words, the system should be able to take stock of its activities from time to time to track performance and assess performance to ascertain whether performance is on course to achieve desired outcomes. Fundamentally, good urban planning systems and planning frameworks, such as strategic, regional, and development plans, should have goals. These goals are key components of the systems and the plans and it is expected that the goals will be achieved at the end of the plan period or the period stated by the planning system. Without the achievement of its goals, a planning system or plan may to a large extent be judged as ineffective or unsuccessful. However, the achievement of the goals of a good urban planning system largely depends on the successful implementation of its frameworks, such as strategic, regional, and development plans, and the achievement of their goals.

For the achievement of the goal of plans, it imperative that the implementation of the activities that are needed to be performed to achieve the goals are constantly monitored and evaluated to ascertain whether performance is up to the required levels and the necessary results being obtained to achieve the goals. There is also a need for evaluation to be undertaken to ascertain the achievement of the goal even if individual activities have been implemented according to plan and the results are at the right levels. Further, the idea of monitoring and evaluation is to help devise and institute alternative courses of action, should the initial strategies for implementation fail to achieve the desired outcomes.

Of course, as discussed previously, monitoring and evaluation of planning activity should be a collective exercise involving stakeholders. However, the exercise should commence with the formulation of plans and making decisions on the goals of the plan. Proper practice demands that the goals set for plans are clearly and specifically stated, measurable, and achievable within a certain time frame. It is also important that clear indicators and benchmarks are spelt out during the goal formulation stage and during the implementation of plans for measuring the achievement of the goals. It is equally imperative for appropriate methodologies to be devised to analyse whether goals have been achieved or otherwise. Additionally, monitoring and evaluation should be able to address other issues, such as determining actual levels of performance, the gap between actual performance and expected performance, causes of failure or gap in performance, alternative courses of action to address failure and the justification, as well as the implications of adopting such alternative courses of action.

4.7 Chapter summary

This chapter discussed indicators of a good urban planning system. It noted that there is no "one size fit all" set of indicators for a good planning system for every part of the world, as conditions across countries are not even. However, the chapter outlined and discussed several considerations, such as the definition of an urban planning system's goals, promotion of optimal urban design, and effective development control as a useful guide for putting in place an effective and efficient planning system.

5 The role of incentives in effective urban planning

A conceptual framework

5.1 Introduction

Compliance with urban planning and development regulations is vital to any successful planning system (Mckay, 2003; Buitelaar et al., 2011). Compliance with regulations can be voluntary or involuntary. Involuntary compliance with regulations is expensive since it requires enormous resources and strong institutions. Furthermore, the processes utilised to ensure involuntary compliance usually do not achieve a desired outcome (Sutinen and Kuperan, 1999). As noted in the previous chapter incentives can play a meaningful role towards achieving a successful planning regime, and significantly voluntary compliance with planning regulations based on incentives has proven to achieve optimum results (Malpezzi and Mayo, 1997; Lai et al., 2007). Voluntary compliance based on incentives can thus be very instrumental to the success of urban planning and development regulations. To trace its role and consequences, there is a need for a lens to perceive the levels of incentives to promote voluntary compliance and how successful voluntary compliance can be achieved.

Economic theories help to draw insights from real-world behaviours. The Austrian economics theory of human action provides an effective explanation of voluntary compliance based on incentives. This chapter therefore devises a conceptual framework using insights from the human action theory to showcase the role and consequences of incentives and voluntary compliance with urban planning and development regulations.

5.2 Towards development of a conceptual framework

Chapter 2 discussed two main components of urban planning theory: namely, the justification and form of urban planning. From an economics standpoint, the chapter also discussed several orthodoxies for planning interventions, including those from the neo-classical, property rights, and transaction cost economics schools of thought. However, it became apparently clear from the discussions in the chapter that there is a lack of consensus on the economic basis for planning intervention in the urban property market, particularly in a capitalist society. That said, Chapter 3 noted that urban planning has become an indispensable tool for the socio-economic development of societies. Nevertheless, the success of any planning regime is dependent on compliance with regulations that underpin the regime (Webster, 1998; Mckay, 2003, 2007; Buitelaar et al., 2011). Compliance with planning regulations means land users or developers act in a manner that is consistent with regulations (Lai et al., 2007).

There is a range of factors that determines whether people will act in compliance with regulation. Consequently, with a full understanding of the factors that motivate people to act in a specific way, it is possible to predict the compliance rate accurately, even before regulation is formulated. People can be compelled by coercive force accompanied by a threat of sanctions or violence to act in a specific way (Scholz, 1997; Tallberg, 2002). Alternatively, people can be impelled by incentives to behave or act in a specific way. Studies, such as Pogodzinski and Sass (1990), Malpezzi and Mayo (1997), Pejovich (1999), Tiesdell and Allmendinger (2005), Lai et al. (2007), and Buitelaar et al. (2011), have provided insights on how incentives can be used to promote compliance with planning regulations.

Threat of sanctions to ensure compliance with regulations, involuntary compliance, is based on traditional deterrent philosophy (McKay et al., 2003). This philosophy is premised on the certainty and severity of sanctions as predictors of compliance with regulation. Thus, compliance with regulation is expected to be high where there is a greater likelihood that violation will be detected, and expeditious, certain, and significant sanction will be imposed (Sutinen and Kuperan, 1999; Winter and May, 2001). Therefore, to promote compliance, regulation must be unambiguous, and agencies charged with the responsibility of enforcement must control regulated entities through a comprehensive programme of monitoring, surveillance, and enforcement. This can be executed through a competent judiciary system with up-to-date courts and effective public machinery with proactive leadership, adequate and competent staff, and logistics in order to detect violation and implement threats of sanctions to ensure compliance albeit with huge financial costs (Tallberg, 2002). Sutinen and Kuperan (1999) note that compliance with regulation based on a deterrent philosophy is the costliest item in natural resource management programmes, accounting for 25% to over 50% of all public expenditure.

The above discussion suggests that jurisdictions with very weak and unreliable justice systems and public administrative set-ups have limited prospects of achieving compliance with planning regulations entirely based on a deterrent enforcement model. In SSAs, the judicial and court systems are weak and under resourced (USA-GOA, 2004; Keith and Ogundele, 2007; Platteau, 2009). Furthermore, they are plagued with bureaucratic and complex court procedures, and high cost of litigation, corruption, and ineptitude (Platteau, 2009). As discussed in the next chapter, planning institutions in the region are weak, under-resourced in terms of both human and material resources, and suffer from political interference in the execution of their functions (UN-Habitat, 1999, 2009; Rakodi, 2001, 2006b; Mwimba, 2002; Kironde, 2006; Aribigbola, 2007; GoG, 2009). This, coupled with an unwieldy legislative mechanism where colonial legislation operates side by side with new laws and customs of the people, has made authorities charged with the enforcement of regulation turn a blind eye to non-compliance to eschew confrontation or promote compromise (Blocher, 2006; Rakodi, 2006c; Platteau, 2009). Even in developed jurisdictions such as the UK, where there are comparatively better justice and public administration systems, studies like Mckay (2003), Mckay et al. (2003), McKay (2007), Lai et al. (2007), Harris (2010) assert that enforcement of planning regulations is weak due partly to poor detection of violation, lack of financial resources, and discretion in enforcement. They argue that the deterrence model does not explain the available evidence very well and its prescriptions are usually not practical as expected small-sized sanctions do not always result in non-compliance (Sutinen and Kuperan, 1999).

Voluntary compliance with regulations based on incentives should thus be given a large scope in any system of urban planning in SSA if it has any chance of success. What constitutes incentives at a point in time and jurisdiction as well as its sustainability are usually not straightforward (Pejovich, 1999; Buitelaar et al., 2011). Also, incentive may be contrived or instinctive. To utilise contrived incentives, planning and urban development regulations must ensure appropriate levels of incentives to impel people to act in compliance. This, for example, may be construed as reduction in title formalisation cost or assistance with cost of developments to ensure compliance with planning regulation. Undoubtedly, promoting this type of incentives could be very difficult and expensive as was the case with such schemes in countries like Uganda, Nigeria, Botswana, and Kenya, which had to be abandoned due to their huge cost implications (UN-Habitat, 1999).

Instinctive incentives offer the more feasible option with a greater likelihood of achieving maximum compliance with planning regulation. Regulation compliance is more likely, if Governments incorporate large doses of instinctive incentives. The human action theory offers an effective explanation of instinctive incentives towards voluntary compliance with planning regulations in SSA, and it is thus employed to devise the conceptual framework. The choice of the human action-based framework also allows the quantification of individuals' choices towards contributing to the wider urban planning policy debate given the increasing discourse across the globe to help make urban planning more effective to address the twenty-first-century development challenges.

5.3 The human action theory

Human action theory is a praxeological theory that emerged from a branch of political economy usually regarded as Austrian economics (Mises, 1949;

Hoppe, 1995; Hülsmann, 2004; Kinsella and Tinsley, 2004; Rothbard, 2004; Carnis, 2009). The theory had long been associated with the core elements of the 1870s economic revolution by Menger (1871), Jevons (1871), and Walras (1877) (Baird, 1998; Rothbard, 2004). However, it was Mises (1949) in *Human Action: A Treatise* who coordinated insights of the theory and formally presented it as an integrated theory. Essentially, human action theory postulates that every human being acts and, from the economic perspective, acts instinctively to achieve a desired end in the cheapest and best possible way if able to do so (Greaves, 1949; Mises, 1949; Rothbard, 2004). For example, a prospective residential property owner will act in the cheapest way either to construct or to buy fully developed property. Therefore, from the standpoint of human action theory, economic propositions should focus entirely on individuals and not groups since groups, such as companies and clubs, do not act as such. Rather, it is individuals among the groups who act on behalf of the group (Greaves, 1949; Mises, 1949; Rothbard, 2004). Thus, there is no group action which does not emanate from individuals (Greaves, 1949; Mises, 1949).

Human action is defined as a purposive behaviour of using means to achieve a desired end (Mises, 1949; Kinsella and Tinsley, 2004; Rothbard, 2004; Carnis, 2009). Human action is distinguishable from mere reflexes and behaviours (Mises, 1949; Kinsella and Tinsley, 2004; Rothbard, 2004; Facchini, 2007). It therefore follows that an action occurs within a means and end framework (Menger, 1871; Baird, 1998). However, the rationale for institution of an action by individuals is to substitute a more satisfactory state of affairs for a less satisfactory state of affairs (Greaves, 1949; Mises, 1949; Baird, 1998; Rothbard, 2004).

A fundamental principle in economics states that people or economic agents act in direct response to incentives (Mankiw, 2011). That is, for individuals to act they must be impelled by incentives (Greaves, 1949; Mises, 1949; Rothbard, 2004). For example, for land or property owners to use their lands or properties in a specific way, there must be an incentive to impel them to use them as such. Since human action takes place within a 'means and ends' framework, individuals intuitively compare the value of ends with the value of means or resources used up or to be used in an action. The positive difference between the values of ends sought by an action and the means deployed to accomplish an action constitutes the prime incentive that drives an action (Greaves, 1949; Mises, 1949; Baird, 1998; Rothbard, 2004).

The value of means or resources used up in an action to arrive at ends constitutes the cost of an action whilst the value of ends sought by an action represents the anticipated benefit from an action (Mises, 1949; Baird, 1998; Kinsella and Tinsley, 2004; Rothbard, 2004). What is noteworthy, however, is that individuals speculate the difference between the value of means used or to be used in an action and the value of ends sought by an action. Thus, individuals speculate on the difference between the cost and the benefit of action (Greaves, 1949; Mises, 1949; Rothbard, 2004). For example, developers in putting their land resource into a particular use will speculate the difference between the value of resources to be expended and the value of that land use to determine whether it is worthwhile to do so. This, therefore, makes perception important as well as crucial in the determination of the kind of action human beings will take (Baffour Awuah et al., 2011c).

Human action further holds that means in an actual sense exist in the universe as elements and not as proper means. As such, it is only when human beings can conceive these existing elements in the universe as important or relevant to the achievement of ends that they become means (Greaves, 1949; Mises, 1949; Rothbard, 2004). In other words, it is the ability of human beings to establish a cause and effect relationship between elements in the universe and the ends they are desirous of attaining. Rothbard (2004) likens this conception of means to discovering technology in the sense of production.

Given the foregoing discussions, human action is contingent on incentives, which are determined through speculation of the difference between the values of means and ends. Additionally, the means applied to attain the ends can be discovered only when human beings are able to establish a cause and effect relationship between them on the one hand and the ends sought on the other hand. This implies that, for there to be incentives to impel an action, means must be discovered: a cause and effect relationship between some elements in the universe and the ends being sought must be established. This further suggests that incorporated in human action are incentives borne out of speculation that the value of the ends for which an action is directed is more than that of the means deployed, and upon the initial discovery of means. This again presupposes that where means are not discovered, there cannot be incentives and without incentives, an action cannot be activated. Even in situations where means are discovered but are not available, an action cannot be activated because it implies a lack of incentives. Fundamentally, insights of the human action theory constitute the bedrock of Austrian economics (Bratland, 2000; Kinsella and Tinsley, 2004). However, apart from Austrian economics, aspects of the insights from human action theory have been applied in several fields of endeavours including political ethics (Hoppe, 1989) and legal theorising (Barnett, 1997; Kinsella and Tinsley, 2004). Even in the field of planning there has been an application of aspects of the theory in Hong Kong (Lai et al., 2007) and in the US (Staley, 2004).

5.4 Application of human action theory

Despite the lingering debate on economic rationale for planning intervention, it is generally accepted that state intervention in the urban property market through planning is to address market failure by reducing negative externalities and promoting positive externalities (Evans, 2003; Klosterman, 2003; Lichfield et al., 2003; Adams et al., 2005; Qian, 2010). Therefore, it is expected that planning will ensure health, safety, convenience, economy, amenity, and aesthetics (Keeble, 1959; Gurran et al., 2008). These expectations of planning as demonstrated by Figure 5.1 ultimately manifest themselves in property value appreciation (Fischel, 1990; Lai et al., 2007). However, in practice planning is exercised through planning regulations (Payne and Majale, 2004; Tiesdell and Allmendinger, 2005; Adams, 2008). This means that to achieve expectations of planning and ultimately derive appreciation in property values there must be compliance with planning regulation. Compliance with planning regulation signifies performance of regulation requirements. These include the zoning and preparation of sub-division planning schemes, acquisition of building permits, and provision of infrastructure, among others (Bertaud and Mapelzzi, 2001; Buitelaar, 2004; Cheshire and Sheppard, 2004; Lai, 2005).

Thus, from the human action theory standpoint and in the context of this book, compliance with planning regulation constitutes human action. This in effect signifies that meeting the requirements of planning regulation, such as the zoning and preparation of sub-division plans, provision of infrastructure, and acquisition of a building permit, constitute human action. Therefore, the value of the ends to which compliance with these planning regulation requirements is directed; expectation of planning reflected in appreciation in property values constitutes benefit of urban planning, while the value of the resources used in meeting the requirements constitutes the cost of urban planning (Figure 5.1).

Insights from human action theory further suggest that for human beings to act, they must be impelled by incentives. That is, there must be a positive difference between the cost and the benefit of action, otherwise known as prime incentives. As applied to urban planning this means that for property owners/developers/land users to comply with planning regulation requirements, the benefit of compliance with these requirements should exceed the cost of meeting these requirements. This means that for there to be compliance with regulation, appreciation in property value resulting from meeting the requirements of regulation must be more than the cost of meeting the requirements of regulation.

However, in accordance with the postulates of human action, for there to be incentives to impel individuals to act, there is a need for individuals to establish a causal relevance between some elements in the universe and the ends to which action is directed. That is, means must be discovered. The implication of this postulation in the context of this book is that property owners/developers must first of all be aware of planning regulation, urban planning, and its relevance to their ends of property value appreciation or socio-economic development (Winter and May, 2001). In other words, the conception of planning regulation as means to the achievement of their ends.

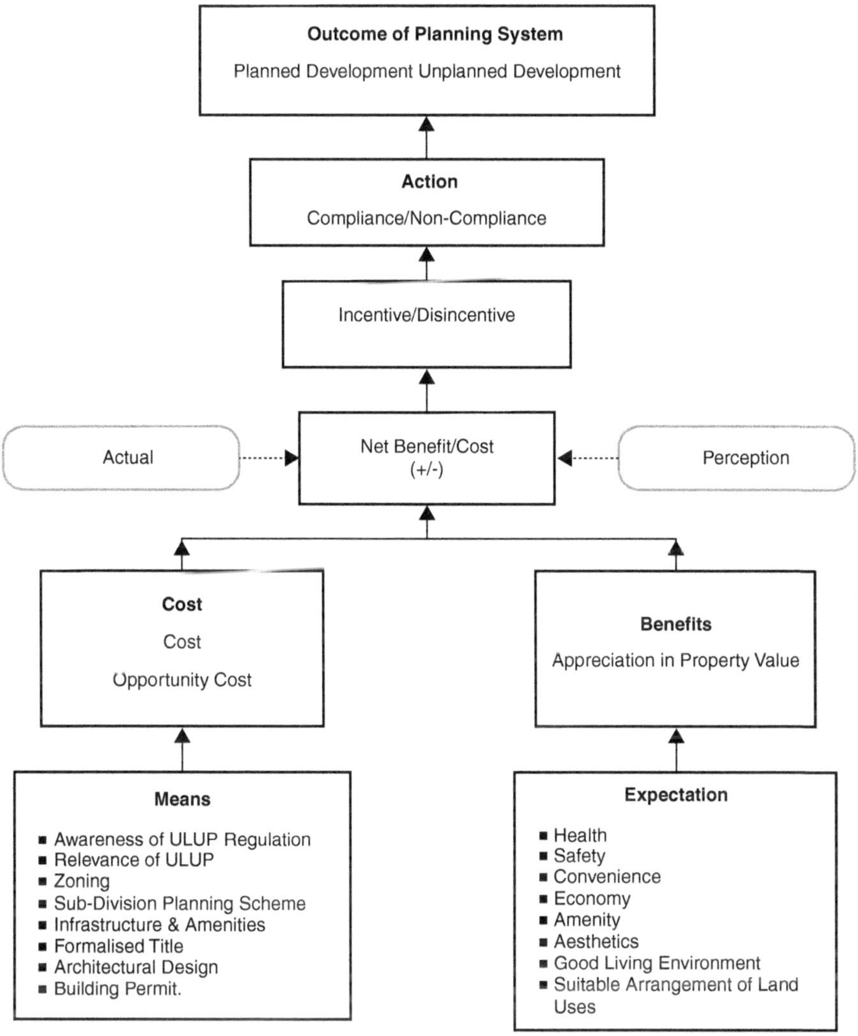

Figure 5.1 Conceptual framework for the role of incentives in urban planning.
Source: Derived from Mises (1949).

In addition, implications from insights of the human action theory reveal that, even where means are established but are not available, action cannot be instituted since it implies lack of incentives. This, as applied to urban planning, suggests that where property owners/developers perceive a positive outcome with respect to the cost and the benefit of compliance with planning regulation requirements yet do not have the means or the resources to meet them, there will be no incentives to comply with them (Winter and May, 2001).

Given these insights from human action theory as applied to urban planning, the logic of the analytical framework as depicted by Figure 5.1 suggests that where an urban planning regime provides incentives there will be compliance with the regime's requirements. This will therefore lead to planned developments devoid of unauthorised and slum settlements and with provision of infrastructure and amenities. Conversely, where a planning regime does not provide incentives, there will be a disregard for its requirements. Consequently, the outcome of such a planning regime will be lack of planned developments with unauthorised developments and lack of infrastructure and amenities.

It is also imperative to acknowledge that the insights from the human action theory as espoused herein are criticised as subjective because the costs and the benefits are relative to individuals who may perceive them differently (Lai, 2005; Egbu et al., 2008). However, objectivity itself may first be derived from subjectivity (Kim, 2009b). It is therefore based on that premise that this book proceeds. Besides, any effort to test the propositions of this framework will dwell on representatives of property owners/developers and not all of them to obtain data. This practice is found to reduce subjectiveness and biases (Lusk and Norwood, 2009). Additionally, extensive use of statistics to establish common trends in such efforts will reduce elements of subjectiveness.

5.5 Chapter summary

This chapter devised a conceptual framework for the role of incentives and its consequences in compliance with urban planning and developments regulations. The chapter noted that the success of urban planning is very much dependent on compliance with its regulations. However, given the ineffectiveness of justice and public administration systems and planning institutions in SSA, involuntary compliance, which is based on coercive force, is not likely to succeed in the region. Rather, voluntary compliance with planning regulations based on instinctive incentives is more likely to succeed. The Austrian economics theory of human action was used to conceptualise voluntary compliance with regulations based on instinctive incentives. The next chapter interrogates urban planning in SSA, identifying the causes of planning failure within the context of the human action theoretic framework.

6 Sub-Saharan Africa's urban planning systems

6.1 Introduction

Evidence shows that no planning system is perfect and that all planning systems are prone to failure. Chapter 3 of this book highlights how urban planning as has been practised over the years is ineffective in the face of twenty-first-century challenges, such as rapid urbanisation and re-urbanisation and the effects of climate change on urban infrastructure. More specifically, non-compliance with planning regulation in the UK (McKay, 2003; Lai et al., 2007), the sprawling of US cities (Schmidt and Buehler, 2007; Ihlanfeldt, 2009), and problems with the implementation of smart growth policies in Canada (Filion and McSppurren, 2007) are some of the failings of planning systems across the world. However, this chapter discusses planning systems and their specific weaknesses in SSA. The chapter commences with a discussion of the nature of SSA planning regimes, their state, and their determinants/causes, situating it within the context of the human action theoretic framework and the current efforts being made by re-engineering planning regimes in the region to produce optimum outcomes.

6.2 Nature of SSA planning systems

Evidence of spatial developments in Africa shows that some form of settlement planning existed in parts of SSA prior to Western Europe's colonisation of Africa at the turn of the nineteenth century. Some parts of SSA, particularly West Africa, had a rich urban tradition prior to colonialism (Mabogunje, 1968, 1990; Wekwete, 1995; Konadu-Agyemang, 1998; Njoh, 2004; Rakodi, 2006a). Urban centres such as Timbuktu in Mali and Zanzibar in Tanzania were already major trading centres with their own spatial configuration (Mabogunje, 1990; Wekwete, 1995; Njoh, 2004). For example, findings from archaeological and other in-depth studies suggest that settlement planning among the Akans, the largest tribe in Ghana, dates to about 3,500 years ago or more (Farrar, 1996).

Although rudimentary at this early stage, planning was implemented by traditional leaders in concert with their people and based on their customs with regard to socio-economic development. Planning in Ghana during this period was, for example, used by traditional leaders as a land management tool to achieve overall socio-economic development (Barbot, 1732; Domfeh, 2001). Barbot (1732) notes that coastal Akan settlements during this period were crooked and irregular, and ended up as wide-open spaces, which were used as markets and meeting grounds for deliberation on the well-being of the settlements. Furthermore, developments were clustered and occupied by related lineages with small lanes and streets in between them. These spatial arrangements were strictly followed by members of these settlements. The rationale was to reduce cost in terms of travel time to pursue economic and related activities at the centre and defend communities against external aggression (Barbot, 1732; Farrar, 1996).

The spatial arrangements in pre-colonial Yuroba settlements in Nigeria (Arimah and Adeagbo, 2000), which were akin to those of the Akan Bonos and Asantes in Ghana (Wilks, 1959; Effah-Gyamfi, 1975), conformed to the same goals as the coastal Akan settlements. These Yuroba, Bono, and Asante settlements, strictly adhering to norms, situated the palaces of their traditional leaders at the centre of their settlements with a vast open space in front for markets and durbars. Besides, one main road, which led to the palaces of the traditional leaders at the centre, divided these settlements into two parts. Contributing to the subject, Keeton and Nijhuis (2019) further provide a litany of examples of planned settlements in Africa prior to colonisation. The city of El-Lahun in Egypt otherwise referred to as Kahun or Ro-hent, which is sometimes regarded as the oldest master planned urban settlement currently known in Africa, is one of them. According to the authors, the gridded street patterns of the city suggest authoritative planning rather than spontaneous occurrence. Another example of a medieval planned African city is Songo Mnara in Tanzania, a fifteenth-century Swahili stone town, which had a highly developed social welfare systems, craftsmanship, and political organisations. The authors also cite pre-colonial Senegalese cities, such as Diakhao (sixteenth century), Kahone (mid-sixteenth century), and Maka, (eighteenth century), which were clearly organised along orthogonal grids, as well as the eleventh-century Edo Benin City in Edo State, Nigeria, which is believed to have been designed, down to its underground drainage, based on fractals and had a centralised and sophisticated bureaucracy, and Harlaa in Ethiopia, which was designed with geometric precision and programmatic spatial divisions that suggest coordinated planning during that period. From the standpoint of SSA evolutionary land tenure thesis (Atwood, 1990; Platteau, 1992; Yngstrom, 2002; Hammond, 2006), since planning is a feature of land markets, it is conceivable that these indigenous planning practices would have evolved over time. Nonetheless, with the advent of colonialism, indigenous planning arrangements were truncated.

6.2.1 Colonial planning systems

Formal urban planning in SSA was instituted by Western European colonialists particularly the British, French, Portuguese, Germans, and Belgians (UN-Habitat, 2009; Watson, 2009a, 2009b; Baffour Awuah et al., 2011b, Silva, 2015; Keeton and Nijhuis, 2019). Planning had emerged in Western Europe and North America in response to adverse effects of industrialisation and urbanisation, imperfections of the urban property market. This was the epoch when Western Europe had colonised Africa (Rakodi, 2001). Therefore, planning arrangements that existed in Western Europe were transplanted to Africa (Mabogunje, 1990; Home, 1990; Njoh, 1997, 2004, 2009; Rakodi, 2001; Musandu-Nyamayaro, 2008; UN-Habitat, 2009).

Planning activities ranged from the passage of minor legislation on health, the preparation of development schemes, site clearance, and the building of infrastructure to the passage of major legislation in the immediate period before and after the Second World War in 1945. In the British colonies, activities such as road improvements, slum clearance, and housing for areas where colonial officials ruled directly were undertaken, while the preparation of layouts and building of administrative headquarters, railway, and mining towns were executed in the areas they governed indirectly. Garden cities were also constructed for white settlers, in addition to the development and conservation of garden suburbs and parks for pre-colonial urban societies and company towns (Home, 1990). Njoh (2004) also catalogues 16 of such planning projects at the turn of the nineteenth century in the French part of SSA. These include the 1890 urban development plans for the capital colony of Dahomey (now Republic of Benin) and the city of Doula in Cameroun; the 1880 design and construction of a military settlement at Saint Louis in Senegal for the French military personnel stationed at the colony; and the first urban development plan for Conakry, capital of Guinea in 1895.

The major planning legislation that was passed, particularly in the British-controlled areas, included Kenya's 1936 Town Planning Ordinance, Nigeria's 1946 Town Planning Ordinance, Malawi's 1948 Town Planning Act, and Tanzania's 1956 Town Planning Ordinance. These planning laws prescribed a welfare model rational comprehensive approach to planning with the use of master plans underpinned by the land use segregation concept (Njoh, 2009; UN-Habitat, 1999, 2009; Bolay, 2015; Silva, 2015; Keeton and Nijhuis, 2019; Mutuku et al., 2019), with its cardinal principles of unifunctional land use, discreet zoning, regulations, and consensus signifying that government decisions were in the interest of the larger society (Baffour Awuah et al., 2010). Colonial authorities based on these planning activities promoted spatial segregation. This meant the physical separation of European settlements where all the infrastructure and amenities were provided and high health standards and building regulations were enforced from those of Africans by 'cordon sanitaire of open spaces with parks and race-courses' (Mabogunje, 1990; Larbi, 1996; Njoh, 2004, 2009; Home, 2012; Bolay; 2015; Silva, 2015; Keeton and Nijhuis, 2019; Mutuku et al., 2019). Examples of this were the creation of threefold urban centre divisions of the native city, the non-European Township, and the European Reservation in Nigeria by the Township Ordinance of 1917, and the allocation of separate zones for railway employees, European and Asian traders, and African labourers in Kenya (Mabogunje, 1990).

Although few areas occupied by the native population were serviced with infrastructure and amenities, such as electricity and roads, these services were to facilitate the activities of colonial government officials like sanitary inspectors, tax collectors, and the police and military personnel (Njoh, 2009). Thus, the provision of infrastructure and amenities was intended to meet the colonialists' health, political, and economic ends via good sanitation, revenue mobilisation, and the maintenance of law and order. Njoh (2009) notes further that, to maintain a full grip on their colonies and assuage nationalistic sentiments, colonialists sited their homes and administrative set-ups on hilly areas to monitor and control the colonised people. Again, planning policies were geared towards economic gains that could be achieved using Africa's cheap labour and restricting the movement of indigene Africans from rural areas to urban areas as an additional way of controlling them (Mabogunje, 1990; Satterthwaite, 1996; Rakodi, 1998; Njoh, 2004, 2009). South Africa and Zambia are some of the examples of colonies where such restrictions were placed on rural-urban migration (Rakodi, 1990; Mwimba, 2002; Home, 2012).

In addition to the above, colonial planning and related policies supplanted indigenous African land tenure systems with systems that were prevalent in Western Europe. The new land tenure systems permitted large-scale commodification of land in Africa and in some cases the vesting of entire ownership in colonial governments (Amin, 1972; Rodney, 1972; Wekwete, 1995; Okoth-Ogendo, 2000; Njoh, 2004, 2009; Home, 2012). A notable feature of the new tenure regime was ensuring control over all land transactions by the colonial governments and making them owners of so-called "unoccupied and ownerless lands" to advance the economic and political ends of the colonialists (Hammond, 2006; Hammond et al., 2006; Njoh, 2009, Home, 2012). For example, on the one hand colonial governments made free grants or introduced additional policies that favoured the few educated indigenes and the politically active group to control them. On the other hand, to ensure the achievement of economic ends, European colonialists promoted large-scale commercial plantations and mining activities in Africa with their home companies as the beneficiaries. This was ensured through colonial governments' generous offer of land either free of charge or at giveaway prices to such companies (Amin, 1972; Rodney, 1972; Hammond et al., 2006; Njoh, 2009).

6.2.2 Post-colonial planning systems

Excepting the Republic of South Africa, which adopted an integrated planning system in 1994 (Musandu-Nyamayaro, 2008; Watson, 2009a), and a few other countries, the literature shows that SSA in general is clinging to colonial planning policies (Rakodi, 2001, 2006a; Watson, 2009a). At independence, mostly in the 1960s, leaders of newly emergent African states were enthusiastic about embarking on rapid socio-economic development. They therefore sought to overhaul colonial structures, including land tenure and development policies (Rakodi, 2006a; Hammond and Antwi, 2010). However, the attempt to review colonial land and planning policies was short-lived (Okoth-Ogendo, 2000; Larbi et al., 2004). Tanzania, for example, made the Arusha Declaration in 1967. This culminated in African Socialism (Ujamaa) as its new political philosophy. As part of that new philosophy, all lands were nationalised and planning was supposed to have been people-oriented, but this could not be sustained (Wekwete, 1995).

The major attempt at planning reforms perhaps occurred towards the latter part of the 1970s. This was when the World Bank linked lending agreements to a review of planning regulatory frameworks (Payne and Majale, 2004; Musandu-Nyamayaro, 2008). That aside, there have been piecemeal attempts to revise planning practice in countries in the region. Governments of countries like Zimbabwe, Zambia, Botswana, Tanzania, Kenya, and Nigeria made attempts to reform their planning regimes with the intention of promulgating flexible planning laws and development standards to suit the needs of the poor and low-income communities. The remainder was intended to relax development control and provide serviced plots of land, funds, and materials for the construction of buildings. Eventually, these arrangements turned out to be unsustainable and were abandoned due to cost implications (UN-Habitat, 1999). What is intriguing is the survival of these planning regimes in SSA, despite numerous criticisms about them being deleterious in nature (Payne and Majale, 2004; Kironde, 2006; Bolay, 2015; Silva, 2015; Keeton and Nijhuis, 2019; Mutuku et al., 2019). Planning regimes in SSA are therefore characterised by a hierarchy of statutory plans and sets of development control regulations which are linked to local government administrative laws and are driven by government and its officials to the exclusion of the larger populace (Wekwete, 1995; Rakodi, 2006c). Having made this exposition, it is now appropriate to look at the case study country.

6.2.2.1 Formal urban planning in Ghana

The institutionalisation of urban planning in Ghana, as in its counterparts in SSA, was undertaken by Western European colonialists, particularly the British (see Afrane, 1993; Gambrah, 1994; Konadu-Agyemang, 1998). Formal planning in Ghana began with the promulgation of the Towns

Ordinance in 1892 (Gambrah, 1994; Baffour Awuah et al., 2011b). Several urban planning schemes were prepared, and regulations on the creation of good sanitary conditions, the prevention of diseases, minimum plot sizes, and alignment of streets, among other things, were passed in the 1900s and 1920s (Gambrah, 1994; Konadu-Agyemang, 1998). The Town Planning Ordinance (1925), for example, was passed for the creation of health boards to promote healthy environments. Some planning schemes were also prepared and implemented in Accra and Kumasi, the capital and second-largest city, respectively, in 1920 and 1927, during Sir Governor Gordon Guggisberg's era (Baffour Awuah et al., 2011b). Similarly, various infrastructure and amenities were constructed (Konadu-Agyemang, 1998). However, it was not until 1945 that the government considered planning a comprehensive activity for the first time (Afrane, 1993; Larbi, 1996; Konadu-Agyemang, 1998; Acquaah-Harrison, 2003; Baffour Awuah et al., 2010, 2011b).

This followed the promulgation of Ordinance No. 13 of 1945, which was based on the British Town and Country Planning Act (1932) (Amissah, 1979; Konadu-Agyemang, 1998; Owusu, 2008; Baffour Awuah et al., 2011b). Ordinance No. 13, which provided for the creation of town and country planning boards with responsibility, inter alia, for ensuring orderly and progressive development of land, was later replaced by Cap 84 in 1954. However, earlier in 1944 the Town and Country Planning Department (TCPD) was set up to prepare draft planning schemes and reports. The Department became a secretariat of the planning board even though this was not expressly provided for by the Ordinance (see Domfeh, 2001; Baffour Awuah et al., 2011b). As in other SSA countries, the urban planning legislation prescribed a rational comprehensive approach to planning and the use of master plans. Consequently, underlying the country's planning regime was the land use segregation concept with its cardinal principles of unfunctional land use, discreet zoning, regulations, and consensus, signifying that government decisions are in the interest of the larger society (Afrane, 1993; Baffour Awuah et al., 2010, 2011b).

Based on these planning activities, British colonialists pursued their comparatively highly valued health, political, and economic ends. For example, as they did elsewhere in SSA, British colonial authorities undertook spatial segregation through zoning to achieve their ends. Consequently, whilst the colonial officials were living in big bungalows in large luxurious compounds in prime areas like the European, Airport, and Cantonment residential areas in Accra, their Ghanaian compatriots lived in deplorable areas like Chorkor and James Town (Larbi, 1996; Konadu-Agyemang, 1998). After independence in 1957, attempts were made to re-orient planning in Ghana under its first president, Dr Kwame Nkrumah. Cap 84 was, for example, revised in 1958 following the promulgation of the Town and Country Planning Act (1958) (Act No. 30) (see Kotey et al., 2004). This replaced the planning boards with the minister responsible for town and country planning (Baffour Awuah et al., 2011b; see further Kotey et al., 2004). The TCPD also became a secretariat of the minister responsible for town and country planning whilst the planning board was completely abolished with the passage of the Town and Country Planning (Amendment) Act (1960) (Act No. 33). These attempts at re-orienting planning in the country were short-lived (Larbi, 1996; Acquaah-Harrison, 2003).

During the period between 1985 and 1990, the country witnessed some planning reforms under the World Bank and the International Monetary Fund Economic Recovery Programme, which was undertaken through three different projects: Urban I, II, and III (Larbi, 1996). This, for example, resulted in the preparation of the 1991 structure (strategic) plan of Accra, which was intended to determine the land development process and growth direction of the city (Larbi, 1996). Furthermore, in 1993 after a protracted period of total central government control, planning was decentralised with the promulgation of a host of legislation, including the Local Government Act (1993) (Act 462), the National Development Planning Commission (NDPC) Act (1994) (479), and the National Development Planning (Systems) (1994) (Act 480). This arrangement, in collaboration with the country's Civil Service Law, Provisional National Defence Council Law (PNDCL 327), also decentralised TCPD. This made former regional and districts outfits of the department part of the regional and district co-ordinating councils and the metropolitan/municipal/district assemblies part of planning authorities (Baffour Awuah et al., 2011b; see further GoG, 1996b; Braimah et al., 2016).

Despite the foregoing, the core colonial urban planning regulatory framework has remained intact (see Grant and Yankson, 2003; Kotey et al., 2004; Owusu, 2008; Oduro, 2010; Cobbinah et al., 2015). The new planning arrangement, as prescribed by Act 462, did not repeal Cap 84. Besides, Act 462, which made local governments planning authorities, has no Legislative Instrument (LI) to dictate its practical workings. As such, Cap 84 and Act 462 operated concurrently and were supported by the National Building Regulations 1996 (LI 1630) (see Domfeh, 2001; Nkum and Associates, 2001; GoG, 1996a, 2009; Baffour Awuah et al., 2011b). Again, studies such as Larbi (1994), Konadu-Agyemang (1998), and Hammond (2006) report that colonial land and planning policies have survived until today because of their provision of incentives for the few elites to control land and its resources.

The urban planning regime in Ghana therefore stipulates that no development should be undertaken in a community/area declared a statutory planning area by the government unless that community or area is zoned and covered by an approved sub-division planning scheme. It is imperative to state that all urban centres in the country have been declared statutory planning areas. That said, the planning regime, as applied to the residential neighbourhood development within a statutory planning area, operates through several processes. First, the community of which the residential neighbourhood is a constituent should be zoned and the residential neighbourhood earmarked as such. The zoning is undertaken by planning authorities – the metropolitan/municipal/district assemblies in their medium-term development plans. Second, a sub-division planning scheme must be prepared to cover the neighbourhood. This sub-division planning scheme must receive the prior approval of the relevant planning authority. Third, prospective developers must acquire a building/development permit prior to the commencement of their developments. Development under the planning regime is defined to include infrastructural works. However, prospective developers require pre-permit items, such as architectural designs; a formalised title; and, in some cases, environmental and traffic impact assessment reports.

Fourth, upon commencement of a development, planning authorities are supposed to check and approve every stage of the construction of the proposed development. They are also supposed to issue a certificate of occupancy prior to occupation of newly constructed buildings. The rationale behind all these requirements is to ensure that building projects are properly screened to meet the minimum acceptable standards (see Afrane, 1993; Baffour Awuah et al., 2011c). Although not expressly stated as a binding requirement, the country's planning regime is also intended to ensure the provision of infrastructure and amenities prior to the commencement of actual residential building developments. Consequently, as in the case of other SSA planning regimes, Ghana's planning model prescribes a plan, service, develop, and occupy principle.

It needs to be pointed out that, through the planning authorities, the government is, under normal circumstances, supposed to prepare and approve sub-division planning schemes, provide infrastructure and certain social amenities, and bear their cost. Private residential building developers under this arrangement are only supposed to obtain building permits to construct their buildings. They also need to receive approval from planning authorities to continue with development at every stage of construction and obtain a certificate of occupancy upon completion. The cost of these activities, including the requirements for building permits – such as architectural designs and the formalised title – are borne by private developers. However, for some time the government was unable to adequately prepare planning schemes and provide infrastructure. Therefore, over years, particularly since the latter part of the 1980s, there have been arrangements where private landowners engage their own consultants to prepare planning schemes (see Konadu-Agyemang, 1998; Arku, 2006; Watson, 2014; Keeton and Nijhuis, 2019; Keeton and Provoost, 2019). These planning schemes are then sent to the planning authorities for the requisite approval. The costs for the preparation and approval of the planning schemes are paid by landowners. The same arrangement pertains to infrastructure and certain social amenities like community parks. Indeed, this is the current situation in practice, and it is very common with private real estate development companies whose influence on the residential housing market has been surging since the liberalisation of the country's economy in the 1980s. Besides, the arrangement for inspecting developments at every stage of construction and the issuance of the certificate of occupancy hardly take place. What is noteworthy is that the preparation and approval of planning schemes, as well as the costs of infrastructure and social amenities, are ultimately transferred onto the individual residential building developer or purchaser. The developments with regard to the above arrangements are prevalent across African cities and towns, and are often referred to as new town developments and gated communities, among other things (Watson, 2014; Murray, 2017; Keeton and Provoost, 2019; see further Section 6.3). In an extensive analysis, Keeton and Nijhuis (2019) concluded that these new urban forms are steeped in twentieth-century planning models, ranging from functionalist Chinese grids to American gated communities. Notwithstanding the preceding discussions, there are ongoing efforts to reform the country's planning regime (see Section 6.4).

6.3 The state of SSA planning systems

Despite the environmental, economic, and social significance of urban planning, as discussed in Chapter 3, planning systems in SSA are inadequate, weak, and ineffective (UN-Habitat, 1999, 2009, 2014; Payne and Majale, 2004; Watson, 2009a). The planning systems are said to have proven incapable of addressing the urban development needs of the region. The inadequacy, weakness, and ineffectiveness of the planning systems in SSA are manifested in the deformities of the region's cities and urban areas, and several linked urban environmental ills. First, the region's cities are typically crowded especially within the central areas with pockets of small and fragmented neighbourhoods, which lack reliable transportation and adequate job opportunities (UN-Habitat, 2014; Lall et al., 2017). This means that the cities are disconnected. Indeed, according to Lall et al. (2017), African cities are 20% more fragmented than their counterparts in Asia and Latin America, and this, in turn, prevents firms from reaping scale and agglomeration benefits. Another challenge associated with African cities, as noted by Lall et al. (2017), is the high costs they impose on households and firms. These are in the form of high nominal wages and transaction costs for doing business in these cities, which serve as disincentives for investors and workers' high food, transportation, and labour costs. SSA cities and urban areas also face many environmental challenges. These include urban pollution and the effects of extreme climate, such as high temperatures and flooding, which the present urban authorities simply do not have the capacity to deal with. The cities are challenged by many natural and man-made hazards such as surface and coastal flooding, drought, extreme temperatures, vector-borne diseases, as well as seismic hazards from local fault lines, air or water pollution, depletion of natural resources, and related health impacts including respiratory illness and waterborne pathogens like cholera (ARUP and Cities Alliance, 2016).

Admittedly, there are a few areas in the region, particularly the prime areas, which are well laid out and where planning requirements are largely adhered to. These areas are mostly occupied by the rich and the elite. But even these areas are being blighted by their co-location with shanty settlements and rapid illegal conversions of land use (Friedmann, 2005). An example of co-located first-class residential areas with shanty settlements is shown in Figure 1.2. Indeed, the growing body of literature demonstrates that new forms of urban development can be categorised into two groups, namely, unregulated urban growth, which is reflected in informal settlements, and planned new towns (Watson, 2014, 2016; Abubakar and Doan, 2017; Murray 2017), but both are not sustainable (Keeton and Provoost, 2019). Various names are used to describe these new towns, or they come in several forms. These include gated communities, satellite cities, and new cities (Watson, 2016). Keeton and Provoost (2019) define these developments as planned urban developments for more than 30,000 residents with mixed programmes on greenfield sites that are developed as a single entity with some degree of political autonomy and contend that most of the developments target the higher-income groups. They also provide several amenities, such as reliable water and electricity, and access to private 24-hour security and horse racing tracks, and most of them are not designed to transform in response to either systemic shocks or incremental socio--ecological changes but are planned as finite products, with little attention to either existing environmental conditions or future threats (Keeton and Provoost, 2019). As stated previously, the authors further state that the developments are inspired by twentieth-century planning models particularly functionalist Chinese grids and American gated communities, and that in the last three decades there has been an increase in the development of these satellite cities partly due to an increase in consumerism, urbanisation, and the growing middle class, resulting in global real estate investments (Watson, 2016; Baffour Awuah and Gyamfi-Yeboah, 2017). Examples of these new town developments or visions are the proposed Hope City in Ghana, the satellite cities surrounding Nairobi, Kenya, and the new urban vision for Kigali, Rwanda (Watson, 2016), Kilamba City in Angola, and Tatu City in Kenya (Keeton and Provoost, 2019).

Commenting on these developments in Nigeria, Lamond et al. (2015) noted that the recent ones are massive in scale and encompass housing, commercial, and transport infrastructure development, and climate change adaptation programmes. The authors further observed that some of the developments are undertaken through partnership with government using joint venture agreement schemes and identified specific developments and initiatives in cities such as Abuja, Calabar, Ibadan, and Lagos. These include the proposed Centenary City Project in Abuja, the Summit Hills

Project in Calabar, the Legacy Estate and Palms Ibadan in Ibadan, and the Lagos Urban Transport Project (LUTP). Although these projects are resulting in or expected to result in huge urban transformation by providing infrastructure, accommodation, and job opportunities, and ensuring effective and efficient functioning of the cities to promote socio-economic development they are not fully responsive to the diversity of needs across an urban area, city, or region (Gandy, 2005; Sawyer, 2014; Lamond et al., 2015). Keeton and Nijhuis (2019), in their study on contemporary African new town developments, also concluded that the developments fail to effectively address the social, ecological, and spatial challenges of individuals, and the contemporary African urban environments. In particular, the study noted that such developments do not have the potential to provide an opportunity for engaging public spaces and necessary facilities to support daily life. Further, they fail to envisage large communities that can develop at their borders, and the intimate social and economic bonds between these two sets of areas. Similar sentiments have also been expressed by studies such as Silva (2015).

The other urban form, which also manifests the planning challenge in SSA, is the unregulated urban growth associated with informal communities where developments do not boast of proper planning and basic infrastructure and services, such as tarred roads, electricity, and pipe-borne water. Although available evidence shows that there is some degree of compliance with issues pertaining to planning and urban development regulations within new town developments in SSA, the urban form under reference connects directly with one of the weakest links of SSA planning systems, which is low compliance with their regulations or requirements. Between half and three-quarters of all new housing in SSA cities is constructed on land that has been supplied through processes that do not adhere to formal legal requirements regarding sub-division, transfer, and development control (Rakodi, 2006b). This implies that there are rising levels of informal developments with poor housing environment (UN-Habitat, 2014; Lall et al., 2017). In fact, evidence suggests that 62.2% of the urban population in SSA live in unauthorised and slum developments with no or less adequate infrastructure and services. This compares against 24% in Western Asia, 27% in Latin America and the Caribbean, 27.5% in South-East Asia, 35.5% in East Asia, and 42.9% in South Asia (UN-Habitat, 2008). Lall et al. (2017) further note that 28% of urban residents in Dar es salaam, Tanzania, live at least three to a room and that the percentage is even higher (50%) in cities like Abidjan, Cote D'Ivoire. Thus, apart from being crowded at central areas they lack adequate infrastructure and services, and this has been compounded by rising levels of urbanisation, signifying that investment in infrastructure, industrial, and commercial structures has not kept pace with the levels of urbanisation. SSA, for example, has the world's least developed infrastructure (Calderon and Serven, 2008; World Bank, 2011). It is even estimated that only 30% of roads in Africa are paved, and a mere 20% of the continent's population have access to electricity or a modern form of energy, compared to 50% in South Asia and 80% in Latin America (Africa Rising 21st Century, 2010). Consequently, the SSA formal planning model of 'plan, service, develop and occupy' has now turned into 'develop, occupy, service and plan'.

6.3.1 Determinants of low compliance with regulations/ planning failure

The preceding discussions have established a low level of compliance with planning regulations in SSA as well as the manifestation of planning failure in the region. This discussion focusses on determinants of this low compliance with planning regulations/planning failure from the viewpoint of regulated entities and property owners/developers/land users, given that the weakness of public institutions responsible for enforcement of regulations in the region is already noted.

Insights from human action theory hold that, for property owners to comply with planning regulations, there should be incentives, that is, a positive difference between the benefits and costs of compliance with regulations to impel them to do so. Prior to that they must be aware of regulations and establish the relevance of regulations to the achievement of their ends. Nonetheless, it is argued that, although planning regimes in SSA provide some window of opportunity for the public to participate in the planning process, in reality urban residents are not involved and therefore are oblivious of regulations (Afrane, 1993; UN-Habitat, 1999, 2009; Nkum and Associates, 2001; Payne and Majale, 2004; Kironde, 2006; Aribigbola, 2007). Even if they were involved in the process, planning regulations are numerous and so complicated that planning officials themselves are sometimes not aware of regulations and their demands (Afrane, 1993; Payne and Majale, 2004; UN-Habitat, 2009). Kironde (2006) established that 98% of developments under the Kinyerezi in Dar es Salaam, Tanzania, were not covered by requisite building permits, a situation which is attributed to lack of awareness. Mensah (2010) also established high levels of unawareness of legal building permit and other land development requirements among unauthorised developers in Aboabo, Kumasi, Ghana. Given that property owners are not aware of planning regulations, compliance with regulations is expected to be low, based on the dictates of human action theory (Habitat, 1999, 2009; Payne and Majale, 2004; Aribigbola, 2007). However, findings from studies such as Arimah and Adeagbo (2000) also show that, despite the high level of awareness of planning regulations – 56%, 73%, and 80% among low-, middle-, and high-income groups, respectively, in the city of Ibadan, Nigeria – compliance with regulation is still low. A study by Boamah et al. (2012) in Wa Municipality in Northern Ghana found that, despite a high level of awareness (76% among respondents) of the legal building permit requirement, compliance with the requirement is low. This therefore suggests continuous enquiry into the issue of awareness of regulations and their compliance.

It is suggested that planning regulation and urban planning are not perceived by most people in SSA as a relevant tool for socio-economic development, given the exploitative colonial antecedents in the region (Rakodi, 2001, Chapter 7). Furthermore, post-colonial African governments have not revised the colonial planning apparatus due to its provision of incentives for the elite and the rich in society to control land resources (Chapter 7). Consequently, planning is seen by most people in the region as a tool for suppression and exploitation of their resources by a few people in society (Wekwete, 1995; Konadu-Agyemang, 1998; Hammond and Antwi, 2010, Chapter 7). From a human action standpoint, this signifies lack of conception of planning as a means by most urban dwellers to promote their socio-economic needs, and thus they are not expected to comply with planning regulation.

Additionally, it is claimed that planning regimes in SSA are largely unbeneficial to most urban dwellers in the region. Although some studies (Asabere, 1981; Arimah, 1992; Anim-Odame, 2008) on urban development processes in SSA demonstrate that planning factors such as government zoning increase property values, planning has not achieved its aim in the region. It is argued that planning in the region is unable to deliver developable lands to most urban populations (Rakodi, 2006b, Egbu, 2007; UN-Habitat, 2014; ARUP and Cities Alliance, 2016). They do not consider development imperatives, such as the rising informal sector, in the region, which provides a means of livelihood for most urban residents (Brown, 2012). For example, while most urban dwellers particularly those in the low-income communities would want to put their homes to multiple uses to earn income, these regimes by their strict land use segregation concept serve as an obstacle to their development needs (Afrane, 1993; Tudzi, 1996; Payne and Majale, 2004). Brown (2012, p. 84) makes the point that municipal governments around the globe do not see the local development potential of informal enterprises. As such, the policy approach towards them has often varied from benign neglect to frequent harassment, fines, and evictions, and noted reports of such approaches in 17 SSA countries, including Benin, Cote D'Ivoire, Ghana, Ethiopia, Tanzania, Zambia, and Malawi.

Apart from these planning regimes' irresponsiveness to the socio-economic development needs of most urban dwellers, their requirements (regulations) also continue to be restrictive. These requirements, as noted earlier, include zoning, approved sub-division plans, infrastructure and planning/building permits as well as pre-permit application items, like a formalised title and architectural design. That aside, the compliance costs of the requirements in terms of financial resources for official and unofficial fees for documentation, time lag, commuting cost, and professional fees, among other things, are enormous. On average it takes over one year for planning permission to be granted in most countries in SSA. A study by Hammond and Antwi (2010) also established that the social cost of land title regulative policies on a 0.23-acre residential plot of land in Ghana is US$5,320.00. What is even more intriguing is that indirect costs, such as unofficial fees paid to public agencies to expedite the action on documentation and the cost of time lag, constituted the bulk, that is, 90%, of this cost. For infrastructure, the situation is even worse. It is estimated that the cost of infrastructure services in SSA is at least twice that in South Asia (Africa Rising 21st Century, 2010). It can therefore be surmised that the cost of compliance with planning regulations in SSA is greater than the benefits and from the standpoint of human action this provides a recipe for non-compliance with these regulations.

Finally, the implications of human action suggest that where there are no means or resources there will be a lack of incentives and to that extent non-compliance with planning regulations by property owners. Therefore, given the rising levels of urban poverty in SSA and the restrictive nature of SSA planning requirements, which a majority of urban dwellers do not have, it stands to reason that compliance with regulation will be low. It is in this vein that Wekwete (1995) writing on planning laws in Southern and Eastern Africa concluded that development control is appreciated by every community, but not when it renders people homeless.

6.4 Efforts to improve SSA planning systems

The role of land policy and development, and resource access and management in economic development has attracted the attention of national governments and international development agencies in the last two decades or more (Larbi et al., 2004; Borras and Franco, 2008). The international community in concert with national governments, especially those in the developing world, has introduced several initiatives to address these development imperatives. These include the launch of the Habitat Agenda at Turkey in 1996 (UNCHS, 1996); the formulation of Agenda 21 at the UN Earth Conference in Rio de Janeiro, Brazil, in 1992; and the establishment of Cities Alliance by the UN-Habitat and the World Bank in 1999, and the UN's millennium development goals and its 'successor-in-title' the sustainable development goals, launched in 2015. In general, these initiatives were/are to ensure adequate shelter for all and promote sustainable urban development (Payne and Majale, 2004; UN-Habitat, 2009).

Following the above interventions there have been several urban planning and development initiatives across the developing world such as the passage of the new national urban policies with the help of the UN-Habitat (UN-Habitat, 2013). For example, Nigeria has embarked on several planning and urban development initiatives. These include: (1) the Urbanisation and Infrastructure Research and Evaluation Programmes; (2) the Evaluation of Nigerian Infrastructure Facility I and II Programmes; (3) the

Growth and Employment in States Project, particularly the third phase that focussed on land administration – Systematic Land Titling and Registration Project; (4) the formulation of Vision: 2020, which is a federal government policy to transform and recommend strategies to develop smart and functional cities for rapid economic growth, and the promotion of good governance in the country's planning system; (5) the promulgation of a National Urban Development Policy in 2012; and (6) the adoption of the Sustainable Cities Programme by the Ibadan, Enugu, and Kaduna states.

Ghana also passed its national urban policy in 2012 (GoG, 2012). Earlier in 1999, the country developed its national land policy and launched a land tenure reform in 2003 under a national land administration project (LAP) (Baffour Awuah and Hammond, 2014). As part of this project a sub-project – land use management and planning, which is to reform urban planning in the country – commenced in 2007. The aim of the project is to develop a coherent, streamlined, and sustainable land use planning and management system, which is decentralised and based on consultative and participatory approaches to effectively manage human settlement developments (GoG, 2009). The objectives include developing and testing models and processes of land use planning and development controls in partnership and with the active participation of communities and customary land owners; developing and drafting a coherent and modernised legal framework for town and country planning, including model guidelines and regulations; and developing information/public awareness campaign strategies and materials to support the implementation of the reformed planning system. The main policy study to underpin the planning reform was completed in 2009. Planning model guidelines and planning standard and development guidelines have also been developed, and a new spatial planning act the 'Land Use and Spatial Planning Act, 2016 (No. 925 of 2016)' was passed in 2016. Fundamentally, as its preamble states, among other things, Act 925 seeks to revise and consolidate existing laws on land use and spatial planning towards provision for sustainable development of land and human settlements through a decentralised planning system. The act therefore promotes the development of spatial development frameworks and the establishment of a hierarchy of plans like the national, regional, and district spatial development of plans as well as a hierarchy of bodies, such as regional and district spatial planning committees. Another significant feature of the act is the establishment of the Land Use and Spatial Planning Authority, which is to oversee and/or assist individuals and institutions involved in spatial plan preparation, implementation, and development of land resources.

A careful examination of these ongoing initiatives shows that they are partly influenced by new planning models such as the communication and the just city planning models and they seek to achieve sustainable urban development and governance, as well as promote equity in urban development and management. However, given the socio-economic conditions in SSA, inter-tribal and land ownership conflicts, the rise in urban poverty, weak civil societies, imbalanced power relations, and rapid urbanisation, among other things, it is debatable whether these prospective planning arrangements alone will improve planning practice in the region (Watson, 2002; Harrison, 2006). Home (2012, p. 42), writing on a related subject, noted, among other things, that the poor in SSA are generally pre-occupied with their day-to-day existence, rather than engaged in time-consuming solidarity activities (*such as deliberative planning process*), while outside elites may manipulate the process to their own advantage. Even in the developed world, such as the UK, the planning system, which, inter alia, hinges on some of these collaborative planning ideals is said to require cultural change on the part of stakeholders to materialise (Shaw and Lord, 2007). Yet not much has been achieved since its implementation (Shaw and Lord, 2009). Keeton and Nijhuis (2019) call for the implementation of adaptive and inclusive planning strategies in Africa. The authors argue that adaptive planning strategies are systematic in operation and cater to both urban form and processes as well as utilise a multi-scalar approach, which considers national development, regional networks and nodes, and local including neighbourhood-level existing qualities. Furthermore, the planning approach is said to allow planners to engage social and environmental realities through more inclusive design and planning processes, leaving room for adaptation of generic principles to the unique characteristics of individual places (Keeton and Nijhuis, 2019). It is, however, unclear how the adaptive and inclusive planning approach addresses the core defects of the collaborative planning model as applied to SSA and discussed above.

Despite the criticisms of SSA urban planning systems and the ongoing planning reforms, little is known of the extent and magnitude of its economic impact on individuals, households, and constituent economies, which signifies that no realistic solution can be proposed. Relevant studies have mainly been descriptive or have focussed on single or few aspects of the urban development processes in the region. The human settlements and land use policy study undertaken as part of the planning reform in Ghana, for example, observed that the cost of compliance with planning regulations is high and is one of the reasons for the high non-compliance rate with regulations (GoG, 2009). However, the study could not outline the extent and magnitude of this cost to inform policy on how much the cost should be reduced. Indeed, there is a dearth of in-depth studies that apply insights from economics to provide a conceptual understanding of the weakness of the region's planning regimes and quantitative notion of their cost and benefits (Egbu, 2007; Egbu et al., 2008). This is despite recommendations by studies, such as Farvacque and McAuslan (1992), and Dowall and Clark (1996), for such appraisal of planning regimes in the developing world for appropriate policy formulation.

That aside, studies such as Bertaud and Malpezzi (2001), Cheshire and Shephard (2002, 2004), and Corkindale (2004) have suggested that planning regimes generate both positive and negative economic impacts.

As such, it would be inappropriate to uphold or dismiss a planning regime without evaluating its extent of economic incentives (Hayek, 1976). It is therefore towards contributing to bridging this knowledge lacuna on lack of evidence on the quantitative notion of the economic incentives provided by SSA planning regimes that this book has been prepared. However, given the discussions so far, this book reinforces its central argument that SSA urban planning regimes are weak and dysfunctional in part with low compliance with planning regulations because they do not provide incentives to property owners/developers.

6.5 Chapter summary

This chapter set out to discuss SSA planning systems; outline their nature, their state and determinants of their failings, and current efforts towards improvement. The chapter began with historical discussions on planning and institutionalisation of formal planning, and their nature in the region. This was followed by a discussion on the state of planning regimes, specifically compliance with planning regulations in the region and its determinants from the perspective of the human action theoretic framework, with property owners/land users as the reference point. In conclusion, the chapter discussed current efforts at improving planning practice in SSA, noting the challenges that confront or may confront the initiatives. The next chapter focusses on how incentives have influenced urban planning particularly from the policy formulation standpoint.

7 Influence of incentives on urban planning practice

7.1 Introduction

Chapter 5 developed the human action theoretic framework with insights into the role instinctive incentives can play to make planning systems effective. The framework was subsequently used to analyse the effectiveness of SSA planning systems based on compliance with planning and urban development regulations. This chapter extends the application of the human action theoretic framework to demonstrate the influence of incentives on the institution and operation of urban planning as a policy interventionalist activity. In so doing, the chapter uses the history of planning and its operation in the UK, Japan, and SSA as reference points. These jurisdictions were purposively chosen just to reflect planning practice in different geographical areas and the different motives of planning at the time of its inception in those jurisdictions. The chapter, after this introduction, outlines the analytical propositions and thereafter uses the propositions to discuss the experiences of the jurisdictions.

7.2 The human action analytic framework propositions

The application of human action analytic framework in Chapters 5 and 6 conceptualised compliance with planning regulation by property owners/land users as a form of human action, which is based on incentives – individual property owners/land users should be aware of regulations, perceive them as relevant to their socio-economic development, speculate a positive difference between the benefit and the cost of compliance with regulations, and have the 'means' (resources) to meet the cost. The logic of the analysis was that where planning regimes provide incentives to property owners/land users, compliance with their regulations will be high, and the outcome of planning systems will be manifested by orderly developments with the provision of the necessary infrastructure and amenities.

However, the analytic framework holds that economic schemes should focus on individuals rather than on groups such as companies since groups do not have an independent existence of their own. Rather, groups are collections of individuals, and group or collective actions are performed on behalf of the group via actions of specific individuals (Mises, 1949; Rothbard, 2004; Facchini, 2007). This presupposes that the conception of land use planning and its implementation are traceable to some individuals and any analysis of them should focus on such individuals. Consequently, this chapter views institutionalisation of urban planning, particularly as a government interventionalist action, as an activity that should be analysed from the standpoint of individuals who constitute government. After all, it is these individuals who enter into some form of agreement with others and in this case citizens of society to act on their behalf. For example, a president of a country assenting to a bill on urban planning in order to make it law is, under normal circumstances, deemed to have been done on behalf of the country's citizens. The chapter further conceptualises urban planning as a 'means', and the logic proposed in this chapter is that institutionalisation of planning and its forms are forms of human action which are dependent on incentives (Chapter 5). The application of the human action analytic framework in this chapter is purely based on historical analysis and covers three main periods: namely, the origins of formal planning up to 1959, the period from 1960 to 1979, and the 1980s–2000s. These periods marked major turning points in the history of urban planning.

7.3 Inception of urban planning

Urban planning is considered as old as human settlements and had existed in several forms (UN-Habitat, 2009). However, what is today regarded as formal urban planning originated in the Western world during the nineteenth century and spread across the world through importation of planning ideas and colonialism (Nadin and Stead, 2008; Watson, 2009a, 2009b).

7.3.1 The UK situation

In the UK, planning emerged following the industrial and agricultural revolutions and their associated ills such as pollution of residential areas, unfit housing, and poor water and sewerage services during the aforesaid period (Simpson et al., 1989; Hall, 2002; Boelens, 2006). Despite the passage of certain laws, such as the Public Health Act (1851), minimal efforts were made to address the ills, and the powers given to public officials under these laws to act were not exercised (Simpson et al., 1989; Mullins and Murie, 2006). This was due to the high cost of government intervention and the unwillingness of government to distort the operations of the market (Mullins and Murie, 2006). This resulted in a situation of lack of incentives for strong intervention in the property market by government to correct the inefficiencies as the cost of such intervention was perceived to be more than the benefits.

The existing ills resulted in several voluntary efforts and working-class self-initiatives in urban control, civic design, and rural rehabilitation. These included Ebenezer Howard' Garden City concept and a movement to address the social and environmental ills occurring around the latter part of the nineteenth century (Malpass, 2000). Additional laws such as the 1890 Housing of the Working Classes Act were passed to enable local authorities to build housing for general needs. This followed the agitations and threats of civil strife from the Labour Movement, which was formed at that time (Mullins and Murie, 2006). The above efforts to address the socio-economic ills of UK society were not enough. Indeed, the country during the 1900s was described as a troubled giant; its economy was stagnating, agriculture was in a long recession, and much of the countryside population was in rural slums, while the industrial towns, home to almost 80% of the population, manifested a lack of amenities; a high level of un-healthiness; widespread overcrowding; pollution; and, 30% of the population living under the 'poverty line' (Simpson et al., 1989). Urban planning was conceived as a 'means' around 1904 for the achievement of good health, amenity, and social contentment by the National Social Reform Council and other environmental groups. Subsequently, the 1909 and 1919 (Addison Act) Housing and Town Planning Acts, and the 1932 Town and Country Planning Act were passed to promote housing (Simpson et al., 1989; Mullins and Murie, 2006; Harris, 2010). The UK Government further promised to build 'homes fit for heroes' after the First World War, but the implementation of this was delayed due to disputes among government departments on the one hand and government departments and local authorities on the other hand. This was compounded by a housing shortage in the decade preceding 1914 and at a time when the working-class population was growing. Further insurrection was in sight, and taking a cue from what had happened in Russia in 1917, the UK government under the 1919 Act earmarked the building of half a million 'low rent' homes over three years (Simpson et al., 1989). In this instance, it was the incentives from addressing housing needs of the working class and the imminent insurrection that led to the intervention, an indication of a form of human action. The period from 1939 to the 1950s witnessed the arrival of a comprehensive planning system, which strengthened the then existing modernist rational planning approach in support of the creation of a welfare state. The prominent regulation, which brought about this comprehensive planning regime, was the Town and Country Planning Act (1947) (McKay et al., 2003; Shaw and Lord, 2009).

Earlier in the 1930s, several land development problems came to the fore, and planning advocates suggested state intervention for their redress. There was, for example, uneven development with a decline in old industrial areas and growth in areas such as the Midlands and the South-East. Developments in the countryside were also in chaos. These developments led to the formation of the Barlow Royal Commission in 1937 to examine the problem, but the state was not prepared to intervene in the operations of the market. However, with the Second World War taking place, especially following the bombing of UK cities, a lot of physical destruction occurred. According to Mullins and Murie (2006), 4 million houses were destroyed during the war. Financial markets were also disrupted while property value kept falling. This demanded swift government intervention for reconstruction and redressing of the 1930s urban development issues. The interest groups (land and financial), which were resolute about perpetuating relatively unregulated urban land market, had their case weakened. Consequently, the 1947 Act was passed. At the heart of the act were three major issues – government control over the planning process, development schemes, and development control (Newman and Thornley, 1996; Corkindale, 2004; Shaw and Lord, 2009). However, government reconstruction efforts benefitted both sections of the manufacturing industry that experienced and profited from a close wartime relationship with the state and the ordinary working and fighting population whose loyalty and commitment were essential for the prosecution of the war (Simpson et al., 1989). For example, this period witnessed the introduction of the national health insurance system, an expansion of education, and mass construction of council houses (Mullins and Murie, 2006). It is therefore the incentives from the reconstruction – ensuring improved quality of life and social welfare – that necessitated the introduction of a comprehensive planning system, a manifestation of a form of human action.

7.3.2 *The Japan situation*

The reason behind the initial planning intervention in the property market in Japan was to build a nation-state. The perceived incentives of turning around a feudal society and exhibiting the power of a modern state culminated in the institutionalisation of urban planning in Japan. The birth of urban planning in Japan is linked to the Meiji Restoration, which marked the genesis of modern Japan (Watanabe, 1980; Shibata, 2008a). The Meiji Government, which came into being following the overthrow of Tokugawa Bakufu in 1868, had two main pre-occupations: the building of a wealthy nation and a strong army (Watanabe, 1980; Shibata, 2008a). Confronted with a lack of resources such as modern technology, natural resources, capital, and skilled labour, the Meiji Government mobilised land taxes to build capital and then decided to import Western technology and pursue enlightenment or civilisation as the West as Western civilisation was at its peak during that period (Shibata, 2008a). According to Shibata (2008a), the mantra then was "Japanese spirit .... Western technology". Accordingly, the ruling elite (Iwakura mission), bureaucrats, and students visited Western Europe (between 1871 and 1873) and imported Western technology (Sorensen, 2002; Shibata, 2008a). Urban planning was embedded in the imported technology. This was conceived as architecture and engineering driven by 'rational' science, which were to drive a massive programme of building infrastructure and industrialisation (Friedmann, 2005; Shibata, 2008a). The importation of urban planning led to the remodelling of cities, particularly Tokyo, the capital, along the lines of Western cities to symbolise modernity. There was a massive programme of infrastructural development and industrialisation. The first rail line, for example, was opened between Tokyo and Yokohama in 1872 while the Ginza Brick Quarters, commercial and residential developments comprising 1,400 two-storey Western-style buildings, were constructed from 1872 to 1877.

Most of the infrastructural facilities that were constructed in Tokyo in the years that followed were, however, made feasible by the Tokyo City-Ward Reform Ordinance passed in 1888. Indeed, the goals of mass industrialisation and infrastructural development were pursued even at the peril of the lives of Japanese. According to Shibata (2008a) the serious pollution problem resulting from the Ashio mine contamination, the organic mercury poisoning (Minamata disease), and the cadmium poisoning (Itai-Itai disease) which occurred in the 1890s did not attract much attention from the Japanese Government. This signifies that the incentive of the modernisation agenda was the rationale behind Japanese authorities' institutionalisation of intervention. In fact, the mass industrialisation programmes the country embarked on brought in its wake unprecedented urban growth and urbanisation. For example, the population of Tokyo grew from between 600,000 and 700,000 in the latter part of 1860s to 7 million in 1940, while the sub-urban and central and inner cities' populations grew by 183% and 94%, respectively, between 1897 and 1920 (Shibata, 2008a). Urban growth and urbanisation led to social and environmental ills, such as poor urban environmental conditions and inadequate housing. It also led to increases in the prices of land and houses (Watanabe, 1980; Shibata, 2008a). Initially, the Japanese authorities were not concerned about this development. Instead, it was recognised that the agitations, which resulted from the external effects from industrialisation in the Western world during the 'industrial revolution', were due to the increased political consciousness of the people. As such, the Japanese government speculated that, in order to avoid similar unrest, there was a need for the people to be educated to sacrifice for the development of the state (Pyle, 1973; Shibata, 2008a).

The first planning act(s), the City Planning Act and the Urban Building Standard, were therefore passed in 1919 (Sorensen, 2002; Friedmann, 2005; Shibata, 2008a). These enactments came into being upon recognition of the difficulty with the continuation of the educational programme in the face of deteriorating socio-economic and environmental conditions and probable civil unrest (Shibata, 2008a). Unfortunately, the City Planning Act was weak and limited in scope and above all created a centralised planning regime. Following the Great Kanto Earthquake in 1923, a Special City Planning Act was promulgated to address the devastating effects of the earthquake (Watanabe, 1980; Evans, 2002; Shibata, 2008a). It can therefore be inferred that while the 1919 Act was perceived as a comparatively cheaper 'means' to address the imminent insurrection for continuation of the country's developmental programme, the Act of 1923 was perceived as a more cost-effective 'means' to deal with the effects of the earthquake, a reflection of human action. The planning arrangement above continued through to the Second World War, during which all efforts were concentrated on the war. The war led to the destruction of many cities. Two-hundred and fifteen cities were air-raided, which was accompanied by food shortages and massive repatriation problems (Watanabe, 1980). The new Ministry of Construction created in 1948 therefore took charge of planning. The Urban Building Standard was replaced with Building Standards Act while the City Planning Act was supplemented by Special City Planning Act (1946–1954). The incentive for all these planning arrangements was to reconstruct damaged Japanese cities through a comprehensive land consolidation programme (Watanabe, 1980; Evans, 2002; Shibata, 2008a) including, for example, providing 300,000 homes for the homeless in the first winter after the war.

7.3.3 SSA context

Chapter 6 traced the history of the institutionalisation of formal urban planning in SSA. The chapter brought to the fore the idea that planning was instituted in the region by Western European colonialist powers at the turn of the nineteenth century. Further, Western Europe's association with Africa had occurred much earlier through trade, which had established some structures that later became the nucleus for colonisation (Njoh, 2009). However, during this period the continent was not opened for exploitation. Colonial officials were confronted with the threat of diseases and nationalistic reprisals from natives, which needed to be dealt with in order to put the colonisation agenda – exploitation of the continent's resources – on course (Njoh, 2009). Urban planning was used as a cheaper means to achieve the ends of Western European colonialists – health, political, and economic aims, which are a manifestation of human action. Thus, human action dictated that colonial officials find a comparatively cheaper means of addressing these challenges, which was found in Planning. The above was partly encapsulated in the 1923 annual address of the president of the Royal Town Planning Institute, cited in Home (1990), which notes that:

> ...we have to remember that many of our members are working in remote parts of the world, confronted with problems very different from those we have at home. Housing, sanitation, and traffic present very distinctive features in India and in our tropical colonies. We have to accept a much more economical scale of housing as reasonable where for

> ten months of the year it is possible, and indeed advantageous, to sleep in the open air, but the established type often leaves much to be desired from the sanitary point of view, and while we struggle to remedy this, the conditions prescribe that our efforts take much simpler and more primitive form than is customary at home. There are numerous endemic and epidemic diseases to be battled with...

The rationale of planning was manifested in the planning practice during the period under reference, which started with the passage of legislation, slum clearance, and the preparation of development schemes, among other things. Ultimately, urban planning ensured that there is spatial segregation between where the colonial officers and the indigenous population lived. This was done through physical separation of European settlements where all the infrastructure and amenities were provided and high health standards and building regulations were enforced, from those for the local communities by 'cordon sanitaire' of open spaces with parks and race-courses. Although some areas occupied by the native population had infrastructure and amenities, these services were meant to facilitate the activities of colonial officials, such as sanitary inspectors, tax collectors, and the police and military, in order to ensure good sanitary conditions, ensure smooth revenue mobilisation, and maintain law and order, respectively (Njoh, 2004, 2009). To enhance further exploitation of the sub-continent's resources, the planning arrangements supplanted indigenous African land tenure systems with those that were popular in Western Europe. These permitted large-scale commodification of land in Africa and, in some cases, the vesting of entire ownership in colonial governments (Amin, 1972; Rodney, 1972; Wekwete, 1995; Okoth-Ogendo, 2000; Njoh, 2004, 2009; Home, 2012). It also ensured control over all land transactions by colonial governments and made the so-called 'unoccupied and ownerless lands' the property of colonial governments to advance their political and economic ends (Hammond et al., 2006; Home, 2012). While colonial governments, for example, made free grants of these lands to the few educated and politically active indigenes to control them, it promoted large-scale plantations and mining with their home companies as beneficiaries. This was executed through a generous offer of land either free of charge or at giveaway prices to such companies (Amin, 1972; Rodney, 1972; Njoh, 2009). Thus, unlike in the UK and Japan, which introduced planning because of market failure and turning a feudal into a modern state respectively, the incentives for securing the health of colonial officials stationed in the colonies, assuaging reprisals from natives and economic exploitation prompted institutionalisation of planning in SSA, a reflection of a form of human action. It is in this vein that Rakodi (2006a) notes that contemporary African cities, excepting a few, were new creations in the colonial period and represent the aims and the vision of the politically and economically powerful – the expatriate colonial entrepreneurs and administrators.

7.4 Urban planning from 1960 to 1979

7.4.1 The UK situation

Although the Town and Country Planning Act (1947) had established the fundamental principles of the UK planning system (Nadin, 2007; Shaw and Lord, 2007; Nadin and Stead, 2008) there were efforts to modify the country's planning system during the 1960s. The 1960s and 1970s witnessed several global development imperatives, such as increasing poverty, the rise of civil societies, post-modernism, and feminism (Campbell and Fainstein, 2003; UN-Habitat, 2009; Watson, 2009a, 2009b). These development imperatives and their impact were present in UK society. For example, Mullins and Murie (2006) report that the country had to grapple with large-scale poverty, which was compounded by mass immigration from the Caribbean and South Asia. This situation resulted in homelessness with its attendant agitations and campaigns from grass-root movements and churches as well as the formation of Shelter, the housing and homelessness charity, and other housing associations. The extant planning arrangement therefore came under immense criticism for not considering the socio-economic context within which planning is practised. The planning system was, for example, said to concentrate on physical development of space – it prevented undesirable developments, but did not promote desirable developments. Further, it did not involve interest groups in the planning process, and promoted suburbia developments separating work from home, among others (Albrechts, 2006).

To address the above weaknesses of the planning system, incremental and strategic planning approaches, which promoted the participation of stakeholders in land development processes, were introduced (Conyers and Hill, 1984; Pennington, 2000; Healey, 2003; Shaw and Lord, 2009, p. 419). Indeed, the acid test for the efficacy of planning at that time was the scope and content of structure plans; the structure plan in relation to other policy-making processes; interagency linkages for development and implementation; public participation; aims, objectives, and problems in planning methodology; and monitoring research and intelligence (Drake et al., 1975 in Shaw and Lord, 2009, p. 418). It was therefore the incentives for addressing the agitations that stemmed from post-modernism in the face of urban development challenges that existed at that time which prompted the modification of the planning approach, a reflection of a form of human action.

7.4.2 The Japan situation

The latter part of the 1950s witnessed the beginning of the recovery of the Japanese economy, manifesting in rapid economic growth. Therefore, contrary to the global poverty crisis, the 1960s through to the greater portions of the 1970s witnessed economic prosperity in Japan. Watanabe (1980) reports that the entire country was intensively developed with heavy industries, highway systems, bullet train lines, new towns, and golf courses. This was followed by rapid urbanisation and the central business districts of cities were inundated with high-rise office complexes while their fringes showcased sprawling sub-urban developments. Thus, although there was material prosperity and physical convenience, the increase in prosperity and rise in massive developments led to increases in land prices, a deteriorated natural environment, and the demise of non-material values (Watanabe, 1980; Evans, 2002). These coincided with the infiltration of civil society activities and post-modernism into the body politic of Japan. Japanese authorities in the face of these urban challenges had to also contend with the opposition of their policies (Evans, 2002; Shibata, 2008b). Consequently, the City Planning Act (1968) known as the 'New Act' was passed to replace the 1919 Act. A new Urban Redevelopment Act (1969) was also passed to consolidate old and new redevelopment programmes. A prominent feature of the 'New Act' was the creation of City Planning Areas, which divided these areas into Urbanisation Promotion Areas and Urbanisation Control Areas. The remainder was the delegation of plan-making functions to the prefectural and municipal levels, and the introduction of a development permission system, public participation in the planning process, a sophisticated zoning system, and the creation of a hierarchy of plans (Watanabe, 1980; Sorensen, 2000; Evans, 2002). Although it is argued that the central government control of the planning system did not change with the above new planning arrangements (Friedmann, 2005), it signalled the beginning of decentralisation and public participation in planning in Japan (Evans, 2002). It is therefore because of the incentives to address the deteriorating environmental conditions and 'contain' the prevailing opposition – civil society activities and post-modernists – that this planning arrangement was put in place, an indication of a form of human action.

7.4.3 SSA context

Most SSA countries had attained independence by the 1960s, and these newly emergent states were enthusiastic to embark on rapid socio-economic development. They therefore sought to overhaul the colonial structures, including land tenure, planning, and development policies. The idea was to operate a state-controlled economic system with state-funded industrialisation as the primary driver of development (Rakodi, 2006a; Hammond and Antwi, 2010). However, as noted in Chapter 6, the modernist planning system – a rational comprehensive planning model with the use of master plans – remained intact and, in some cases, consolidated. For example, Ghana, after gaining independence in 1957 adopted a welfare economic model of development, which sought to achieve growth and development through state-led industrialisation (Car, 2008). However, attempts to integrate policy planning with land use planning under the country's first president Dr Kwame Nkrumah to promote development was short-lived (Hammond and Antwi, 2010). Similarly, as reported in Chapter 6, Tanzania in 1967 made the Arusha Declaration, which led to the introduction of African Socialism (Ujamaa) as its new political philosophy. As part of that new philosophy, all lands were nationalised and land use planning was supposed to have been people-oriented, but this could not materialise. Analyses by studies such as Wekwete (1995), Okoth-Ogendo (2000), Hammond et al. (2006), and Home (2012) demonstrate that the colonial land use planning policies could not be revised because they ensured control of land and its related resources by the few: the elites and powerful individuals in government and their agents. This served as incentives for them to maintain the planning arrangement, a reflection of a form of human action.

7.5 Urban planning from the 1980s to the 2000s

7.5.1 The UK situation

The 1980s witnessed the neoliberal turn in planning and urban development (Evans, 2001; Allmendinger and Haughton, 2012). This ensured that urban development became private sector or market driven (Anderson, 1990; Robinson and Shaw, 1994). During this period it was argued that state controls and subsidies were responsible for the then economic decline in the UK. Economic liberalism through the 'free market' was offered as a mechanism to bring about prosperity. The rationale was to enhance physical and economic regeneration in rundown areas. The presumption was that such regeneration will stimulate wider economic and social benefits – the so-called 'trickle-down effect' (Robinson and Shaw, 1994). To ensure the implementation of this agenda, the idea of enterprise zoning was introduced with the establishment of Urban Development Corporations (UDCs) to take over some key areas of the planning system (Anderson, 1990; Robinson and Shaw, 1994; Marshall, 2009). Enterprise zones created around this period included Dudley, Clydeback, Hartlepool, and Salford, while an example of UDCs established was the London Docklands. Several other private sector-friendly policies were also introduced. These included simplifying planning procedures whereby developments, which conformed to the rules for each of the zones, did not require individual planning permission; enhancing capital allowances against corporation and income tax liabilities for investment in industrial and commercial property; and exempting property from local business rates. It thus became evident that local authorities were technically and dramatically weakened (Marshall, 2009). However, with the re-occurrence of economic crises, particularly the property market crash in the late 1980s, which led to the collapse of several companies that were to lead developers under the UDC projects, (for example, the Canary Wharf developers Olympia collapsed in 1992) some of these neoliberal policies were reversed. It can therefore be argued that it was the incentives for promoting the 'ends' of free market 'apostles' and their adherents which led to the formulation of the 1980s planning policies.

Following the 2004 Planning and Compulsory Purchase Act, the UK planning system was beyond the traditional land use planning system to spatial planning system (Shaw and Lord, 2007, 2009; Tewdwr-Jones et al., 2010; Allmendinger and Haughton, 2012). This spatial planning arrangement is said to bring together and integrate policies and programmes which influence the nature of places, and how they can function (Nadin, 2007; Shaw and Lord, 2007; Tewdwr-Jones et al., 2010). Although some of its features may not be different from planning arrangements since the post-Second World War period, Nadin (2007) identifies five major themes which drive the planning system. These are to support timely plan and decision-making processes to enable planning authorities to positively shape outcomes rather than report them; to promote community and stakeholder participation throughout the plan-making to ensure widespread understanding of difficult decisions at the heart of planning practice; to create an integrated mechanism by which private stakeholders, public service providers, and community groups can have their activities for place-making designed; to encourage and promote development rather than restricting development; and to ensure that policies are clearly rooted in evidence. Clearly, this new planning arrangement subscribes to a collaborative approach to planning (Allmendinger and Haughton, 2012). According to Shaw and Lord (2009) the historical antecedent of the above planning paradigm is traced to the post-1997 public service 'Modernisation Agenda' and the political philosophy of the 'Third Way' – so-called collaborative working with the possibility to reconcile parties previously thought to have competing objectives. The aforesaid planning paradigm is also partly attributable to the European Union's 'Territorial Agenda' – European Spatial Development Perspective (ESDP) and developments in planning in continental Europe (Nadin, 2007; Tewdwr-Jones et al., 2010). Tewdwr-Jones et al. (2010) outline three motivations for the adoption of this new planning paradigm in the UK. These are the need to respond to increased expectations of planning delivering at various spatial scales, within and outside existing territories; to sign unto the ESDP and benefit from the EU Structural Fund as well as attract significant investments; and to promote economic growth and contribute towards improved economic performance of all regions beyond traditional local government boundaries with an emphasis on strong community involvement in the planning process at the local level through Local Development Frameworks to address social inclusion, economic and environmental issues and their spatial implications and inter-relationships – the idea of sustainable communities. Allmendinger and Haughton (2012), however, argue that the aim of the planning paradigm to promote engagement and ensure legitimacy is superficial while its processes for participation are carefully choreographed to minimise the potential for offering people with dissenting views a hearing. This signifies that the incentives from attracting funds and significant investments from the EU and addressing concerns over the environment in a competitive globalised world prompted this new planning arrangement, a reflection of a form of human action. Now that the UK is making the necessary arrangements to leave the EU, it remains to be seen what future planning arrangements will be.

7.5.2 Japan situation

Evans (2002) notes that the 1980s witnessed a gradual extension of decentralisation in planning and that the concept of district planning was introduced in 1980, which, among other things, allowed a measure of citizen participation – land owners and residents were given the opportunity to participate in district plans' preparation. Nevertheless, the main policy during this period was 'Urban Renaissance'. Shibata (2008b) recounts that Japan suffered economic crises in the early 1980s due to an expansion of the social welfare programme and huge investment in public works in the 1970s. This, coupled with the rise of neoliberalism in the country, led to a policy change – the introduction of the 'Minkatsu Policy', which made private enterprise the driver of economic development. This policy ushered neoliberal planning in Japan particularly in the area of urban development. Shibata (2008b) further reports that the 'Minkatsu Policy' sought to promote market-led land development to stimulate the then stagnant economy and deregulate land use controls to provide motivation for land developers. However, unlike the UK where rundown areas in urban centres were targeted, land use in these urban centres was not considered as the 'highest and best use' by business elites and the Japanese Government – central bureaucracy. Consequently, the Japanese Government introduced measures, for example, to convert Category I Exclusive Residential Zone areas, which were reserved for low-rise residential buildings only, to high- and medium-rise development areas. Public lands were also sold for urban regeneration and construction of quality high-rise residential and office buildings. It was thus an incentive to attract investments and to satisfy neoliberal forces to rescue an ailing economy that brought about this planning arrangement, a manifestation of a form of human action.

The neoliberal planning policies adopted by the Japanese Government led to a short-term boom, which later turned into a bubble that was destined to burst. For example, the country's total stock of property values was nearly four times the value of the total property stock in the US and constituted about 20% of the world's wealth in 1991 (Shibata, 2008b). However, this bubble burst in the early 1990s as a result of the Government's macroeconomic mismanagement, speculative land investment, and poor development control measures (Friedmann, 2005; Shibata, 2008b). The economic mismanagement created financial and administrative stringencies at the heart of Government, which meant a disincentive for Government to centralise planning. By this time also the activities of civil societies were becoming entrenched in Japan. Coupled with the Great Hanshin-Awaji Earthquake in 1995, which exposed the social and environmental excesses of decades of pursuing development, the Government decided to strengthen democratisation of planning through vigorous decentralisation (Evans, 2002; Friedmann, 2005; Shibata, 2008b). This process started with the 1992 amendment of the City Planning Act, which required all cities within earmarked City Planning Areas to prepare their own master plans based on citizens' opinions. Subsequent amendments extending this democratisation process occurred in 1999 and 2000 (Evans, 2002). The democratisation process is being pursued through 'Machi-zukuri'. This is a form of community planning (Evans, 2002; Sorensen, 2002; Friedmann, 2005; Shibata, 2008b) which espouses the core principles of the collaborative planning model. Based on the foregoing discussions, it can be argued that the Government's disincentive to pursue a centralised planning arrangement on the one hand and the incentive to respond positively to civil societies and address decades of social and environmental excesses on the other hand gave rise to this planning arrangement – a reflection of a form of human action.

7.5.3 SSA context

SSA during the latter part of 1970s suffered persistent socio-economic problems and by the early 1980s the region was in deep socio-economic crises, which compelled most constituent economies to adopt the IMF- and World Bank-sponsored Structural Adjustment Programmes (SAPs) (Konadu-Agyemang, 2000, 2001; Owusu, 2001). At the heart of these SAPs were neoliberal prescriptions, which required, among other things, the cutting of government expenditure on social services, re-entrenchment of public sector workers, devaluation of currencies, and removal of all forms of price controls. Planning systems in the region were not immune from these policy prescriptions. Indeed, the World Bank linked its lending agreements to the reform of planning regulatory frameworks in the region (Payne and Majale, 2004; Musandu-Nyamayaro, 2008). The prescriptions of the World Bank, inter alia, sought to decentralise planning and promote public-private sector partnership in urban development. Several attempts were therefore made at reforms. For example, the Governments of countries such as Tanzania, Kenya, Zimbabwe, Zambia, Botswana, and Nigeria made attempts to reform their planning regimes. These were to be done through the promulgation of flexible planning laws and development standards to suit the needs of the poor and low-income people. The remainder was to relax development control and provide serviced plots of land, funds, and materials for the construction of buildings (UN-Habitat, 1999; Baffour Awuah et al., 2011c). In Ghana, several urban projects were undertaken between 1985 and 1990 (Larbi, 1996). Eventually, the Local

Government Act (Act 462), which sought to decentralise planning, was passed in 1993. However, these attempts at planning reforms in the SSA were sporadic and short-lived. Consequently, except for the Republic of South Africa, which had adopted an integrated planning approach in 1994, constituent economies were still stuck in colonial planning arrangements (Musandu-Nyamayaro, 2008; Watson, 2009a). Thus, while the incentives for attracting development assistance to address development imperatives led to sporadic planning reforms in SSA, the incentives to control land and related resources by the few elite and their cronies have continued to ensure the prevalence of colonial planning arrangements. For example, in analysing the Ghanaian situation Konadu-Agyemang (1998, p. 145) notes:

> The continuous existence of the colonial planning apparatus in the country for over four decades since independence should not be misconstrued to mean it is effective and acceptable. Rather, its continuous survival has been made possible thanks to the few rich and elites in society who are afraid that any changes will adversely affect their role in the administration of land and its resources.

However, as noted in Chapter 6 several countries are currently undertaking planning reforms in the SSA as part of wider land tenure reforms but something concrete in practice is yet to be achieved, which is far from the dictates of the colonial planning arrangements.

7.6 Chapter summary

This chapter has demonstrated how human action and by extension incentives has influenced urban planning practice particularly at the policy formulation level in three major jurisdictions. The chapter shows that incentives have a major role to play in urban planning policy formulation and that planning's role in ensuring sustainable, safe, inclusive, productive, and liveable urban centres may not materialise without the appropriate doses of incentives. The next chapter demonstrates how to calibrate incentives.

8 Economic evaluation framework

8.1 Introduction

The previous three chapters demonstrated the significant role which incentives, as outlined by the human action theoretic framework, can play in urban planning practice and more importantly in helping planning systems to be effective. However, to determine the quantum of incentives inherent in a planning system or whether a planning system offers incentives, there is a need to devise a suitable evaluation framework. This chapter devises a suitable measuring framework to calibrate the extent of economic incentives of a planning system from the perspective of the individual property owner. The chapter commences with a discussion on economic evaluation methodologies and subsequently devises an economic evaluation framework for measuring incentives based on the propositions of the human action theoretic framework discussed in Chapter 5.

8.2 Economic evaluation methodological review

Several approaches exist for the economic evaluation of policies (Armstrong and Taylor, 1985). According to Hammond (2006) and Hammond and Antwi (2010), the evaluation of policies can be examined from several perspectives. For example, from the standpoint of knowledge claims, the economic evaluation of policies, such as planning policies, can be examined either from quantitative or from qualitative perspectives (Evans, 1996; Clarke and Dawson, 1999; Forss et al., 2002; Khakee, 2003; Corkindale, 2004; Brueckner, 2007). The evaluation of policies can also be approached, inter alia, from the standpoint of ex ante or ex post, depending on whether the evaluation is prior or subsequent to the implementation of policies (Lichfield, 1966, 1996; Clarke and Dawson, 1999; Alexander, 2006); an economic perspective in terms of macro- and microeconomics (Adams et al., 2005; Hammond, 2006; Hammond and Antwi, 2010); and the nature of the effects of policies, for example, on consumers or suppliers (Pogodzinski and Sass, 1990). The thrust of this discussion, however, centres on quantitative economic impact methodologies in view of the aim of this book.

Three main economic evaluation methodologies are identified in the literature for an examination of the economic impact of planning policies. These are: (i) the multiplier-based; (ii) revealed preference; and (iii) the stated preference methodologies.

8.2.1 *The multiplier-based methodologies*

The multiplier-based economic evaluation methodologies are several. These include economic-based, Keynesian income-expenditure and input-output (Leontief, 1966; Miernyk, 1982; Hertsgaard et al., 1984; Armstrong and Taylor, 1985; Lichfield, 1996) and export-based (Miernyk, 1982; Bergstrom et al., 1990; Hughes, 2003) models. Fundamental to these economic evaluation methodologies, as their categorisation suggests, is the multiplier. The multiplier, as a concept, was originally developed during the great depression in the 1930s by Keynes to provide justification for public spending to stimulate national economies towards employment generation (Wang, 1997). Despite its original purpose, the multiplier concept is now being used even by industries to demonstrate their contributions to national and regional economies (Wang, 1997). The multiplier-based economic evaluation methodologies work on the macroeconomic level. They calibrate the economic impact of interventions, such as policies, on an aggregate basis proxied on variables such as employment, per capita income, GDP and housing, among others (Armstrong and Taylor, 1985; Crompton, 1995; Wang, 1997; Donnelly et al., 1998; Gelan, 2003; Hughes, 2003; Lee and Taylor, 2005).

Given the complexities associated with multiplier-based methods, their requirement of huge volumes of organised data (Crompton, 1995; Hughes, 2003; Hammond and Antwi, 2010), and the focus of this book on quantifying individual choices regarding planning requirements, these methods are not discussed. Therefore, the chapter turns to a discussion on microeconomic impact methodologies.

8.2.2 *The revealed preference methods*

These methods operate based on actual behaviour of people or market participants. For example, how much people pay for goods and services which is considered the value or benefit they derive from the goods and services (Kula, 1997; Cheshire and Vermeulen, 2008; Wijen et al., 2009). As applied to urban planning, this can be conceived as how much people pay for planning variables, such as approved sub-division planning schemes, tarred roads, electricity, formalised titles, and building permits. The most known and used revealed preference method is the hedonic price model (Bertaud and Malpezzi, 2001; Cheshire and Sheppard, 2004; Egbu et al., 2007; Cheshire and Vermeulen, 2008; Wijen et al., 2009).

8.2.2.1 Hedonic price model

Although the hedonic price model has a long historical antecedent, its theoretical foundation is credited to Rosen (1974). This followed inspirational works from Griliches (1961), who developed the earlier works further into an approach for estimating commodity price changes as price indices. Subsequently, Lancaster (1966) provided the model's microeconomic foundation for estimating the value for utility-generating attributes with its natural application to housing (Brachinger, 2002; Sirmans et al., 2005; Hammond, 2006).

The method works on the premise that goods are valued based on their utility-bearing attributes or characteristics. Thus, embedded in a good are several attributes, which are valued based on the utility consumers derive from them (Rosen, 1974). It therefore operates by decomposing a good into its different attributes and assigning implicit prices to each of them (Rosen, 1974; del Saz-Salazar and Garcia-Menéndez, 2005; Sirmans et al., 2005). These prices are known as hedonic prices and reflect the maximum amount consumers are willing to pay for a unit of an attribute. This is revealed to them from the observed price of differentiated goods and the specific amount of the attributes associated with them (Rosen, 1974).

Theoretically, the method can be estimated as a single- or double-stage equation(s). The first stage entails econometrically estimating the implicit price of attributes through regression analysis. That is, it estimates the effect of a product's attributes on its price by regressing the price on the attributes. At the second stage, the model then estimates the structure of the demand and supply of the attributes (Rosen, 1974; Sirmans et al., 2005). However, in practice the method usually takes the single-stage approach (Brachinger, 2002; Sirmans et al., 2005), which sets the functional relationship of the model. This can be illustrated as follows:

Let $x = (x_1,...,x_K)$ where x is a set of ordered attributes of any good. This means that preferences of economic agents regarding the good are solely determined by its corresponding attributes vector. This further means there is a functional relationship f between the price of the good, ρ, and its attributes, x, written as:

$$\rho = f(x) \tag{8.1}$$

Given the above functional relationship, the implicit prices of the attributes are assessed as partial derivatives of the hedonic function in Equation 8.1. This is written as:

$$\frac{\partial \rho}{\partial x_k}(x) = \frac{\partial f}{\partial x_k}(x) \quad (k = 1, \ldots, K) \tag{8.2}$$

The hedonic price (implicit price), $\frac{\partial f}{\partial x_k}(x)$, all things being equal, indicates how much of the price of the good, ρ, changes, if it is endowed with an additional unit of the attribute, ∂x_k.

In its simple form a typical hedonic function can be expressed as follows:

$$\rho = \beta 0 + \sum_{k=1}^{K} \beta k x_k + \varepsilon \tag{8.3}$$

where ρ is the price of the good; $\beta 0$ is the normal regression intercept; βk $(k=1, \ldots, K)$, the coefficient of the regression, is the marginal change in price with respect to a change of the kth attribute, x_k, of the good; ε is the stochastic term that takes care of the anticipated measurement error.

Comparatively, the hedonic price model is said to be rigorous due to its dependence on the actual behaviour of economic agents (Cheshire and Vermeulen, 2008; Wijen et al., 2009). However, there are theoretical and practical difficulties that affect its usage. To begin with, the model may be expressed in a linear and a non-linear form, and can employ countless attributes. This poses a practical problem as to the appropriate functional form of the hedonic model in any given situation (Kula, 1997; Brachinger, 2002; Sirmans et al., 2005). Besides, the methodology's huge data requirements and the presumption of arm's-length market transactions could be problematic. This is due to the difficulty in satisfying conditions for such transactions (Kula, 1997; Wijen et al., 2009; Herath and Maier, 2010).

Despite these problems, the hedonic price model has extensive application in the developed world, especially in the US and the UK, in areas such as the calculation of consumer price indices, tax assessment, the valuation of cars and computers (Herath and Maier, 2010). However, most of its applications have been in urban development processes and real estate sectors, particularly the housing market (Sirmans et al., 2005; Herath and Maier, 2010). Within these sectors, attributes usually employed in the hedonic model include age of a building, land size, number of storeys, number of bedrooms and rooms, number of bathrooms, kitchen, and garage size. The rest are closeness to natural bodies; location in terms of neighbourhood; and its environmental characteristics, such as crime rate and distance from the CBD, and location with respect to public facilities like schools and sewers (Brookshire et al., 1982; Sirmans et al., 2005). From the standpoint of urban planning, relevant impact studies dwelling on the hedonic model use marginal prices of planning attributes of a property as its value, hence the benefits (Cheshire and Sheppard, 2004; McConnell and Walls, 2005; Cheshire and Vermeulen, 2008).

Related approaches have been in the use of actual sale values of properties or the hedonic price indices to establish prices of properties and develop an ordinary least square (OLS) regression equation with the sale price as the dependent variable and its determinants as independent variables based on a partial equilibrium framework to analyse the economic impact of planning policies. A typical functional form of such equations is given below:

$$\rho x = \beta 0 + \beta_1 a + \beta_2 b + \beta_3 c + \cdots + \beta_n p + \varepsilon \tag{8.4}$$

where ρx is the nominal price of the property; $\beta 0$ is the normal regression intercept; a is all the variables that determine the sale price of the property except planning determinants; $b \ldots p$ are the planning variables; $\beta_1 \ldots \beta_n$ are the coefficients of the variables; and ε is the stochastic term that takes care of the anticipated measurement error. Given this equation, if all the sale price determinants are the same or controlled for properties under enquiry except one, any difference in price is attributable to that determinant and is seen as the value or impact of that determinant. A similar reasoning is also used to assess the impact of planning policies on the supply of land and housing or the number and cost of constructions. Studies such as Bramley and Watkins (1996) and Bramley and Leishman (2005) in the UK and Quigley and Raphael (2006), Ihlanfeldt (2007, 2009), and Glaeser and Ward (2009) in the US, in the main, dwelt on this approach. In fact, due to differences in planning policies among jurisdictions in states in the US, studies like Quigley and Raphael (2006) and Glaeser and Ward (2009) examined the impact of land use regulation restrictiveness, calculated as an index and then incorporated it in the regression.

The use of hedonic and related methodologies in the urban development process and real estate sectors in the developed world, such as the UK and the US, has been made possible due to the availability of huge volumes of organised data and articulate property markets. Indeed, the studies outlined in the preceding paragraph, for example, relied heavily on rich archival time series data from building societies and government departments. However, such situations are hardly encountered in SSA (Hammond, 2006; Egbu, 2007; Egbu et al., 2007; Hammond and Antwi, 2010). Apart from that, the approaches are mostly oriented towards examining positive impacts, that is, benefits of planning policies, and are therefore incapable of addressing other issues, which are germane to SSA urban planning policies, such as bureaucratic delays. In addition, there have been many disagreements over these approaches and their findings even in the developed world (Quigley and Rosenthal, 2005). For example, the controversy on attributing the value of planning to planning constraints or amenity from the standpoint of these approaches still lingers (Ihlanfeldt, 2007, 2009). This therefore makes examination of the stated preference methodologies imperative.

8.2.3 *The stated preference methods*

The stated preference methods are usually used for the valuation of goods and services which have no known existing markets, such as public goods (Brookshire et al., 1982; Adamowicz, 2004; Lusk and Norwood, 2009; Wijen et al., 2009). The main method from this group of economic impact methodologies is the contingent valuation method (CVM) and the conjoint analysis technique (Roe et al., 1996; Wijen et al., 2009). However, the application of the conjoint analysis technique has mainly been in the area of marketing research (Roe et al., 1996; Green et al., 2001). This discussion therefore focusses on the CVM.

8.2.3.1 The contingent valuation method

The origin of the CVM is traced to Ciriacy-Wantrup's (1938) work on the benefits of soil erosion prevention (Akwansivie et al., 2010). The earliest application of the method is credited to Davis (1963) who used the method to determine the value and lovers of a recreational area (Kula, 1997; Hammond, 2006; Akwansivie et al., 2010). The method is based on 'value theory' and works on the presumption that individuals value their own consumption in a rational manner. That is, they will seek to maximise consumption or utility and minimise their expenditure, as best as possible, subject to constraints like income and other socio-economic factors (Kula, 1997; Abeka, 2005; Hammond, 2006). It therefore seeks preference measurements from individuals who are affected by non-marketed goods based on the notion of compensating and equivalent variations or the concept of willingness to pay (WTP) and willingness to accept (WTA) (Brookshire et al., 1982; Adler and Posner, 1999; Lusk and Norwood, 2009; Wijen et al., 2009). Fundamentally, it is a process of eliciting people's preference in terms of how much they are willing to pay for a satisfaction from a non-marketed good, seen as benefit, or how much they are willing to accept for a loss in satisfaction from a non-marketed good. In the context of urban planning it means how much property owners/developers will be willing to pay for planning variables like a sub-division planning scheme, a formalised title, a building permit, and vice versa when these variables are not available.

In eliciting responses for WTP for a benefit or accept payment for a loss, the method, in the main, uses questionnaire surveys (Brookshire et al., 1982; Alberini et al., 1997; Kula, 1997; Akwansivie et al., 2010). The rationale is to simulate a market for the good which has no market and generate its value based on the hypothetical market created and presented to respondents (Bravi and Curto, 1997; Hammond, 2006; Akwansivie et al., 2010). As applied to this work, this may be vividly describing the planning variables and the applicable market conditions. The method requires respondents to be well informed about the good (Bravi and Curto, 1997; Kula, 1997; Akwansivie et al., 2010). Additionally, since the method works on the presumption that individuals seek to rationally maximise their satisfaction subject to their socio-economic constraints, the survey usually collects the socio-economic characteristics of respondents to enhance the data analysis (Bravi and Curto, 1997; Kula, 1997; Akwansivie et al., 2010).

There are several approaches to eliciting bids from respondents on WTP and WTA. These include the open-ended elicitation method, the bidding game, and the dichotomous choice method, which is sometimes referred to as the referendum method (Bravi and Curto, 1997; Akwansivie et al., 2010). The open elicitation method has to do with the precise assessment of individuals' own reservation price based on introspection analysis. An example of the question to elicit this bid is:

> How much will you pay for a standard 3-bedroom house in Kwabenya, Accra if it is covered by an approved building permit?

The bidding game also usually takes the form:

> Will you pay X amount for a standard 3-bedroom house in Kwabenya, Accra if it is covered by an approved building permit? No.....will you rather pay Z amount?

This process continues until the respondent submits a bid. The dichotomous choice method comes in two forms – single- and double-bound choices – and has gained popularity among contingent valuation practitioners lately due to its simplicity in the use of collected data (Calia and Strazzera, 1998; Hammond, 2006; Akwansivie et al., 2010). With regard to the single-bound method, respondents are required to answer yes or no, if they are willing to pay a given amount for a non-marketed good. However, for the double-bound method if the answer is in the negative, a further question is posed with a lower bid, and vice versa, until an acceptable bid is reached.

Following Davis (1963), CVM gained wide application, initially in the field of environmental economics (Brookshire et al., 1982; Akwansivie et al., 2010) and subsequently in the social policy arena (Bravi and Curto, 1997; McGranaham et al., 2001; Wijen et al., 2009; Akwansivie et al., 2010). The method's wide application is not limited to the developed world, but in the developing world too it has seen substantial application. For example, Abeka (2005) used the method to determine the benefits of individual household place on waste collection services in the four depressed communities of Sukura, Nima, Ussher Town, and Teshie in Accra, Ghana. Akwansivie et al. (2010) also used the method to estimate the willingness of residents of Kumasi and Accra, Ghana, to pay for the cost of improving water quality in these areas.

This upsurge in the use of the CVM has been due to its rigorousness (Brookshire et al., 1982) and versatility to incorporate different components of value of a good and make respondents aware prior to submitting bids (Bravi and Curto, 1997; Wijen et al., 2009), a situation which is not possible under the hedonic model. Besides, the scope of the methodology is broad and does not depend on the availability of data on peoples' actual behaviour (Wijen et al., 2009). That said, the method is said to suffer from hypothetical biases. This situation arises where there is a potential discrepancy between what people say they are willing to pay in a contingent market survey and what they pay when confronted with the real situation (Cummings et al., 1986; Bravi and Curto, 1997; Kula, 1997; Lusk and Norwood, 2009). In fact, it is observed that such behaviours are pervasive and, on average, people tend to overstate their WTP by a factor of three in hypothetical settings compared to the actual situation where money is involved (List and Gallet, 2001; Little and Berrens, 2004; Murphy et al., 2005). Related to this problem are social desirability biases, where respondents answer questions to please researchers or answer questions to conform to some social norms (Lusk and Norwood, 2009). Another problem with the method has to do with the considerable resources involved in carrying out the contingent valuation survey. Apart from the financial resources, the time required to brief respondents about the good and to fill questionnaires may be enormous. This in turn may not allow respondents to complete their decision-making process towards submitting a bid (Cousey et al., 1987; Abeka, 2005; Hammond, 2006).

It has been argued that a well-designed and carefully executed contingent valuation survey can produce accurate and useful information on household preferences (Cummings et al., 1986; Abeka, 2005; Hammond, 2006; Akwansivie et al., 2010). Several solutions have been prescribed to address the problems with the methodology. For example, it is suggested that hypothetical and social desirability biases are due to strategic behaviour to free ride and derive utility, respectively (Hammond, 2006; Lusk and Norwood, 2009). Methods such as framing appropriate questions, the adoption of ex post calibration, the use of cheap talk to make respondents aware of these biases, and making people submit bids for others to avoid subjectiveness and biases are recommended (Abeka, 2005; Hammond, 2006; Lusk and Norwood, 2009).

8.2.4 Cost estimation methods

The methods discussed so far for calibrating the economic impacts of planning policies are oriented towards estimating the positive impacts of planning policies. They are, in the main, amenable to estimating the benefits of planning policies. However, policies have both positive and negative economic impacts: benefits and costs. Therefore, any meaningful economic impact exercise should compare both impacts for proper decision-making. This presupposes that the examination of methods for estimating adverse impacts of policies or intervention is inevitable. Traditionally, the idea of determining and comparing the positive and adverse impacts of policies has been within the welfare economic framework (Harberger, 1971; Garber et al., 1996; Pinkerton et al., 2002; Khakee, 2003; Cheshire and Vermeulen, 2008). Several methods have thus been developed from this perspective over the years. These include highly aggregated methods, like cost-benefit analysis and cost-effective analysis; intermediate methods, like planning balance sheet (Lichfield, 1966, 1996) and multi-criteria evaluation (Vreaker and Nijkamp, 2006); and highly disaggregated methods, like positional analysis (Khakee, 2003). Despite its several criticisms, it is the cost-benefit method that provides a uniform basis by reducing all impacts into monetary value

(Adler and Posner, 1999; Stevens, 2004; Guo and Gandavarapu, 2010) and is therefore discussed in this book. The main technique for estimating cost from this framework has been the Harberger (1954) Triangle and the concept of deadweight loss.

8.2.4.1 The Harberger Triangle

The Harberger Triangle methodology emerged from the seminal work of Harberger (1954). The technique uses partial equilibrium analysis to estimate the social cost of regulation/policies by means of deadweight loss (Harberger, 1954; Tullock, 1967; Posner, 1975; Wenders, 1987; Yoon, 2004; Hammond, 2006; Gümüs, 2007). The rationale behind the technique is that regulations like planning policies emerge because of minority interest, such as monopolists. Monopolists rent seek to bring about regulations, and since such regulations result in an increase in the price of goods and services above the competitive price, society loses in terms of reduction in consumer surplus. Figure 8.1 illustrates the technique as applied to planning policies.

From Figure 8.1, P_e and Q_e are price and quantity demanded of a real estate product, say, a three-bedroom residential house under competitive market conditions. If, for example, the government should introduce a regulation, say, the acquisition of a building permit from planning authorities prior to construction that ends up increasing the price of such a house to P_f, the quantity demanded will reduce to Q_f. This reduces consumer surplus by $\left(P_f - P_e\right)$ and creates a deadweight loss of triangle XYZ known as Harberger Triangle, the social cost of the regulation with the additional effect of preventing some other people in society from enjoying the product.

While several studies on social cost estimation of regulations (Stigler, 1956; Tullock, 1967; Posner, 1975; Wenders, 1987; Antwi, 2000; Hammond and Antwi, 2010) have adapted or are rooted in the Harberger

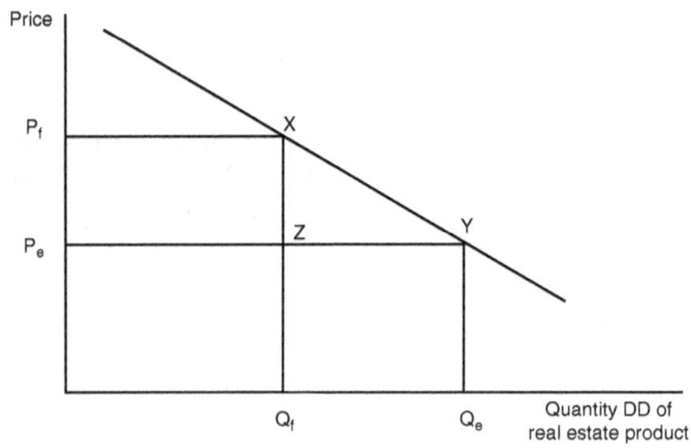

Figure 8.1 Social cost of planning regime requirements.
Source: Adapted from Harberger (1954).

Triangle technique, the method has not gone without criticism. Studies such as Tullock (1967) and Posner (1975) argue that monopolists, to get regulation passed or undertake certain activities to enjoy monopolies, spend resources that are a waste to society. Consequently, the abnormal profit, that is, the area of rectangle XZP_eP_f in Figure 8.1, supposed to be enjoyed by monopolists' feed back into rent-seeking activities and thus must be calculated as part of the social cost. Again, to neutralise the efforts of monopolists to get regulations passed, which will escalate the prices of goods and services, consumers also rent seek and waste society's resources to prevent price increases. This, according to Tullock (1967) and Posner (1975), can double the social cost of regulation (Wenders, 1987; Gümüs, 2007). However, data to authenticate these claims or otherwise are hard to come by (Gümüs, 2007).

Perhaps one of the greatest problems to this partial equilibrium estimation of the social cost of regulation is the usually unknown nature of demand, that is, the elasticity of demand for goods and services that the regulation impinges on (Bertaud and Mapelzzi, 2001; Quigley, 2007). Indeed, Hammond and Antwi (2010), in their work on the economic impact of SSA real estate policies, for example, assumed the nature of demand for real estate products. However, to circumvent the data difficulties, Bertaud and Mapelzzi (2001) propose the Bertaud Model. The mechanics of the model is illustrated by Figure 8.2.

Figure 8.2 represents the demand and supply situation for a common land use, road. P_x L_s, and D are the price, the ideal supply of land (ideal baseline), and demand, respectively, for road. Given the demand for road, should a public authority regulate the supply of land for road to, say, L_r, the social cost of such regulation can be calculated as $ABCI - ACE$. This is because more land is being devoted to road utilisation than what society wants. However, ACE (the nature of demand) is not known and $P_x(L_r - L_s)$ will not be a good measure of social cost because it abandons ACE. However, should the ideal supply on the basis of some international standards or local practices be shifted to L_b, the actual baseline, then area $ACGH$ will not count but will imply a cost of AFG, which is equally neutralised by the sized benefit of GHE neglected. Consequently, $P_x(L_r - L_b)$ or area $FBHI$ is considered an approximation of $ABCI - ACE$ and hence the social cost of land use regulation. The approach therefore sets limits for regulations/policies based on criteria, which can be local or international and estimates social cost as additional requirements of existing regulation, which may include the value of land and infrastructural costs, as well as service charges.

Even though the method looks simple and straightforward, and its use is not without precedent, having been used in countries like Malaysia, India, Thailand, Peru, Senegal, and Russia, it requires considerable amount of resources (Bertaud and Mapelzzi, 2001). Besides, the setting of baseline standards can be an onerous task, especially where different local

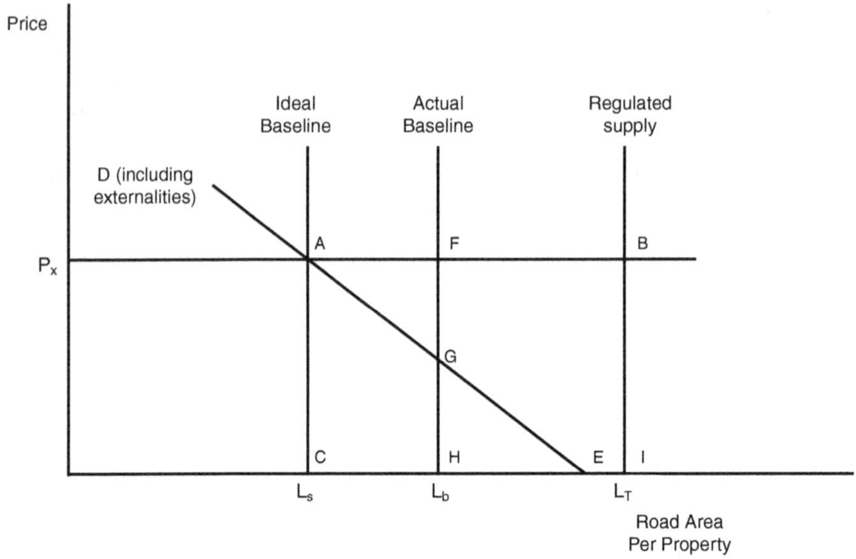

Figure 8.2 Approximation of cost of planning regime requirements.
Source: Adapted from Bertaud and Malpezzi (2001).

conditions in terms of standards in the informal land market exist. That said, questions have been asked as to whose cost and benefits do all these economic impact methodologies seek to address: is it individuals, companies, or local authorities? Which costs and benefits, in geographical terms, should be taken account of? Should the decision relate to efficiency or equity and social justice? (Lichfield, 1996). Even from the new institutional economics perspective and with reference to transaction cost, there is no clear methodology for its measurement (Buitelaar, 2004; Musole, 2009), perhaps due to the controversy associated with the concept. Buitelaar (2004) outlined a procedure for its measurement using experience from the urban development processes in the Netherlands but did not subject it to empirical testing noting that transaction cost alone may not be useful unless compared with an appropriate barometer. Egbu (2007) and Egbu et al. (2008), applying insights from Buitelaar (2004), ended up measuring the transaction cost in time lag with respect to the number of days it takes for a development right to be granted in Nigeria and a description of the other transaction cost activities.

Given these numerous methodologies, their data requirements and complexities, it is therefore not surprising that there is a lack of clear understanding of the economic impacts of planning policies, even in the developed world, due to disagreements over findings from relevant studies (Fischel, 1990; Pogodzinski and Sass, 1990; Pollakowski and Wachter, 1990; Foley, 1992; Keogh and Evans, 1992; Evans, 1996; Bramley, 1996; Adams et al.,

2005; Quigley and Rosenthal, 2005). Consequently, a bespoke methodology(ies) drawing on insights from these conventional methodologies and the conceptual framework, as well as data peculiarities in SSA, is required. This is outlined in the subsequent sections.

8.3 Evaluation framework(s) development

Insights from the human action theoretic framework (Chapter 5) espouse that for planning policies to achieve the desired outcomes, they must provide incentives. The prime incentive is the positive difference between the value of resources expended to adhere to planning regimes' requirement(s) and the value of the end of such adherence from the standpoint of individual property owner/developer (Figure 8.3). Figure 8.3 demonstrates the typical variables that should feed into the costs and benefits of compliance with SSA planning regime requirement(s) (Chapter 6). It is noted that costs and benefits associated with compliance or otherwise with planning regime requirement(s) may go beyond an individual property level. This, for example, may include positive and negative externalities to adjoining planned and unplanned developments' neighbourhoods (Corkindale, 2004) and planning authorities' administrative running costs and benefits. However, these impacts, as indicated by Figure 8.3, are beyond the scope of this book too. Similarly, zoning and certificate of occupancy requirements are beyond the scope of this book. Consequently, the linkage of the summation of costs on all the cost variables to the summation of all the benefits of the benefit variables is what is required.

Given the complexities associated with methodologies used in the developed world and their huge volumes of data requirements, a practical and innovative way should be adopted to calibrate these values considering the merits of the methodologies and SSA data peculiarities. This may require, for example, building cost from scratch and combining different methodologies.

8.3.1 Cost estimation

Compliance with SSA planning regime requirement(s) regarding urban development is a continuum of activities (Chapter 6). These range from the preparation and approval of a sub-division planning scheme to the acquisition of a building permit prior to the commencement of development, which are undertaken at both public and private sector institutions. It is also evident from the literature that, to expedite action on some of these activities, developers make follow ups at these institutions and often make extra out-of-pocket payments to officials at the public institutions (Farvacque and McAuslan, 1992; Antwi, 2000; Hammond and Antwi, 2010). These costs, which tend to swell the overall cost of complying with these planning regimes requirement(s), need to be considered where appropriate.

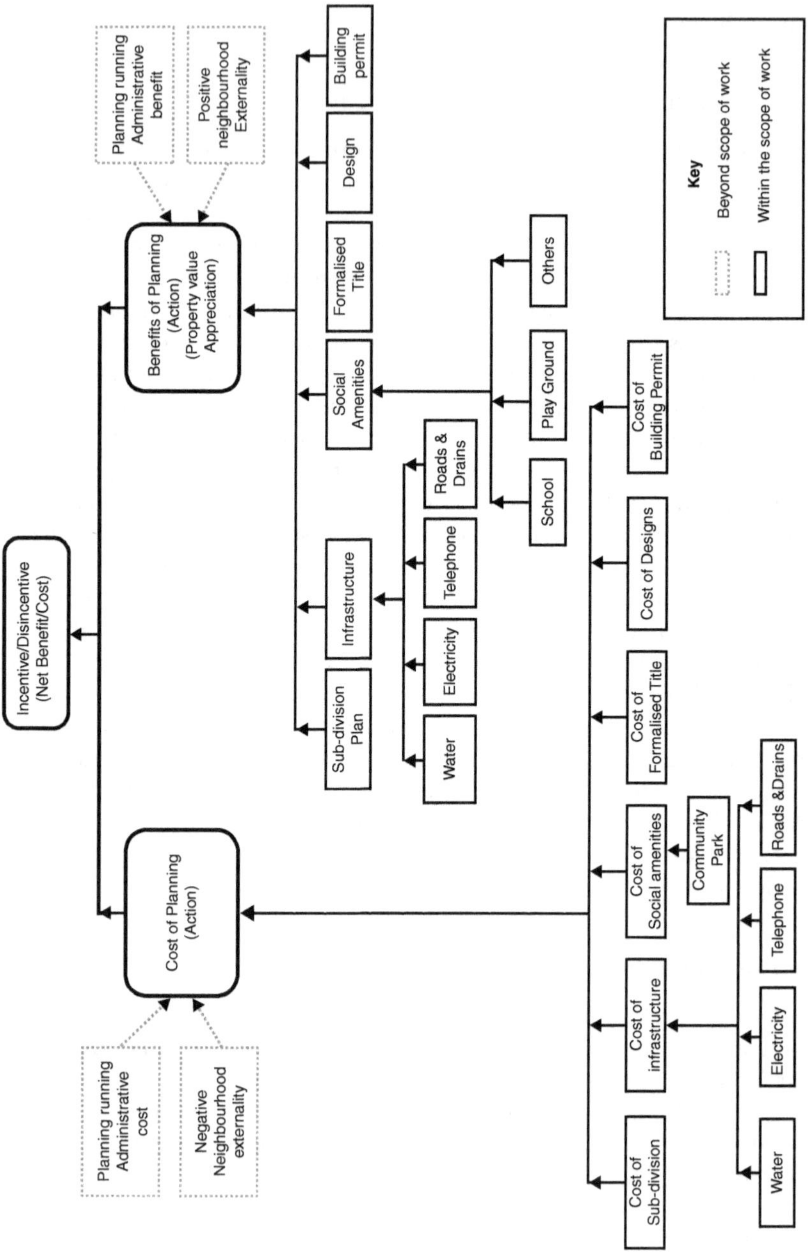

Figure 8.3 Determination of economic incentive.
Source: Author's own creation.

Additionally, it is noted that in a typical planned neighbourhood there are common or ancillary land uses, such as infrastructural facilities, which benefit individuals and institutions within the neighbourhood. It therefore stands to reason that the cost of these land uses under normal circumstances should be apportioned among the beneficiary land uses.

Typical SSA planning regime compliance requirements from Figure 8.3 are approved sub-division planning schemes, infrastructure and amenities, architectural designs, formalised titles, and building permits. Denoting the cost of these activities as ω_1, ω_2, ω_3, ω_4, and ω_5, respectively, the planning regime requirement(s)' compliance cost per property can be calculated as follows:

1. **Approved sub-division planning scheme (ω_1)**

$$\omega_1 = \frac{\kappa}{\delta} \times \left[(\alpha \times \gamma) \times (1+i)^n\right] + \varepsilon \qquad (8.5)$$

   where ω_1 is as previously defined; κ is the area of land for the property and is less or equal to δ; δ is the total area of land with uses that are subject to approved common land uses' cost allotment under an approved sub-division planning scheme and is less than γ; α is the approved sub-division planning scheme cost per hectare land under an approved sub-division planning scheme; γ is the total land area under the approved sub-division planning scheme. $(1+i)^n$ is a compounding factor that takes account of the cost of time lag, that is, the time value of money and has i as the capitalisation rate signifying cost of capital and n as time lag. ε is the error term that takes account of all measurement errors.

2. **Infrastructure and amenities (ω_2)**

$$\omega_2 = \omega_{2_1}, \ldots, \omega_{2_j} = \frac{\kappa}{\delta} \times \left[\phi + (\mu \times \vartheta) \times (1+i)^n\right] + \varepsilon \qquad (8.6)$$

   where ω_2, $\frac{\kappa}{\delta}$, $(1+i)^n$, ε are as previously defined, for example, $\omega_{2_1},\ldots,\omega_{2_j}$ is a range of particular infrastructure/amenity ω_2 can take on at a time; roads and concrete drains, electricity, community park; ϕ is the land cost for particular infrastructure/amenity; μ is the cost of a particular infrastructure/amenity per unit area of land under a sub-division planning scheme; ϑ is the extent of land area a particular infrastructure/amenity occupies under a sub-division planning scheme.

3. **Architectural design (ω_3)**

$$\omega_3 = (\sigma + \lambda + \upsilon)(1+i)^n + \varepsilon \qquad (8.7)$$

   where σ, λ, υ are the architectural design charge per property, commuting/transport cost for follow-ups on a qualified architect or draughtsman per property design to ensure design completion and collection, and professional fee per property design for engagement of a property consultant to contract an architect/draughtsman to design and ensure completion of design respectively. All other variables are as previously defined.

4. **Title formalisation (ω_4)**

$$\omega_4 = \left(\varphi + \sum\nolimits_{\chi=1}^{i} \chi\right)(1+i)^n + \varepsilon \tag{8.8}$$

where φ is the official fee for formalisation of deed per property at public agency(ies); $\chi_1, \chi_2, \chi_3, \ldots, \chi_i$ are variables, such as the cost of deed per property, the commuting cost for follow-ups to expedite action on deed preparation, the unofficial fee for formalisation of deed per property at public agency(ies), the commuting cost for follow-ups to expedite action on title formalisation activities. All other variable(s) are as previously defined.

5. **Building permit (ω_5)**

$$\omega_5 = (\varphi + \tau + \pi + \upsilon)(1+i)^n + \varepsilon \tag{8.9}$$

where φ, τ are official and unofficial fees per property paid at public agency(ies) towards acquisition of a building permit; π is the commuting cost per property for follow-ups at public agencies to expedite action on the processing of building permit; and v is the professional fee per property for engagement of a property consultant to pursue procurement of a building permit. All other variables are as previously defined.

Given the foregoing, a typical SSA planning regime requirement(s) compliance cost per property can thus be assessed as:

$$UR_c = \sum \left(\omega_1 + \omega_{2_1} + \ \ldots + \omega_{2_j} + \ \ldots + \omega_5\right) + \varepsilon \tag{8.10}$$

where UR_c is the planning regime requirement(s)' compliance cost per property. All other variables are as previously defined.

8.3.2 Benefits estimation

The benefits of urban planning in the context of economics are reflected in property prices or values (Chapter 5). Thus, the benefits of a typical SSA planning regime's compliance requirement(s) upon their execution are reflected in property prices or values. This means that the planning regime requirements' compliance benefit can be extracted from property prices or values through the compliance requirements outlined by Figure 8.3 as variables. These are an approved sub-division planning scheme, infrastructure (tarred roads and drains, electricity, pipe-borne water), social amenities (school), community, convenience shop, architectural design, formalised title, and building permit. The cumulative benefit of compliance with planning regime requirement(s) and value or benefit contributions of each of the variables can be calculated. However, given data constraints, two approaches to the estimation of the planning regime requirement(s)' compliance benefits are proposed:

1. Approach one
   Approach one initially proposes the use of the CVM to procure property value data to determine the value contribution of each of the variables through OLS regression. Subsequently, the individual values are summed to obtain the overall planning regime requirement(s)' compliance benefits. Thus, with this approach, real estate valuers and agents guided by the recommended procedures for the CVM can be asked to give their professional opinions as to the value of a prescribed property in a study area, even if it is in an area not provided with all the planning regime requirement(s)' compliance variables. Thereafter, they should be asked to provide their opinions of value for the prescribed property if it is in an area provided with or covered by a specific planning regime requirement to the exclusion of the other requirements. Real estate valuers and agents are recommended to be used as respondents because they are better placed by their training to provide comparatively more informed opinions of value. Besides, it will assist in reducing the biases and subjectiveness that may occur with reliance on actual property owners.

   The values that will be obtained from the CVM can be analysed with OLS regression: Equation 8.4 is re-stated so as to obtain the benefits of the individual variables:

$$\rho\chi = \beta 0 + \beta_2 b + \beta_3 c + \ldots + \beta_n p + \varepsilon \qquad (8.11)$$

   where $\rho\chi$ is the price or the reported values of the property if it is associated with only a particular variable and all other variables are as previously defined. The planning regime requirement(s)' compliance benefits per property can thus be expressed as:

$$UR_b = \sum (\beta_2 + \beta_3 + \ldots + \beta_n) + \varepsilon \qquad (8.12)$$

   where UR_b is the planning regime requirement(s)' compliance benefit per property, which is a conglomerate of a range of benefits, and $\beta_2, \beta_3, \ldots, \beta_n$, the coefficients of Equation 8.12, are the planning requirement(s)' compliance benefit(s), and all other variables are as previously defined. It is imperative to make the point that the practice of adopting the CVM to procure data for analysis using regression models, such as the above approach, is not without precedent in the extant literature. Hammond (2006) and Hammond and Antwi (2010) applied similar approaches relative to their studies on the calibration of economic impact of SSA real estate policies. Such was also the approach used by Bertaud and Mapelzzi (2001) in their assessment of costs and benefits of land use regulation in Malaysia.

2. Approach two
   The second approach also proposes the use of CVM, but the real estate valuers and agents should be asked to give their professional opinion of value of the prescribed property if it is associated with all the planning regime requirement(s) and if it is not, assuming other value determinants are the same. The difference in means of the two different groups of the reported values can then be adopted as the benefit of the planning regime.

   From the discussions, pitting the planning regime requirement(s)' compliance benefit with the planning requirement(s)' compliance cost to ascertain whether the planning regime provides a prime incentive can thus be written as follows:

$$P_i / P_d = UR_b - UR_c \tag{8.13}$$

where P_i / P_d is the prime incentive/disincentive, an indicator of economic incentives/disincentives. If UR_c is less than or at least equal to UR_b, that is, where planning regime requirements' compliance cost is less than or at least equal to planning regime requirements' compliance benefit then there is prime incentive (P_i) This signifies the planning regime's provision of economic incentives. Alternatively, should the planning regime requirements' compliance cost exceed that of its compliance benefit then a prime disincentive (P_d) arises, an indication of the planning regime's provision of disincentives.

8.4 Chapter summary

This chapter set out an economic evaluation framework capable of measuring incentives provided by urban planning systems, particularly those in SSA. In so doing, the chapter commenced with discussions on conventional economic impact methodologies often employed in the developed world. However, due to the complexities often associated with the conventional methodologies and their numerous data requirements, which are hardly encountered in SSA, bespoke evaluation framework(s) were developed considering data paucity in the region. Using insights from the developed framework(s), the next chapter reports on an outcome from a case study in Accra, Ghana, to provide some evidence relating to whether the country's planning system provides incentives to property owners.

9 Evidence from a case study on the provision of incentives under a planning system

9.1 Introduction

Chapter 8 devised methodologies for estimating the extent of economic incentives provided by a planning system from an individual property owners' perspective and within developing countries, where organised data is often difficult to come by. This chapter presents the outcomes from an application of the methodologies (determination of prime incentives) to a case study – a planned development in Kwabenya, a suburb of Accra, Ghana's capital city. In so doing, the chapter initially gives summarised discussions on a research methodology/paradigm and the appropriate research methodology, strategy, and data collection methods, among others, employed to obtain data. This is followed by an overview of Accra and then the profile of the case study. Subsequently, findings from the case study are presented before the narrative in the chapter is summarised.

9.2 The research paradigm

Paradigm is an elusive concept and appears to lack a clear definition (Guba, 1990; Kerlinger and Lee, 2000; Ellis and Crookes, 2006). The originator of the term – Kuhn (1970) – is said to have applied the term in 21 distinct perspectives (Guba, 1990). Paradigm, therefore, has wide discipline coverage. However, in the context of discipline enquiry, the paradigm question seeks to address the general principles or the philosophical realm within which a research should be undertaken (Guba, 1990; Clarke and Dawson, 1999; Creswell, 2007, 2009; Pansiri, 2009; Abdulai, 2010).

Several philosophical considerations are known in the extant literature to drive the discipline of enquiry. However, in the main, five of such considerations are often rehearsed. These are ontology, which delves into what constitutes reality (knowledge), its nature and its origin; epistemology, which is the scope of knowledge construed in terms of the relationship between the researcher (knower) and the phenomenon under enquiry; and methodology, which is how to find knowledge (Guba, 1990; Clarke and Dawson, 1999; Creswell, 2003, 2007, 2009; Pansiri, 2009). The rest are axiology, the value make-up of knowledge, and rhetoric, which is the language by which knowledge is communicated (Creswell, 2003, 2007, 2009). Based mainly on the first three philosophical considerations, two research paradigms – the quantitative and the qualitative research paradigms – are often identified in the field of social science (Guba, 1990; Clarke and Dawson, 1999; Ellis and Crookes, 2006). However, a third paradigm known as mixed methods or multi-methodology is increasingly gaining popularity (see Creswell, 2003, 2009; Johnson and Onwuegbuzie, 2004; Abdulai, 2007, 2010). Having outlined these research paradigms, it is now expedient to examine them and display how the paradigm for this work was selected.

9.2.1 The quantitative research paradigm

The quantitative research paradigm, also known as scientific, traditional, and conventional research methodology (Guba, 1990; Kerlinger and Lee, 2000; Khakee, 2003; Hammond, 2006; Abdulai, 2010), dominated research until the 1970s (Clarke and Dawson, 1999; Khakee, 2003). The paradigm is originally rooted in positivist claims to knowledge, which is underpinned by an empiricist tradition (Guba, 1990; Clarke and Dawson, 1999; Kerlinger and Lee, 2000; Creswell, 2009). These claims to knowledge advocate that the rationale for research is to expand verifiable knowledge. That is, knowledge allows explanation, prediction, and understanding of empirical reality construed as the only reliable knowledge that can improve human condition (Nachmias and Nachmias, 1996; Khakee, 2003). This notion is based on realist ontology, which posits the existence of a single objective reality in the world: absolute truth driven by immutable natural laws independent of human perception (Guba and Lincoln, 1981; Guba, 1990; Clarke and Dawson, 1999). However, with the emergence of post-positivism following nineteenth-century works from the likes of Comte; Durkheim; Newton; and, more recently, Phillips and Burbles (2000), the quest to achieve absolute truth – being 'positive' – is said to be non-realisable (Creswell, 2003, 2009, p. 7). Phillips and Burbles (2000), for example, argue that knowledge is conjectural and anti-foundational, which signifies that evidence discovered in research is usually imperfect and fallible. Therefore, absolute truth is never attainable.

Despite pessimism about the achievement of absolute truth, post-positivists still acknowledge the existence of a single objective reality (Guba, 1990; Creswell, 2003, 2009). This single objective reality is, however, conceived as convergent, fragmentable, and capable of being broken down into separate parts for examination. It is also deterministic, the existence of a cause and effect relationship in a social problem (Babbie, 1990; Clarke and Dawson, 1999; Kerlinger and Lee, 2000; Winter, 2000; Creswell, 2003, 2009). Consequently, to post-positivists acquisition of knowledge on the single objective reality should be based on careful observation and measurement (Glesne and Peshkin, 1992; Creswell, 2003, 2009). This signifies the need for application of rational methods involving the generation of numeric measurement of observation and verification of laws and theories that govern the single objective reality (Boyd, 1991; Bogdan and Biklen, 1998; Clarke and Dawson, 1999; Creswell, 2009).

Driven by the foregoing positivist and post-positivist ontological creeds, advocates of the quantitative research paradigm epistemologically adhere to an objective stance in enquiry. This requires detachment of inquirers from the subject matter of enquiry (Clarke and Dawson, 1999; Creswell, 2003, 2009). The essence is to prevent all forms of biases and subjectiveness in enquiry (Babbie, 1990; Nachmias and Nachmias, 1996; Hammond, 2006). Essentially, therefore, the quantitative research paradigm subscribes to a deductive approach to research, where causal explanation and prediction of outcome of phenomena follow a deductive logic form. The research commences with a theory comprising a set of interconnected general propositions that sets its hypotheses on the premise of logical reasoning. This is followed by the prescription of an operationalisation procedure for variables or constructs in the hypotheses. The hypotheses are then tested upon collection of empirical data to authenticate or otherwise the theory (see Babbie, 1990; Denzin and Lincoln, 1998; Clarke and Dawson, 1999; Kerlinger and Lee, 2000).

9.2.2 *The qualitative research paradigm*

The qualitative research paradigm, in contrast, emerged over five decades ago as an alternative to the traditional quantitative or scientific research paradigm (Guba, 1990; Khakee, 2003). This research paradigm is underpinned by varied philosophical assumptions (Guba, 1990; Creswell, 2007, 2009; Pansiri, 2009). The paradigm is also described variously – naturalistic, constructionist, interpretivist, post-positivist, holistic-inductive (Clarke and Dawson, 1999) – and comes in several designs (see Wolcott, 1992; Denzin and Lincoln, 2005). These include grounded theory, ethnography, case studies, narrative, and phenomenology (Creswell, 2007, 2009). However, the qualitative research paradigm, in the main, is driven by social constructionist and interpretivist claims to knowledge (Guba, 1990; Clarke and Dawson, 1999; Creswell, 2003, 2009). These claims to knowledge rest on relative ontology (Guba, 1990), which construes reality as multiple, divergent, and interrelated (Guba and Lincoln, 1981, p. 57, 1990; Creswell, 2003, 2009). Thus, unlike positivists' claims to knowledge, it rejects the notion that there is a single objective reality out there in the world. The philosophical consideration underlying the qualitative research paradigm therefore professes that reality is not located in an objective external world or the subjective mind of the knower but within dynamic transactions between the two (Barone, 1992, p. 31). Consequently, social constructionists hold the view that truth is a very elusive concept and cannot be objectively ascertained. Furthermore, it is perceived that reality is not a single entity.

Rather, individuals and groups will construct their own versions of reality depending on their own socio-economic, political, and cultural background and experiences. It is thus not for the researcher to identify which of them is close to the truth, but accurately record and report all the versions (Clarke and Dawson, 1999).

Epistemologically, social constructionists based on their ontological position describe as untenable the detachment of researchers from the object of research to avoid biases and achieve objectivity (Clarke and Dawson, 1999). In fact, social constructionists argue that the idea of undertaking value-free and neutral enquiry, in which the investigator becomes detached from the investigated, is a hoax. This is because quantitative researchers usually return to the human world as active participants to find an explanation for their outcomes (see Torgerson, 1986, p. 36, 40). To this extent, the qualitative research paradigm advocates that getting close to the object or actors in an enquiry to understand their point of view and the social world is imperative. This signifies a clear case of scientific objectivity as in quantitative research and phenomenological subjectivity, as in a qualitative research paradigm (Clarke and Dawson, 1999). What is worthy of note is that this epistemological viewpoint of qualitative research paradigm advocates, among others, and rests on the notion that there is a fundamental difference between natural and social phenomena. As such, the method adopted to investigate natural phenomena may not necessarily be suitable for social phenomena. Therefore, the qualitative research paradigm is inclined to an inductive approach to research in which data is not collected to test hypothesis but to derive a broad generalisation from observed data (Clarke and Dawson, 1999; Creswell, 2007, 2009).

9.2.3 The mixed-methods paradigm

The mixed-methods paradigm, otherwise known as multi-methodology, is a comparatively recent development (Johnson and Onwuegbuzie, 2004; Creswell, 2009; Abdulai, 2010). The paradigm basically conceived as combination of the first two paradigms (Abdulai, 2007, 2010) predominantly comes in three designs: sequential, concurrent, and transformational (Creswell, 2003, 2009; Abdulai, 2010). Although connected to several philosophical considerations, the central philosophical consideration that drives this paradigm is pragmatism (Creswell, 2003, 2009; Johnson and Onwuegbuzie, 2004). The pragmatic philosophical stance rejects the existence of a single objective reality out there in the world as acknowledged by positivists and posits that enquiry, among others, takes place within a historical, socio-economic, and political context. From this philosophical standpoint, truth is what works at a point in time (Creswell, 2003, 2009). Consequently, researchers within this paradigm lay emphasis on the social problem at hand and its solutions. Therefore, the paradigm subscribes to an amalgamation of philosophies, strategies, and data collection techniques to ensure a solution of social problems at hand (see Creswell, 2003, 2009; Johnson and Onwuegbuzie, 2004; Morgan, 2007).

9.2.4 *Choice of research paradigm*

The paradigm question has been a longstanding controversial issue described variously as the great paradigm wars (see Gage, 1989; Johnson and Onwuegbuzie, 2004) and paradigm problem (Chambers et al., 1992) relative to the appropriateness of one paradigm over the other. However, there has been a shift in thinking to the effect that the paradigm question should not be about the superiority or inferiority of one paradigm to another (Guba, 1990; Creswell, 2003, 2009; Ellis and Crookes, 2006; Hammond, 2006; Abdulai, 2010). This is because the various paradigms have their own merits and demerits. Consequently, it remains a moot point to say that one paradigm is better than the other (Hammond, 2006). In practice, certain paradigms are also more suitable to addressing some research problems than others. For example, it is argued that the application of different methods to the same research problem will yield different results. Therefore, the adoption of an inappropriate method is likely to lead to misleading outcomes with serious repercussions for the application of such outcomes (Clarke and Dawson, 1999; Ellis and Crookes, 2006). Additionally, the adoption of a specific paradigm to address a research problem enables a consistent and systematic appraisal of the research and its findings (Ellis and Crookes, 2006). A research paradigm thus guides the process of enquiry and forms the basis for the practice of science (see Kuhn, 1970). It directs researchers to appropriate research strategies and methods given the nature of the phenomenon under investigation. Consequently, while there is a need to select a research paradigm, such a selection defies conventional logic of choice of alternative courses of action based on their strengths and weaknesses. Rather, such choices must be based on the availability of resources; time; research audience; experience of the researcher; and, most importantly, the research problem (Creswell, 2003, 2009; Hammond, 2006; Abdulai, 2010).

This present work, right from the outset, sought to devise a suitable analytical framework to investigate compliance with planning regulations and evaluate in quantitative terms the economic incentive/disincentive provided by SSA urban planning systems regimes using Accra, Ghana, as the case study. This task required measurement of real-world numerical data (see Evans, 1996) to test the framework devoid, to a greater extent, of biases. Given the preceding discussions, the quantitative research paradigm comparatively is more suitable to addressing the core issue underlying this work. Consequently, the quantitative research paradigm was adopted. Based on an evaluation of the relevant extant literature, a suitable theory was adopted to devise an analytical framework from which general propositions were developed. Subsequently, the central argument of the work

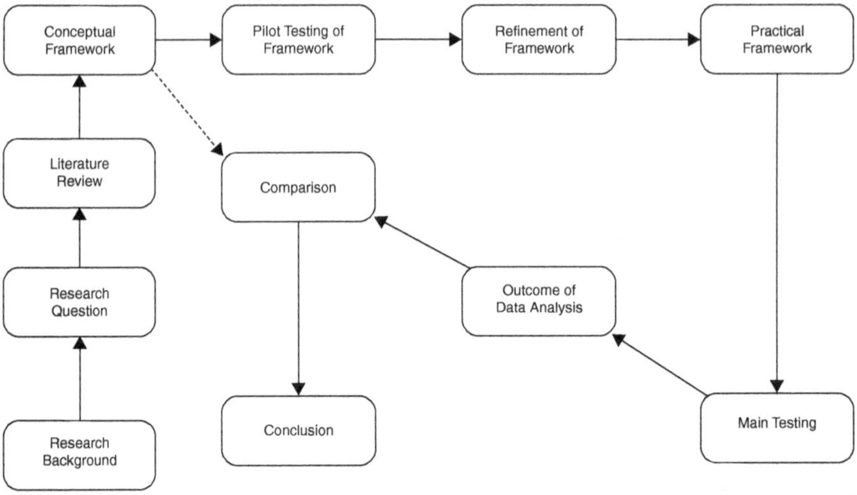

Figure 9.1 The research process adopted.
Source: Author's own creation.

was constructed through logical reasoning. Then, the operationalisation procedure was outlined and the research variables measured to test the central argument for validation or otherwise of the analytical framework. The research process, as outlined in Figure 9.1, therefore began with a background to the research to obtain insights into the issues under reference. Guided by the background insights, the relevant literature was evaluated to identify a suitable theory based on which the conceptual framework of the research was crafted. The framework was pilot tested, refined, and ultimately subjected to the main testing upon collection and analysis of real-world data after which conclusions were drawn. It is imperative to note that the acknowledged research paradigms and the designs they prescribe are based on models in the developed world where, for example, there are up-to-date postal systems and an availability of organised data. However, as indicated elsewhere in this work, such conditions are not the usual norm in the developing world. This means a practical technique, suitable to the conditions of SSA, was required to put the practical aspect of the research in motion. This thus leads to a discussion on the strategy adopted for the research.

9.3 Strategy of enquiry

Several research designs pertain under the quantitative research paradigm (see Babbie, 1990). However, two of such designs usually encountered in the extant literature are the experimental and survey designs (Babbie,

1990; Nachmias and Nachmias, 1996; Clarke and Dawson, 1999; Creswell, 2009). The experimental research design is broadly classified into experimental and quasi-experimental designs (Nachmias and Nachmias, 1996; Clarke and Dawson, 1999). Although these research designs also have their sub-classifications, in general the idea of experimental designs is to determine the impact or outcome of an intervention (Campbell and Stanley, 1963; Abdulai, 2010). For example, it may be to determine the impact of a planning policy or regulation on housing production. In its strongest form, which is usually associated with natural sciences, experimental designs are undertaken under a randomised experiment (Nachmias and Nachmias, 1996; Clarke and Dawson, 1999). This operates with control and experimental groups. That is, with this design objects or participants under investigation in a research are randomly assigned to two groups: control and experimental groups. The experimental group is then manipulated through administration of the intervention. Consequently, any observed difference compared to the control group is attributed to the intervention (Babbie, 1990; Nachmias and Nachmias, 1996; Clarke and Dawson, 1999). The idea of randomisation is to ensure that each object or participant has an equal chance of being selected into any of the groups and control extraneous variables in order to promote accuracy and internal validity. Therefore, it is to ensure that same or similar results will be obtained using the same barometer and will promote common agreement in observation (Nachmias and Nachmias, 1996).

Despite its seemingly watertight approach, the application of the experimental design has not passed without criticisms. It is argued, for example, that not all observed changes established with experimental groups can be attributed to intervention. Factors not necessarily connected to intervention can cause observed changes, a situation that threatens internal validity (Reichardt and Gollob, 1989). In addition, the procedure for extracting observed changes following administration of intervention has been questioned. The practice has been that the difference between experimental and control groups is not only compared, but inferences are also made on the observed difference. This means that inferences may be subject to inferential errors capable of affecting the internal validity of research findings (Mark and Cook, 1984, p. 75).

Beyond the foregoing, several other adverse concerns have been raised over the usage of experimental designs. These include the procedure for selecting research objects/participants, attrition, and maturation problems (see Campbell and Stanley, 1963; Mark and Cook, 1984). Of grave importance, however, is the general unsuitability of the design for studying social science phenomena. That is, studying phenomena in their natural setting and the huge cost implications for constituting control and experimental groups (Babbie, 1990; Clarke and Dawson, 1999; Creswell, 2003, 2009; Abdulai, 2010). This is further reinforced by the generally uniform planning policies and their application in SSA, and, therefore, their unsuitability for constitution of control and experimental groups (see Monk and Whitehead, 1999; Hammond, 2006; Hammond and Antwi, 2010). Recourse was therefore made to the survey design.

Survey design generally operates by soliciting information from people in their natural setting through answering questions posed by researchers or their representatives. The idea, inter alia, is to use the information gathered to describe and generate numerical tendencies and causal relationships of phenomena under enquiry (Totten et al., 1999). The design occurs in two forms with varying attributes that inform a choice depending on the exigencies of an enquiry. These are cross-sectional and longitudinal designs (Babbie, 1990, 2001; Nachmias and Nachmias, 1996; Abdulai, 2010). According to Babbie (1990, 2001) cross-sectional designs collect information at one point in time, usually within the shortest possible time. The information so obtained is analysed with respect to the same time frame. The longitudinal design, conversely, comes in three different forms: trend, cohort, and panel designs. However, in the main, longitudinal designs comparatively collect and analyse data on phenomena over a long period of time. For example, in trend design, data is collected on the general population at different points in time for a long period to determine trends (Babbie, 1990, 2001; Nachmias and Nachmias, 1996).

Due to time and resource constraints, the cross-sectional design was adopted. This means that the requisite information was solicited from the subject research participants at one point in time (from May 2011 to November 2011) and then the description and numerical tendencies and relevant relationships established with respect to the said time frame. The choice of the cross-sectional design was also reinforced by its comparatively inexpensive nature and the timely manner with which data is collected (Totten et al., 1999; Babbie, 2001; Creswell, 2009; Abeka, 2005; Burton and Mazerolle, 2011). It is also flexible with data collection and analysis, and capable of measuring latent constructs, that is, variables that researchers cannot observe directly or quantify (Burton and Mazerolle, 2011). Despite these advantages, the cross-sectional design, like all survey designs, suffers from dealing with extraneous variables, unlike experimental designs (Clarke and Dawson, 1999). Besides, with survey design there is always the potential for respondents to misinterpret or misunderstand survey questions (Turocy, 2002; Burton and Mazerolle, 2011). Consequently, in implementing the cross-sectional design in this work, carefully designed sampling and data collection methods were employed to counteract these problems to ensure validity (see Babbie, 1990; Nachmias and Nachmias, 1996; Creswell, 2003, 2009).

9.4 Research population and sampling

The aim of this research is to evaluate in quantitative terms the economic incentive/disincentive provided by SSA planning regimes using empirical data from Ghana as the case study. However, as intimated in the preceding section, studying the entire country is impossible due to time and resource constraints. This therefore required samples to be drawn from the research population and then estimates and inferences made to the population. The literature generally identifies two types of sampling: probability and non-probability sampling (Babbie, 1990, 2001; Czaja and Blair, 1996; Kerlinger and Lee, 2000; Abdulai, 2010). Probability sampling works on probability theory (Czaja and Blair, 1996; Kerlinger and Lee, 2000). This emphasises the achievement of true representation. That is, sampling a given population by enabling each member of the population to have equal chance of selection to be part of the sample. The idea is to reduce biases if not to eliminate them from the selection process. The probability sampling is also of different types. In the main, four types are usually encountered in the literature. These are simple random, systematic, stratified, and cluster sampling (see Czaja and Blair, 1996; Nachmias and Nachmias, 1996; Teddlie and Yu, 2007 for detailed discussions).

Non-probability sampling does not employ systematic techniques, such as randomisation in the selection of samples, to eliminate biases. Thus, it is sometimes perceived as weak (see Nachmias and Nachmias, 1996; Kerlinger and Lee, 2000; Abdulai, 2010). However, this perceived weakness can be addressed by extensive knowledge and expertise of the researcher with regard to the issue under investigation, tact and care in sample selection, and by replicating studies with different samples (Czaja and Blair, 1996; Kerlinger and Lee, 2000; Abdulai, 2010). The non-probability sampling also comes in four main forms: purposive, quota, snowball, and accidental or convenience sampling. Purposive, snowball, and accidental sampling were used in this study fundamentally because of the lack of reliable sample frame and the need to ensure that the right kinds of participants are selected for the study.

Purposive sampling draws sample members/units on purpose. It operates where samples are intentionally drawn from a given population based on knowledge of the population, its elements/members, and the aim of the research, and with the belief that the sample drawn will be representative of the population (Czaja and Blair, 1996; Paton, 2002; Teddlie and Yu, 2007). This sampling procedure is usually used in market research and case studies. Its greatest snag, however, is that it may be prone to researcher bias (Abdulai, 2010). According to Rubin and Babbie (2009), snowball sampling is usually resorted to in circumstances where the research population is uncommon or dispersed but has unique characteristics. The idea is to identify members of the given population by asking a few known members of the population. The technique proceeds by first identifying a member or few members of the given population who then lead(s) the researcher onto known member(s) of the population, who also subsequently provide such leads to the researcher. This process continues until the researcher gets the requisite information. The procedure works well when members of a given population know themselves and becomes more useful where sample frames are not available or are inadequate. Its problem, however, is that isolated members of the population may be excluded from the sampling exercise (Abdulai, 2010). Accidental or convenience sampling is often regarded as the weakest of all the sampling procedures. This sampling procedure is used to describe situations where researchers use readily available members of the population or, even better, still use volunteers to draw samples (Teddlie and Yu, 2007). This sampling procedure could be fraught with biases. Besides, there is the likelihood that samples drawn may not be representative of the population (Abdulai, 2010).

9.4.1 *Sample size determination*

Beyond the sampling technique adopted, or to be adopted, it is also imperative for researchers to consider the sample size for their research. Statistically and from the standpoint of probability sampling, sample size is usually determined by:

$$n = N / \left(1 + \left(\alpha^2\right) N\right)$$

where n = Sample; N = Total Population; and α = Margin of Error. This means that to calculate a sample size, particularly in probability sampling, there is a need for researchers to know the extent of the population or sample frame. While, in general, it is known that the larger the sample size, the closer the sample data is to the population (Nachmias and Nachmias, 1996; Kerlinger and Lee, 2000), in practice researchers need to ascertain how many responses will give them sufficient precision at an affordable cost (see Field, 2005; Abdulai, 2010). The logical implication from the foregoing is that the determination of appropriate sample size for a study does not follow any prescriptive method. However, such an exercise should be underpinned by how accurate and confident a researcher wants to be and the budget for the research (Abdulai, 2010). Apart from relying on non-probability sampling techniques, the above insights helped in the choice of suitable sample sizes as detailed in the subsequent sections.

9.4.2 *Area selection*

The phenomenon under investigation focuses on urbanism. This makes urbanisation a major issue for consideration in selecting an area for the research. Accra and, for that matter, the Greater Accra Metropolitan Area (GAMA) is the most urbanised city region in Ghana, where urban planning, development, and management issues are most prevalent. The city region was therefore purposely selected for this work.

9.4.2.1 *Overview of the city of Accra*

Accra is the capital city of Ghana and at the same time is also the capital of the Greater Accra Region, one of the 16 regions in Ghana. From a small coastal settlement with a nucleus of three settlements, namely, James Town,

Ussher Town, and Osu, the city became the capital of Ghana (in 1877). Accra has grown to become a large city (Parker, 2000; Oduro, 2010). From a comparatively small land area of 10 km^2 in the latter part of the nineteenth century, by 2000, Accra occupied a land area of about 777 km^2 with a population of 1,657,856 (Oduro, 2010). Apart from being the political, administrative, and commercial seat of Ghana, Accra is the second-most industrialised city and serves as a home to major manufacturing; recreational services, including key ICT services; and economic activities. The economic and political functions of Accra have made it a global investment destination, attracting people and economic activities from within and outside the country, and have pushed its frontiers outwards as well as maintained a significant role in Ghana's development.

Accra has grown to engulf its adjoining districts, which together with the core city form GAMA (Figure 9.2). The constituent areas of GAMA are the Accra Metropolitan Area; the Tema Metropolitan Area; and Ledzokuku Krowor, Ashiaman, Adentan, Ga East, Ga West, and Ga South Municipal Areas. Although Accra Metropolis and the other districts are separate administrative jurisdictions, they are so physically and functionally integrated that many residents are unaware of the existence of administrative demarcations. Accra Metropolis has become the employment and service centre, while most of the communities in the adjoining districts are conceived as

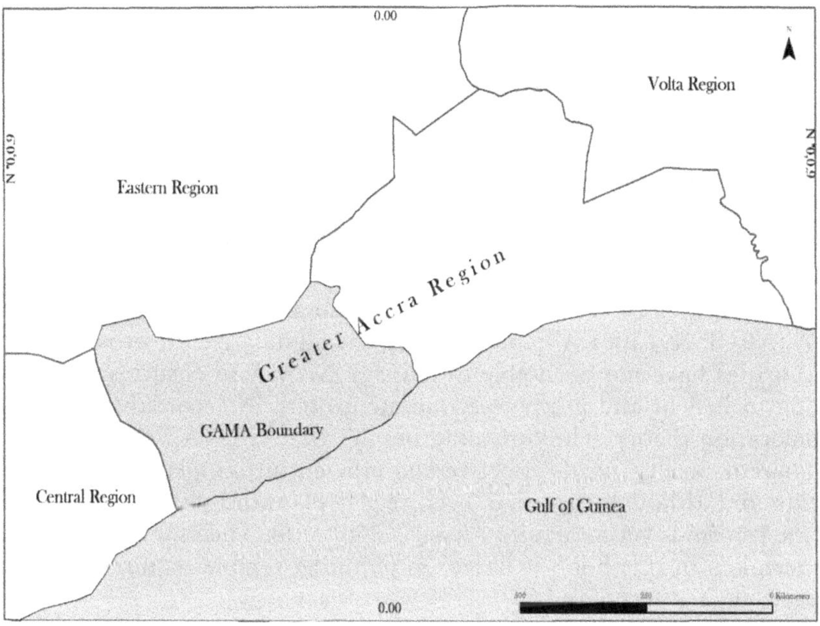

Figure 9.2 Boundary plan of the Greater Accra Region showing the boundary of GAMA.

Source: Extracted from maps at Ghana's survey & mapping division (lands commission).

'dormitory towns' for both the waged workers and the self-employed. Consequently, the name 'Accra' is usually used for the Metropolis itself and the contiguous built-up and developing areas (Oduro, 2010).

GAMA is the most dominant and influential urban region in Ghana and accounts for 25% of GDP and 83% of all foreign direct investment in the country and contributes 32% and 28% of all formal and informal employment, respectively (World, 2016). Like many other SSA countries, Ghana is undergoing rapid urbanisation. The country's population doubled between 1984 and 2013, with an urban population growth rate of 4.4% per annum and a rise in urbanisation rate from 31% to 51% (World Bank, 2015). GAMA is where Ghana's current spate of urbanisation is most intense. Between 1985 and 2000, GAMA's population increased by 50% and the urban extent increased by 160% (World, 2015). However, the growth rate and expansion of GAMA have outrun the capacities of city authorities and governance institutions, resulting in several urban ills, such as increasing insecurity, poverty, inadequate urban planning and land use management, slums and squatter settlements, increasing environmental deterioration, and inadequate urban infrastructure and services (GoG, 2012). For example, it is estimated that 55% of GAMA's population live in informal housing and that the limited access to land means that urban poor households are displaced to rapidly expanding slums in environmentally fragile flood plains and hazard zones in and around the urban region (ARUP & Cities Alliance, 2016). GAMA is also challenged by many natural and man-made hazards, such as surface and coastal flooding, drought, extreme temperatures, vector-borne disease, as well as seismic hazards from local fault lines, air or water pollution, depletion of natural resources and related health impacts including respiratory illness and waterborne pathogens like cholera (ARUP & Cities Alliance, 2016). Further, limited infrastructure connectivity both within the metropolitan area and between Ghanaian cities has reduced local economic efficiency, and the transport costs for goods are relatively high, resulting in Ghana being ranked 100 out of 160 survey countries in the Logistics Performance Index, only slightly above the average for SSA (ARUP & Cities Alliance, 2016). The cumulative effect is that city authorities have not been able to manage GAMA to ensure sustainable living to benefit and promote economic growth in accordance with agglomeration theory. The foregoing implies that GAMA, like the rest of Ghanaian society, needs effective and efficient urban planning arrangements and although there has been recent planning reform, the impact of the reform is yet to manifest itself (Chapter 6). Therefore, the analysis undertaken in this book is based on planning regime requirements discussed in Chapters 6 and 8.

9.4.2.2 Profile of the case study

Kwabenya community, a suburb of Accra, is the case study (refer to Box 9.1 for profile). The community was purposively selected for several reasons.

First, the urban transition taking place in Ghana, particularly in the city of Accra, is on the fringes. Given the focus of this book, which relates to urban transition-connected issues, there is a need for a peripheral community(ies) that reflects the characteristics of the current urban transition in Accra. It is known, however, that districts, such as Tema Metropolitan Area and Ledzokuku Krowor and Ashiaman municipalities, are already fully built and integrated into Accra (Oduro, 2010). However, portions of Ga East Municipality, particularly Kwabenya, and its environs are under transition. This makes the community suitable for a case study in this book. Second, unlike other peripheral communities, which are not covered by approved planning schemes, Kwabenya community is covered. Further, since Kwabenya and its adjoining areas are under transition, areas close to the community without certain planning regime requirements were available as comparable to enable the application of the contingent valuation method to obtain information for the estimation of the benefits of planned developments, especially given that organised data in Ghana is often difficult to come by. Additionally, accessing data on urban development activities from urban development and management stakeholders on already built-up areas is usually difficult because they may have forgotten their experience due to effluxion of time. Comparatively, such data can easily be accessed on Kwabenya since the stakeholders may have dealt with such developments activities not long ago or may be dealing with them currently. Last but not the least, the choice of Kwabenya was influenced by the author's deep insight into urban development activities in Kwabenya and access to official documentary data on the community.

Box 9.1 Profile of Kwabenya community

Kwabenya is a community located on the fringes of the city of Accra and falls within the Ga East Municipality, the political and administrative jurisdiction. The community is about 25 km east of the city of Accra and about 16 km west of Abokobi, the capital of Ga East Municipality. Kwabenya used to be a small rural farming community, which was clustered around its present-day main vehicular terminal. Kwabenya, as of the 1980s, was classified as semi-urban (GSS, 1984). However, the community has seen growth and expansion over the years. It has now become part of Accra as an urban area. According to Ghana's 2000 population and housing census, the population of Kwabenya as of 2000 was 3,862. This consisted of 2,033 males and 1,829 females. People with a tertiary level of education were 113 compared to 672 who had no formal education; 544 of the population were engaged in formal sector employment out of 2,110 people who were were employed. The rest were engaged mainly in informal economic activities. Over the years, Kwabenya has seen massive growth and expansion to integrate with adjoining communities, such as Pokuase on the north, Musuku and Ashoman on the south, and

Dome on the west. The community also continues to grow towards Brekuso on the north-east and east. This massive growth and expansion corresponds with Accra's urban growth and expansion occurring at the periphery. The community has an undulating topography and is covered by three different planning schemes: the North Dome Residential Area Planning Scheme (TCPD/N/Dom/88/1) prepared in 1988, the New Ashoman Residential Area Sector Two Planning Scheme (TCPD/GA/Ashoman/97/1) prepared in 1997, and the West Ashoman Planning Scheme (TCPD/GD/WA/2000) prepared in 2000. The North Dome Residential Area Planning Scheme comparatively covers a large section of the community.

Apart from the indigenous settlement, developments in the community mainly began in the 1980s. Residential land use dominates land utilisation in the area. These are interspersed with commercial land uses, such as shops and pubs especially for developments along the main Dome–Kwabenya–Brekuso Road that divides Kwabenya. The residential developments are mainly three–four-bedroom detached sandcrete block properties. Two gated communities constructed by Regimanuel Gray Company Limited, a real estate development company, are also located in the community. These gated communities referred to as Kwabenya Housing Estate and Baloon Gate Estate are about 1 km to the south-west of the indigenous Kwabenya community. The gated communities comprise detached and semi-detached two- & three-bedroom estate-type residential houses as well as four-bedroom executive houses. The Baloon Gate Estate additionally has a multi-storey block of flats. The community is connected to infrastructural facilities, such as electricity, water, and telephone facilities from the public mains. However, such facilities are yet to be connected to areas of the communities, towards Pokuase and Brekuso on the north and the north-east. Even in the main community where these facilities are available, water supply is not regular, and many properties are not connected to fixed line telephones. Ancillary land uses, such as schools, are few, while others, like community park(s), are non-existent partly due to encroachments.[1] Similarly, road networks within the community are in poor condition. Excepting the Dome-Kabenya- Brekuso Road, which is tarred, all the remaining community roads are not tarred. Records at Ghana's Lands Commission indicate that land ownership within Kwabenya and its environs are mainly family lands belonging to families, such as Nii Odai Ntow, Onamrokor Adain, and Evans and Peter Mensah Anteh Families. Family lands come under private lands in a broad classification of land ownership in Ghana as public and private. Public lands are lands whose ownership is vested in the state (Republic of Ghana), while private lands are customary lands whose ownership is vested in communities represented by stools/

skins and families/clans. Within public lands there is specie of land known as vested lands, which falls in between public and customary lands. This specie of land is associated with duality of ownership: legal and equitable. The legal ownership is vested in the state while the equitable ownership is vested in stools/skins and families/clans. There is also another strand of land within the customary land ownership grouping known as private individual lands. Private individual lands are lands which have their ownership vested in private individuals. Consequently, Ghana can be classified into state, vested, stool/skin, family/clan, and individual lands. However, several hierarchies of interests or ownerships, such as allodial, the highest interest in land in Ghana, estate of freehold, customary freehold, leasehold, and tenancies exist in these lands. However, the analysis in this book focusses on family lands in terms of land ownership.

9.4.3 *Selection of research participants*

The crafted conceptual framework for the research in Chapter 5 outlined that the examination of the phenomenon under investigation is to be done from the standpoint of individual property owners/developers. This implies that individual property owners/developers within the geographical limit for the research constitute the unit of analysis and thus the research population. However, the literature discussions and the information obtained from the informants established that most of the unit of analysis in SSA do not comply with planning regimes' requirements. The situation in Ghana is not different (Boamah et al., 2012; Baffour Awuah and Hammond, 2014). Besides, those who even comply with the requirements usually engage the services of professionals or may not remember aspects of the issues involved in complying with the requirements. Given the foregoing, obtaining all the requisite information from the actual research population was not feasible. As such, professionals involved in the urban development processes were sampled as proxies to property owners in this work. These professionals were relied on because they deal with urban development activities on a regular basis. Therefore, the presumption was that they are very much abreast with planning regime requirement issues and are comparatively better placed to provide the requisite information for the research.

Research participants were selected based on the major themes for the surveys. Four different surveys were undertaken (Table 9.1). In so doing, members of the professional categories who have the experience and often dealt with the subject matter of each of the surveys in the urban development processes in the study site were selected as participants. Thus, in the surveys, to estimate the cost of compliance with planning regime requirements, real estate valuers, real/land estate agents, and lawyers were used as participants for the title formalisation cost survey. For cost relating to architectural design survey, real estate valuers, real estate managers, and then real estate agents were used as participants. It is imperative to state that architects and draughtsmen were not used as participants because they deal with only an aspect of the cost under reference – design cost. It was also noted that most architects usually find it difficult in the study site to indicate a charge for a design on a standard three-bedroom house, given the comparatively small magnitude of work involved. As such, it was considered most appropriate to rely on professionals who had experience with all the aspects of architectural design cost. In the case of acquisition cost for a building permit survey, real estate valuers, real estate officers/managers, real estate agents, lawyers, and architects/draughtsmen were used as participants. For each of the three surveys, a total of 100 respondents were sampled. Apart from giving enough prediction, the above sample sizes were adopted because of time and resource constraints.

The survey relating to the benefit of planning regime requirements used real estate valuers and real estate agents who had a minimum of five years' working experience as participants. Five years' working experience was used as the criterion because it is the working duration for which professional members of the Ghana Institution of Surveyors (GhIS), the accredited professional body for real estate valuers, upon completion are assumed to be matured and can practise on their own. A total of 103 of these respondents were sampled. However, given the predictor variables for examination, which were 12 in number (Table 9.3), a sample size in excess of 300 was required for precision based on the use of ordinary least square (OLS) regression as an estimator or an analytical tool (Field, 2005). Practically, this was unattainable, given the time and resource constraints as well as the unavailability of requisite respondents. That said, questions that solicited data on these variables were mutually exclusive of each other. As such, responses on the variables were treated as observations, which were larger and suitable for the requisite analysis given the prediction that the study envisaged. Consequently, for every response on a variable, additional 11 responses were generated on the other variables through dummying the response on the actual variable as '1' and '0s' for all the other variables. One hundred and two responses were obtained regarding questions on each variable. Again, since the design for this particular survey was a repeated measure design, there was a need for a prior controlled variable based on which the effect of the predictor variables could be measured (Section 9.6.1). Thus, for responses from question on the controlled variable, all the predictor variables were dummied as '0s'. This meant that 13 questions were asked, and 103 responses were received for each of the predictor variables, signifying a total of 1,339 observations. This practice of using responses as observations is common in the real estate finance literature (Francis et al., 2007; Price et al., 2010). It is to be noted that the 1,339 observations were used solely for the OLS regression, approach one (Chapter 8).

Table 9.1 gives details of the breakdown on the size and composition of samples for the research. The surveys focussed on Accra and its environs

Table 9.1 Research participants

Survey	*Research Participant(s)*	*Sample Size*
1	Real estate valuers Real estate/land agents Lawyers	100
1a	Real estate valuers Real estate officers/agents	100
1b	Real estate valuers Real estate officers/managers Real estate/land agents Lawyers Architects/draughtsmen	100
2	Real estate valuers Real estate/land agents	103

1 = Survey on estimation of title formalisation cost, 1a = Survey on Estimation of architectural design cost, 1b = Survey on acquisition of building permit cost and 2 = Survey on estimation of planning regime requirements' compliance benefits.

and, as noted earlier, relied on a combination of purposive, accidental, and snowball sampling techniques due to the lack of adequate and reliable sample frames. The existence of the yearly list of professional members in good standing published by professional institutions, such as GhIS, the Ghana Bar Association, and the Ghana Institute of Architects, was noted. However, these lists are usually not up to date and come without forwarding addresses or the location of members. Apart from that members of these institutions have their own specialisation and locations they focus on. This means that some members' areas of specialisation may not necessarily be the subject matter of this research. Therefore, relying on such sample frames could lead to selection of members who may have no idea of the subject matter of the research.

Ordinarily, a single survey should have been undertaken for the professionals involved in the urban development processes to minimise the duplication of efforts. However, as noted in Chapters 6 and 8, compliance with the requirements of the subject planning regime entails numerous distinct activities. This meant that most of the categories of professionals were not going to be in a position to provide the requisite information for the study. Even with regards to the professionals real estate valuers and agents, it was realised that most of them specialise in their practice. Therefore, it was not possible for them to provide the requisite information on all the various activities. Also, designing a single questionnaire survey for such numerous but distinct activities would have been complex, apart from the fact that individual questionnaires would have been bulky. This in effect would have adversely affected the questionnaire administration and the response rate (Clarke and Dawson, 1999; Totten et al., 1999). Confronted with such practical difficulties and based on discussions with relevant informants, undertaking four distinct surveys was more expedient to target relevant

Table 9.2 Institutional research participants for the study

Institution	*Number of Participants*	*Remarks*
DUR	2	GEMA[1] Municipal Roads Engineer Municipal Roads Quantity Surveyor
DPG	2	GAR[2] Director GAR Estimator
TCPD	2	GAR Director Urban Planning Officer
ECG	2	Schedule Engineer for GEMA Schedule Estimator for GEMA
VGL	2	Schedule Engineer for GEMA Schedule Estimator for GEMA
GWCL	2	GAR Engineer/Manager GAR Operations Manager
Total	12	–

[1]GEMA means Ga East Municipal Assembly.
[2]GAR means Greater Accra Regional.

professionals to obtain the requisite information for the study. In so doing, administration of the questionnaire for all the four surveys was undertaken concurrently to reduce the duplication of efforts. The possibility of using some of the respondents in more than one survey was recognised. However, this was not anticipated to affect the validity of the study given that the four surveys were distinct and dealt with different issues. Besides, where it was anticipated to affect the validity of findings, appropriate statistical tools were used to rectify the necessary anomaly(ies).

In addition to the above participants, several state and quasi-state agencies and departments were involved in the research. These agencies are the Department of Urban Roads (DUR), the Department of Parks and Gardens (DPG), and the Town and Country Planning Department (TCPD). The remainder is the Electricity Company of Ghana (ECG), Vodafone Ghana Ltd (VGL), and Ghana Water Company Ltd. (GWCL). Overall, schedule officers for the research area and officers with expertise on the subject matter of the enquiry from these institutions were used as participants. Table 9.2 gives details on the institutional participants.

9.5 Research variables

Table 9.3 exhibits the research variables. The table gives the variables for compliance with planning regime requirements' costs and benefits.

In the case of planning regime compliance costs, apart from sub-division planning scheme and infrastructure and amenities costs, all the other requirements virtually had the same variables, though they needed explanation. The cost of deed refers to expenditure on site plan, the drafting of deed, and their related costs of making a deed acceptable for processing towards formalisation. Official fee for formalisation is the statutory fee

Table 9.3 Research variables used in the study

No.	*Dependent (Outcome) Variable*	*Predictors*
1	Formalisation of title to land cost	Cost of deed Official fee for formalisation Unofficial fee for formalisation Commuting cost Cost of time lag Professional fee
1a	Architectural design cost	Cost of design Commuting cost Cost of time lag Professional fee
1b	Acquisition of building permit cost	Official fee for permit processing Unofficial fee for permit processing Commuting cost Cost of time lag Professional fee
1c	Sub-division planning scheme	Cost of scheme/unit land area Land size
1d	Infrastructure & community park cost	Cost of infrastructure/community park/unit land area Land cost
2	Planning regime requirement compliance benefit	Sub-division planning scheme Tarred roads & concrete drains Electricity Pipe-borne water Telephone facilities Community park Worship centre School Convenience shop Formalised title Architectural design Building permit

charged at public agencies for formalisation, while the unofficial fee is extra out-of-pocket payments made at public agencies towards formalisation. Commuting cost has to do with cost of travel associated with formalisation and the cost of time lag, the time value for money, and reflects the cost of capital. Professional fee refers to the fee charged by professionals for working on behalf of property owners to deal with parties and institutions involved in formalisation of title and ensuring that their clients' titles are formalised. Official and unofficial fees, as defined herein, are applicable to building permit acquisition cost (dependent variable), while the commuting cost, cost of time lag, and professional fee are also applicable to both design and acquisition of building permit costs (dependent variables). The sub-division planning scheme cost is the expenditure on the preparation and approval of the sub-division planning scheme.

Finally, the independent variables for infrastructure and amenities are the same as that of planning regime requirements' compliance benefits outlined in Table 9.3. The only difference, however, is that the infrastructure and amenity costs did not consider costs on worship centre, school, and convenience shop. This position was premised on the extant practice where such properties are not regarded as communally owned but are for private individuals and institutions. As such, they must bear their cost.

9.6 Research methods

The literature identifies several methods for data collection within the quantitative research paradigm. These basically include questionnaire instruments; extraction of existing data (archival data), which may or may not be pre-determined performance-based data (Babbie, 1990; Creswell, 2003, 2009; Abdulai, 2010); and participant observation (Hammond, 2006). Of course, as discussed elsewhere in this chapter, choice of any of these data collection methods is guided by the research problem and other practical peculiarities, such as time, logistical constraints, and the availability of existing data.

The surveys took six months, from May to November 2011. However, in view of the afore-mentioned peculiarities, questionnaire instruments and extraction of existing data were used to procure data for the research.

9.6.1 Questionnaire instruments and administration

Questionnaire instruments were used in all the surveys. Table 9.4 gives a summary of these instruments. The questionnaire for survey no. (1) was targeted at real estate valuers, real estate/land agents, and lawyers. It was to solicit information from respondents for assessment of formalisation of title to land cost in the study area. This instrument was categorised into three sections 'A'–'C': Section 'A' had questions on the background of respondents and solicited information, such as gender, profession, years of experience of respondents, and experience in formalising title to lands in the study area as well as type of land holding usually dealt with; Section 'B' dwelt on the processes involved in formalisation of title to lands in the study area.

Table 9.4 Survey instruments used in the study

Survey	*Instrument*	*Remarks*
1	Questionnaire	Title formalisation cost
1a	Questionnaire	Architectural design cost
1b	Questionnaire	Building permit acquisition cost
2	Questionnaire	Planning regime requirement compliance benefit

It focused on information relating to duration for the processes and the follow-up respondents, on average, make to expedite action on a process at a vendor of land premises and public sector institutions as part of the title formalisation process. The remainder was usual charges for formalisation of the title products and services, such as deed cost and unofficial fees at public sector institutions, the usual commuting time and cost per follow-up, waiting time per follow-up, and professional fee usually charged for service delivery; and Section 'C' requested the comments of respondents on urban planning in Ghana, if any, and whether they would be interested in receiving copies of the research findings. The questionnaire for survey no. (1a) was earmarked only for real estate valuers and real estate officers/agents. Conversely, the questionnaire for survey no. (1b) was for real estate valuers, real estate officers, real estate agents, lawyers, and architects/draughtsmen. These two latter instruments were structured like the instrument for survey no. (1) and sought information along its lines for the assessment of architectural design and the acquisition of building permit costs. The questionnaire for survey no. (2) was on planning regime requirement compliance benefits and targeted real estate valuers and agents. It had three sections 'A'–'C' and was designed as a repeated measure design instrument: Section 'A' solicited background information on respondents, such as gender, profession, and years of professional experience; Section 'B' elicited benefits of planning regime requirements proxied on property values. As a repeated measure design instrument (see Kerlinger and Lee, 2000; Field, 2005) the same respondents were asked to give their professional opinion of value of a specified property (Chapter 8) in the study area. Subsequently, they were asked to give their professional opinion of value if it is associated with a particular planning regime requirement to the exclusion of the other requirements. The same exercise was done to elicit their opinion of value when the specified property is associated with all the requirements, and Section 'C', the last section, requested respondents' comments, if any, on planning in Ghana and whether they would be interested in receiving copies of the findings from the research.

9.6.1.1 Administration of questionnaire instruments

9.6.1.1.1 PRELIMINARY ACTIVITIES

Due to weak electronic and postal address system in the study site and the need to ensure adequate understanding of questions, to avoid validity problems, a face-to-face administration of the instruments was undertaken with the assistance of a team of research assistants. A team of four research assistants was recruited and trained. These research assistants were BSc (Hons) Land Economy graduates who had just completed their post-graduation national service with the Accra office of Ghana's LC and aspired to become fully qualified real estate valuers and professionals in the built environment. They were, thus, already familiar with the basic issues involved in urban development processes. In addition to the aforementioned strength, the essence of the research, what each questionnaire was about, the meaning of terms in the questionnaire instruments, and how the instruments ought to be administered, among other things, were explained to them. For example, as of the time of the survey, four public land sector agencies, namely, the LC, the Land Valuation Board (LVB), the Survey Department (SD), and the Land Title Registry (LTR), had merged into a new LC pursuant to the promulgation of a new Lands Commission Act (2008) (Act 767). These agencies had been turned into divisions called the Public and Vested Lands Management Division (PVLMD), the Land Valuation Division (LVD), the Survey and Mapping Division (SMD), and the Land Registry Division (LRD) of the new Commission. However, in practice the operations of these divisions were as before, and their operations were undertaken in the same old premises. Besides, members of the public knew the agencies by their old names. Therefore, the questionnaire instruments and, indeed, the entire research used the old names. This had to be clearly explained to the research assistants.

9.6.1.1.2 INSTRUMENT ADMINISTRATION

The administration of instruments was preceded by pretesting of the instruments. Findings from the pretesting of the instruments led to a slight revision of the instruments. To minimise duplication of effort in the face of resource and time constraints, the questionnaires for all the four surveys were administered concurrently. However, to also ensure that the target populations were reached, as much as possible, a combination of two approaches was adopted. First, respondents were targeted at the offices of the public sector institutions/agencies responsible for land title formalisation and acquisition of a building permit. These public sector institutions were the LC, LVB, SD, LTR, and the Ga East Municipal Assembly (GEMA). These locations were selected because they are places most of the respondents visit regularly to put in new applications for formalisation of title and building permits or expedite action on pending applications. Since the researcher together with the recruited research assistants were five, each of them was assigned to one of the public sector institutions to target the respondents.

The second approach partitioned Accra Metropolitan Area into four zones: Accra north, south, east, and west. Although GAMA is the larger urban region, based on the information obtained from informants, it became evident that most of the respondents' offices were in Accra Metropolitan Area. Using the 'Kwame Nkrumah Circle', a popular roundabout in Accra (now interchange) named after Ghana's first president, as a reference point, the four zones were created. The areas to the north of the roundabout, which is along the 'Accra-Nsawam Road', were designated as Accra north. Those from the roundabout to 'Accra Central' were designated as Accra south while the areas from the roundabout towards the Odorkor community along the 'Kaneshie-Odorkor Mallam Highway' were labelled as Accra west. Finally, the areas from the roundabout to East Legon community, along the 'Circle-Tetteh Quarshie-Madina Road' were labelled Accra east. The creation of these zones was to ensure smooth administration of the questionnaire instruments as well as reach the respondents in a cost-effective and timely manner. Each research assistant was assigned a zone while the researcher switched in between the zones to ensure smooth instrument administration.

The two approaches for the questionnaires' administration were used in turns on a weekly basis. The actual questionnaire administration was executed based on insights from purposive, snowball, and accidental sampling. Respondents were identified at the offices of the public sector institutions. Subsequently, an introduction and the purpose for the contact with them were made known. At this point the research, what it sought to achieve, and the benefits respondents stood to gain upon their participation were communicated to them. They were told that participation was voluntary. Also, enquiry was made as to which of the surveys they had the experience to partake in after which their responses were solicited based on the questionnaires, that is, where there was an agreement to participate in the study. Finally, they were asked about other known respondents and their location, and then thanked for making time to participate in the study. Within the zones, areas where offices of the respondents were concentrated were targeted and respondents identified. The questionnaire administration followed the same procedure as those which were undertaken at the public sector institutions. The questionnaire administration was undertaken during normal working days of the week (Mondays to Fridays and from 8:00 am to 5:00 pm).

9.6.2 *Extraction of existing data*

Extraction of existing data from the institutional databases was done in two different forms. The first one involved retrieving archival data from public and private sector institutions, as well as examining their records. Data obtained by this approach were pieces of legislation on statutory (official) fees for the processes involved in formalising titles to land and acquisition of building permits. These legislations included, for example, the Fees and Charges (Miscellaneous Provisions) Act (2009) (Act 793) and the Ga East Municipal Fee Fixing Resolution (2011). The remainder of the extracted data was planning standards, Government of Ghana-approved consultancy rates, and cost of capital, among others. The institutions, which were contacted for these archival data, included the Lands Commission (LC), Land Valuation Board (LVB), Survey Department (SD), and (Land Title Registry (LTR); the Greater Accra Regional (GAR) directorate of Town and Country Planning Department (TCPD); the Planning and Works Departments of Ga East Municipal Assembly (GEMA); the Land Use Management and Planning (LUMP) Office; and the Ghana Institute of Planners, the Bank of Ghana (BOG), and Architectural and Engineering Services Limited (AESL). In addition, some of the records of these institutions, like the LC and LVB, were examined to ascertain whether, for example, official fees stated in applicable legislations were the ones being paid by property owners.

The second form of extraction of data entailed the process below:

1. A prototype sub-division planning scheme was sent to infrastructure and social amenities agencies;
2. Based on the prototype planning scheme, cost data were obtained from the infrastructure and social amenities agencies; and
3. The cost data were further discussed with scheduled/relevant officers and based on the additional information obtained, the necessary adjustments were done to arrive at a unit cost rate for their products. This approach was adopted because infrastructural and social amenities projects are capital-intensive projects, which are undertaken by or under supervision of such agencies, but not on the individual property owner level. This meant that it was not feasible to obtain such information through a questionnaire. Responsible institutions, which were contacted in this regard, were TCPD, DUR, DPG, ECG, VGL, and GWCL.

9.7 Data analyses

Analyses of the research data took several levels with several analytical tools. With regard to the survey data, responses from respondents were first checked to ascertain consistency and to rectify anomalies. Subsequently, the responses were coded and entered in a data analysis programme – Statistical Package for Social Sciences (Version 16). At this stage too, the data was explored, screened, and cleaned. Further to this, descriptive statistical analysis was run on the data. Thereafter, the distributions of the responses were checked to ascertain their normality by carrying out a normality test with Kolmogorov-Smirnov's test and homogeneity of their variance test with Levene's test to determine the direction for the subsequent levels of analysis. Based on the outcome of these tests, the Mann-Whitney and Kruskal-Wallis tests were undertaken based on the planning regime requirement's compliance cost data, generated from the survey of professionals involved in the urban development processes. Both Mann-Whitney and Kruskal Wallis tests are non-parametric tests. However, the Mann-Whitney test is invoked when differences in two situations and different participants are to be tested. It is the equivalent of the independent *t*-test (Field, 2005). It works by ranking actual data generated from a survey and carrying out the analysis on the ranked data instead of the actual data. The Kruskal Wallis test works along similar lines, but under this arrangement independent participants or groups are usually several. It is the equivalent of the one-way independent ANOVA (Field, 2005). The cost data on the variables obtained at this stage was then transported to Microsoft Excel for further analyses using the operationalisation procedure(s) in Chapter 8 to calibrate the cost of the subject planning regime requirements' compliance.

For the planning regime requirements' compliance benefit, both the OLS models, developed as Equations 8.11 and 8.12 in Chapter 8, were activated. All the assessments carried out were based on the levels of significance used in the social science mentioned earlier. However, it needs to be pointed out that the regression was re-run on Stata (Version 11) to enable the standard errors to be clustered, since the standard errors were biased due to the research design (see Field, 2005; Petersen, 2008; Cheah, 2009). For the data procured from relevant institutions on the cost of sub-division planning schemes and infrastructure and social amenities, they were assessed with Microsoft Excel based on their relevant models in Chapter 8 to determine their cost. Subsequently, all the costs and benefits relating to the individual "cost and benefit" items were summed up independently as cost of the planning regime and benefit of the planning regime, and compared to address the central argument of this work.

9.8 Ethical issues in research

Researchers must be guided by some form of ethics in the execution of their work (Shrader-Frechette, 1994). Shrader-Frechette (1994) asserts that research ethics specifies conduct that researchers ought to demonstrate during an entire process of research. This conduct and its related issues have attracted attention over the years, so much so that they are being addressed as an integral part of research proposals (Creswell, 2003, 2009). The relevance of research ethics has made several organisations and institutions to develop standards, guidelines, and principles for research ethics.

Based on the Practice of Responsible Research, this research was subjected to ethical processes and standards. The requisite permission of all the participating institutions was sought. The research also ensured that the rights of participants, their values and needs were upheld. This was done through disclosures to participants regarding the purpose of the study, those who were involved, and how findings were to be disseminated. Further, participants were given prior information that participation in the study was at their own volition, and they had the right to walk out of the study at any time. In the same vein, they were assured of anonymity and confidentiality through, for example, not disclosing their names in the research reports. Regarding the public sector institutions, since there was the likelihood of coming across confidential materials from extraction and examination of their records, the highest level of discretion was maintained to safeguard them against leakages to the public particularly the local press.

9.9 Cost and benefit calculations

To determine whether the planning system in Ghana regarding Kwabenya provides incentives for property owners, there was a need to analyse the cost of compliance with requirements for a planned development and compare it with its benefits. The analysis was conducted at the margins – when a single additional planned residential house is developed. This is because in economics, decisions are taken at the margins. Further, the data used in the analysis are mainly 2011 figures. As stated previously, the variables or requirements that were used to assess the cost of compliance with the planning requirements of a planned development are sub-division planning scheme and infrastructure and social amenities – roads and concrete drains, telephone facilities, electricity, pipe-borne water and community park, architectural design, title formalisation, and building permit acquisition.

To ensure systematic cost assessment, the following activities were undertaken:

1 The sub-division planning scheme of Regimanuel Gray's Baloon Gate Housing Estate, which falls under planning scheme number TCPD/N/Dom/88/1 stated in Box 9.1, was used as a guide for the assessment of the sub-division planning scheme and infrastructure and amenities costs. The boundary plan of the land for the subject housing estate, which is 16.20 hectares (40 acres), is shown herein as Figure 9.3.

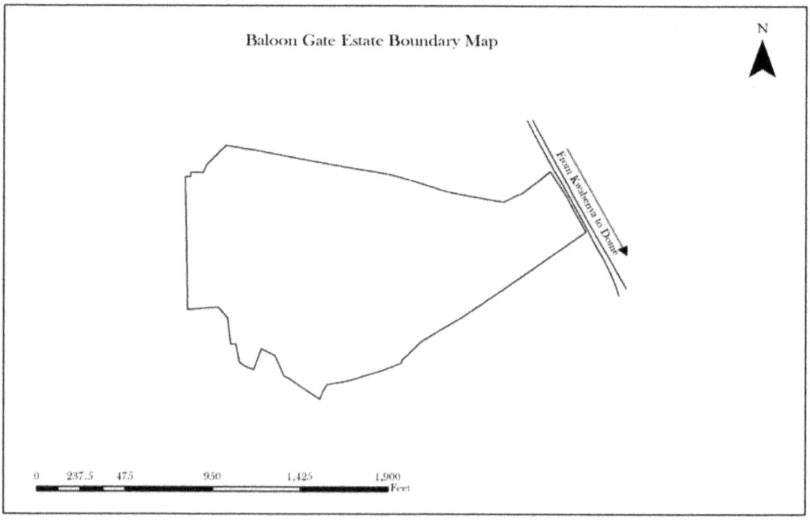

Figure 9.3 Baloon Gate Housing Estate boundary map.
Source: Extracted from GEMA planning department records.

Table 9.5 Adapted land use distribution

Land Use	*Allotted Land Size*	*% of Overall Land*
Residential	9.72 hectares (24 acres)	60
Commercial	0.32 hectare (0.8 acre)	2
Roads	1.62 hectares (4 acres)	10
Community Park	1.62 hectares (4 acres)	10
School	1.3 hectares (3.2 acres)	8
Worship centre	0.5 hectare (1.2 acres)	3
Electricity	0.4 hectare (1 acre)	2.5
Pipe-borne water	0.4 hectare (1 acre)	2.5
Telephone	0.32 hectare (0.8 acre)	2
Total	16.20 hectares (40 acres)	100

Source: Author's field survey – May–November 2011.

2 Ghana's Planning Standard and Development Guidelines (1990) was used. Based on the guidelines and discussions with the erstwhile GAR Secretariat of the TCPD, land use distribution was arrived at. Table 9.5 summarises the land use distribution adopted.

3 A standard three-bedroom house of 254-m^2 floor area on 0.065-hectare (0.16-acre), 50 or more years' leasehold land was used as a basis for analysis. The floor area of the residential development was based on the standard three-bedroom residential developments provided by Ghana's State Housing Company. Although this may not be the average size of a three-bedroom residential development in Accra, it is well known among professionals in the built environment and, therefore, was suitable as a reference development for this work. It was also assumed that nearby settlements will provide land uses, such as refuse dump and cemetery, to serve the envisaged planned community. Further, the land for uses such as commercial, school, and worship centres will be taken up by private individual or entities just as the residential use and not service lands like those for roads or electricity.

4 Cost of capital of 27.5% was adopted. This was the actual average cost of capital that was being charged by commercial banks in Ghana (average lending rate) as at the time of the surveys within the property/construction sector. The rate was obtained from BOG (http://www.bog.gov.gh). In adopting this rate, the average one- and two-year BOG Bond and GOG 91-day Treasury bill rates as well as the overall average Ghana Stock Exchange yield were examined. However, given that the subject matter of this book relates to the built environment, the most appropriate option under the circumstance was to use the actual passing rate in the industry, hence the adoption of the subject rate. Similarly, the Ghana cedi (GH¢) exchange rate to the US dollar (US$) that was prevailing at the time of the survey was adopted to convert monetary assessments in

GH¢ to US$. The exchange rate adopted was US$1.00 = GH¢1.50. This was also obtained from BOG (http://www.bog.gov.gh).

5 Based on the extant practice where three-quarters and in some cases all contract fees for a service are paid in advance, all payments were assumed to be in advance.

6 The cost assessments for the infrastructure were based on the 'mains' and for infrastructure, such as fixed line telephone cost, pipe-borne water, and electricity, they were determined from the shortest possible distance within which the facility can be connected from a main transmission line or station onto the guide estate.

Based on the analysis undertaken, the compliance cost of planning requirements per property was assessed at GH¢56,087.58[2] or US$37,391.72. The breakdown of the subject planning regime requirements' compliance cost per property is given in Table 9.6.

The subject planning regime requirements' cost per property is huge relative to the socio-economic conditions of most people in the case study country (Table 9.6). Indeed, the cost is about 71.54% of the mean value of a standard three-bedroom planned residential development in the study area, in addition to the time lag. The planning regime requirements' costs, however, ranged from a minimum of GH¢545.60 (US$363.73) to a maximum of GH¢23,824.33 (US$15,883). The bulk of the cost came from pipe-borne water connection, tarred roads, and concrete drains costs, which cumulatively constituted almost 70% of the cost. The cost of connecting pipe-borne water per property was the highest: 42.48%. This finding corroborates the evidence of the comparatively high cost of access to water supply in SSA (IIED, 2016). The finding is even more understandable because of the topography of the study area, which is hilly in nature and called for special interventions to ensure a continuous supply of pipe-borne water. The express legal requirements for development rights, approved sub-division planning, architectural design, formalised title, and building permit accounted for 13.83% of the

Table 9.6 Breakdown of planning requirements compliance cost per property

Planning Requirement	*Cost/Property (GHC)*	*Cost/Property (US$)*
Approved sub-division planning scheme	545.60	363.73
Tarred roads & concrete drains	15,410.50	10,273.70.
Fixed line telephone	3,385.03	2,257
Electricity	3,875.00	2,583.33
Pipe-borne water	23,824.33	15,883
Community park	1,835.00	1,223.33
Architectural design	1,835.00	574.67
Title formalisation	4,810.72	3,207.15
Building permit acquisition	4,810.72	1,026.27
Total	**56,087.58**	**37,391.72**

Source: Author's field survey – May–November 2011.

cost. The formalised title cost constituted the bulk of this cost, which alone accounted for 8.6% of the entire cost. Curiously, about 95% of this cost was accounted for by cost other than statutory official fees.

Given the above findings, it can be said that infrastructure and amenities are major drivers of the subject planning regime cost. This may be one of the reasons why the government in the case study country has not been able to adequately provide these facilities. The implication, however, is that any effort to reduce planning regime requirements' compliance cost must critically look at ways of reducing the cost of these facilities, pipe-borne water, and tarred roads and drains. It also implies that there is a need to examine the continuous suitability of some of these requirements taking cognisance of the urgent needs of residential land users and the socio-economic conditions prevalent in the country.

Regarding the cost of express legal requirements for development, although it constituted 13.83% of the entire cost, a substantial part of it emanated from cost other than the statutory fees – indirect cost. This was particularly evident in title formalisation cost. Commuting cost and cost of time lag – 25% and about 22%, respectively – constituted a large portion of the cost. In any event, cost other than the statutory fees, in the main, are traceable to excessive time lag. In fact, excessive time lag implies more time is required to execute the activities involved in complying with these planning requirements. This means that a lot of follow-ups need to be made to expedite action on the activities. These in effect translate into increases in commuting cost and professional fees due to productive time and energy spent by professionals on the activities. Besides, an excessive time lag provides the enabling conditions for payment of unofficial fees and exacerbates the cost of capital. This presupposes that the excessive time lag should be critically looked at in any policy discourse to address the weakness of the subject planning regime.

9.9.1 Benefit estimation

The benefit of the subject planning system was estimated using the benefit methodology(ies), more precisely approach one (Chapter 8). The data that was used for the benefit analysis was obtained from a contingent valuation survey of professional valuers and agents in Accra. The survey therefore obtained the valuers' and estate agents' opinion of values for the standard three-bedroom house of 254-m^2 floor area on 0.065-hectare (0.16-acre) land without the planning requirements. Thereafter, their opinions of value for the subject property were solicited, if the property within the subject area was provided with or covered by a specified planning requirement to the exclusion of the others. Finally, value opinions of the specified property given its location within an area provided with and covered by all the planning requirements were solicited. The planning requirements, which were used to calibrate the benefits, are approved sub-division planning scheme, tarred roads and concrete drains, fixed line telephone, electricity, pipe-borne water, a community park, a worship centre, a school, a convenience shop, architectural design, a formalised title, and a building permit. The benefit of the subject planning regime requirements per property was assessed at GH¢31,161.85 or US$20,774.57. Table 9.7 presents the benefit of each requirement and their percentage of the overall benefit.

Table 9.7 shows that the approved sub-division planning scheme contributes GH¢2,029.13 to the value of the specified property. Although there appears to be no precedent work on the contribution of the approved sub-division planning scheme to property values in the case study country, Asabere (1981) established that government zoning appreciates land values in Accra, although it has not been estimated in monetary terms. Given that zoning begets a sub-division planning scheme, it can be surmised that the result is consistent with Asabere's (1981) observation. Further, this revelation also supports the general acknowledgement in the case study country that where an area is covered by an approved sub-division planning scheme, property values in the area tend to appreciate, all things being equal.

Infrastructural facilities, tarred roads and concrete drains, a fixed line telephone, electricity, and a pipe-borne water connection to a residential neighbourhood contribute greatly to appreciation in property value. As per the specified property, tarred road and concrete drains contributed GH¢9,553.40 (US$6,368.93), the highest of all the contributions, while a fixed line telephone, electricity, and pipe-borne water contributed GH¢742.00 (US$494.67), GH¢5,183.01 (US$3,455.33), and GH¢4,773.80 (US$3,182.53), respectively.

Table 9.7 Overall details of planning requirements benefit

Planning Requirements	*Benefit/ Property (GH¢)*	*Benefit/ Property (US$)*	*% of Overall Benefit per (GH¢)*
Approved sub-division planning scheme	2,029.13	1,352.75	6.51
Tarred roads and concrete drains	9,553.40	6,368.93	30.65
Fixed line telephone	742.00	494.67	2.38
Electricity	5,183.00	3,455.33	16.63
Pipe-borne water	4,773.80	3,182.53	15.31
Community park	509.00	339.33	1.63
Worship centre	-145.63	-97.09	–
School	807.88	538.59	2.59
Convenience shop	912.62	608.41	2.92
Architectural design	788.88	525.92	2.53
Formalised title	5,196.12	3,464.08	16.67
Building permit	811.65	541.1	2.60
Planning requirements benefit	31,161.85	20,774.57	

Source: Author's field survey – May–November 2011.

These results are consistent with findings from Asabere (1981), who combined these facilities as site service and established that they have the tendency of increasing land values in Accra. Arimah (1992) also established a similar relationship between these infrastructural facilities and residential property values in the city of Ibadan, Nigeria. Further studies, such as Anim-Odame et al. (2006) and Anim-Odame (2008), in the case study country which collapsed these variables into location again established a similar relationship. However, this book disaggregates the contribution of the variables to property values and their extent of value in monetary terms.

Beyond that, findings from studies in the developed world, such as the UK (Cheshire and Sheppard, 2002, 2004) and the US (Sirmans et al., 2005), buttress the positive contribution of infrastructural facilities to residential property values. That said, the relatively high valuation of roads and concrete drains was expected and emphasises the premium placed on accessibility in real estate valuation theory and practice regarding value determination (Shapiro et al., 2009). Conversely, the low valuation of pipe-borne water compared to electricity, for example, was not anticipated. The possible reasons may be easy accessibility to water in rubber sachets and the proliferation of residential property owners constructing bole holes and water-wells outside their homes.

The fact that social amenities, such as school and convenience shops, contribute to residential property values was consistent with the above-mentioned earlier studies. However, the value contributions of such amenities in the case study country are rarely analysed on an individual basis. Furthermore, as community parks are hardly encountered in residential neighbourhoods, analyses such as those undertaken by the above-mentioned studies tend to overlook them. This book demonstrates that the value of a community park regarding the specified property is GH¢509.00 (US$339.33), the least valued planning regime requirement apart from a worship centre, while the likes of school and convenience shops are GH¢807.88 (US$538.59) and GH¢912.62 (US$608.41), respectively. The relative low valuation of community park spaces was expected since it is not the norm in the case study country to visit community green spaces as a source of recreation or for preserving greenbelts compared to the developed countries, such as the UK or the US. Perhaps people who have sentiments for this requirement are those within the elite class. This may account for the massive encroachments of earmarked greenbelt sites in urban areas in the case study country. Even the relative low valuation of schools compared to convenience shops was not surprising and may be one of the possible reasons again for encroachment of school sites.

The value contribution of a worship centre was negative: GH¢ (–145.63). This result was not expected considering the religious nature of Ghanaians. The possible reason may be the general nature of religious activities in the case study country, which tends to generate a lot of noise, and the observation that people are not necessarily deterred from travelling a longer distance to their favourite place of worship. For architectural design, its value contribution as per the specified property was GH¢788.88 (US$525.92), while that of a formalised title was GH¢5,196.12 (US$3,464.08). Comparatively, not much was expected in terms of value contribution of architectural design. This is because real estate valuation is usually undertaken 'rebus sic stantibus', that is, as the property stands and not the architectural design is what matters. The value of a formalised title was the most valued planning regime requirement apart from road and concrete drains. The possible reason for the value of a formalised title is that the value of real estate, in the main, stems from a good and perfect title, and not the brick and mortar per se. Consequently, with a formalised title, the value of real estate is generally expected to appreciate especially within jurisdictions where title formalisation is low against the backdrop of rising land ownership conflicts.

Lastly, the value of a building permit with respect to the specified property is GH¢811.65 (US$541.1). The higher valuation of a building permit compared to architectural design, a school, and a convenience shop may be a result of the anticipation of the consequences of non-compliance with the requirement and the common practice of its usage by property owners to support claims of land ownership (Boamah et al., 2012), in an environment where land ownership conflict is rife.

9.10 Evaluation of economic incentives

Insights from the human action theoretic framework suggest that to ensure compliance with planning requirements, planning systems should provide incentives to impel property owners to act in compliance. The prime incentive proposed by the framework as the main driver of compliance with planning requirements is economic incentives (Chapter 5). Based on stipulations in Chapter 8, to evaluate the economic incentives of the subject planning regime, the planning regime requirements' compliance cost per property must be compared with its benefits. Table 9.8 summarises the planning regime requirements' compliance costs and benefits of the individual planning regime requirements, as well as the entire planning regime requirements' compliance cost and benefit.

From Table 9.8 the subject planning regime generates a prime disincentive of GH¢24,925.33 or (US$16,616.89). This disincentive constituted about 31.8% of the mean value of a typical standard three-bedroom planned residential development in the study area at the time of the survey. The disincentive is even exacerbated by an extreme time lag: for example, 12.25 months for title formalisation and 6 months for building permit acquisition, which were found at the time of the survey. Thus, there is enough evidence to support the argument that the subject planning regime does not provide economic incentives for residential property owners.

Notwithstanding the above, further examination of the individual planning regime requirements' costs and benefits from Table 9.8 reveals that the approved sub-division planning scheme, electricity and formalised title recorded positive variances of GH¢1,483.53, GH¢1,308, and GH¢385.40, respectively. This revelation raises an issue as to why a significant number of urban developments in the case study country are not covered by approved sub-division planning schemes, and titles to these developments are not formalised. This has been explained in Chapter 5 and acknowledged somewhat in Chapter 6.

Insights from the conceptual framework profess that without means or resources, action cannot be instituted, even though awareness and conception of means as well as the prime incentive may be ascertained. However, it is known that about 30% of Ghanaians live under the poverty line (GH¢370.89 or US$403.14 per annum) (GSS, 2007; World Bank, 2012b), with rising levels of urban poverty (GSS, 2007). Besides, the country's daily minimum wage as at 2012 was GH¢3.73 (US$2.49) (www.ModernGhana.com, 2012). Further, the minimum wage is not always complied with in certain sectors of the economy, particularly the informal sector. Therefore, landowners may not be able to meet planning requirements, including those that provide a prime incentive, such as approved planning schemes. Consequently, lands are sold to individuals who, together with other land/property users, are also confronted with the same challenge and are not even able to formalise titles to their parcels, despite its provision of prime incentive. With regard to real estate development companies, which are presumed to have the comparative financial resources, the extant practice, in the main, has been to acquire land, prepare a sub-division planning scheme over it, open up a comparatively cheaper earthwork road and connect the same to electricity, and then sell the land or do some developments and sell them without meeting the other planning regime requirements. Even so, their target markets are people in the middle upper class and the upper class who are comparatively few (Centre for Affordable Housing Finance in Africa, 2010).

Table 9.8 also shows the benefit-cost ratios for tarred roads and concrete drains, and pipe-borne water are 0.62 and 0.20, respectively. However,

Table 9.8 Planning regime requirements' cost and benefit

Requirement	*Benefit (GH¢)*	*Cost (GH¢)*	*Variance (GH¢)*	*B/C Ratio*
Sub-division planning scheme	2,029.13	545.60	1,483.53	3.72
Tarred roads and drains	9,553.40	15,410.50	-5,857.10	0.62
Fixed line telephone	742.00	3,385.03	-2,643.03	0.22
Electricity	5,183.00	3,875.00	1,308.00	1.34
Pipe-borne water	4,773.80	23,824.33	-19,050.53	0.20
Community park	509.00	1,835.00	-1,326.00	0.28
Architectural design	788.88	862.00	-73.12	0.92
Formalised title	5,196.12	4,810.72	385.40	1.08
Building permit	811.65	1,539.40	-727.75	0.53
Planning regime Requirements (benefit & cost)	31,161.85	56,087.18	-24,925.33	0.54

Source: Author's field survey – May–November 2011.

these two planning requirements form part of the four planning requirements which were considered most valuable to residential development in the study area. In fact, tarred roads and drains was the most valued planning requirement (Table 9.7). The foregoing suggests it is imperative for measures to be taken to reduce the cost on these two planning attributes if planning is to be made more useful to residential development in the study area. Further, the benefit-cost ratios for the other planning requirements, apart from a sub-division planning scheme, electricity, and a formalised title, reinforce the need to review the planning requirements. These requirements were not valued greatly, yet their costs were comparatively higher. To this extent, the obvious question that must guide policy-makers is whether these requirements are still relevant.

9.11 Chapter summary

This chapter presented findings from the evaluation of a case study in Ghana to determine whether the country's planning system provides prime incentives, based on methodologies developed in Chapter 8 and on empirical data. It was established that the subject planning system does not provide incentives to land users/property owners and partly explains the massive disregard for planning and urban development regulations in Ghana. Based on discussions in this and the previous chapters, this book now proceeds to its final chapter, which offers conclusions and proposals for improvement.

Notes

1 Records at the erstwhile Town & Country Planning Department (TCPD) of the GEMA indicate that the planning schemes for the Kwabenya community have not been fully complied with areas earmarked for ancillary land uses such as schools and roads suffering the worst violations.

2 Ghana cedi – the currency of Ghana.

10 Summary, conclusions and proposal for improvement

10.1 Introduction

This final chapter presents a summary of discussions in this book, conclusions, and recommendations for improvement in planning systems in SSA and indeed across the developing world. The chapter commences with a summary of the discussions based on which conclusions are drawn and recommendations for policy formulation and practice made. This is followed by assumptions and limitations of the book and recommendations for further discussions and research.

10.2 Summary of discussions

Chapter 1 introduced the discussions in this book. It demonstrated the direction of current wisdom relating to the need for sustainable development in the twenty-first century, especially within the built environment of developing economies such as those of SSA. The chapter acknowledged that sustainable development requires cities and urban centres to be inclusive, resilient, liveable, and productive, as outlined by Goal 11 of the UN 17 SDGs, developed from the 2030 UN Agenda for Sustainable Development in 2015. It emphasised that the quest for sustainable urban development and management is also borne out of rapid urban growth and urbanisation, rising levels of urban informality, poverty, and social exclusion, among others, especially in SSA and other developing countries.

Additionally, Chapter 1 noted that like their counterparts across the globe, cities and urban areas play an important role in the socio-economic development of African countries. Further, the role of cities and urban areas on the continent can be strengthened and enlarged if the current urbanisation and urban growth taking place on the continent is managed sustainably. However, urbanisation and urban growth are occurring under weak economic conditions and are characterised by several ills. The chapter moreover established that urban planning systems, which are to ensure appropriate management of urban areas and deal with the development challenges that confront SSA, are weak and dysfunctional. This signifies that SSA planning systems do not provide the right dose of incentives for the effective and efficient performance of the systems, and that this book explored incentives capable of enhancing the effectiveness of the planning systems based on the Austrian economics theory of human action.

Chapter 2 discussed planning theory with a focus on economic justification of urban planning intervention in property markets, and the forms of planning intervention. The chapter established that several conventional economic theories, such as the neo-classical, welfare, and recently neo-institutional with its various strands of transaction cost, property rights, and public choice, have been used to examine the case of urban planning, but it is still unclear what the economic rationale for planning intervention is. This has therefore resulted in frequent use of several orthodoxies to analyse urban planning intervention in property markets. That said, the chapter also discussed the various forms of urban planning practice noting the conventional rational comprehensive (master) planning model and the recent planning models especially the collaborative planning model. The discussion recognised that, although the rational comprehensive planning model has several weaknesses, a lot of effort may be required to ensure that the collaborative planning model, which hinges on the introduction of democratic credentials in the planning process, succeeds in SSA, given the severity of unbalanced power relationships in the region.

Chapter 3 highlighted the relevance of urban planning in socio-economic development. The chapter noted that although planning can be used to pursue individual and group interests, existing evidence shows that planning performs critical socio-economic and ecological functions in societies, and it is the central tool for addressing the two major challenges of the twenty-first century: urbanisation and climate change. However, urban planning as it is currently being used in practice, in broad terms, is incapable of addressing the above challenges and others, such as the effects of globalisation. This has resulted in several urban ills, such as poor urban environmental and housing conditions, the rise of informality and poverty, inadequate infrastructure, and social segregation and exclusion, among others, especially in the developing world.

Chapter 4 discussed factors that can promote effective and successful planning systems. The chapter concluded that a comprehensive and effective legal regime; an institutional system including a judiciary system, coupled with adequate resources both human and material; and monitoring systems to detect non-compliance with planning regulations and enforce compliance are essential. The chapter noted that the use of incentives is also necessary.

Chapter 5 devised a theoretical framework of how incentives can be used to enhance the effectiveness of planning systems based on the Austrian economics theory of human action. The chapter highlighted that the success of planning regimes is contingent upon compliance with their planning regulations, which can be achieved through coercive force (involuntary compliance) or incentives (voluntary compliance). Compliance through coercive force requires up-to-date state institutions, such as the judiciary, the legal system, and planning institutions, and a huge amount of resources, which are hardly encountered in SSA. Voluntary compliance based on incentives can be contrived or instinctive but given that contrived incentives to promote compliance with regulations also require huge resources and have largely not been successful in SSA, compliance based on instinctive incentives stands a better chance of success in SSA. Human action theory, which was first put together as an integrated theory by Mises (1949), provides an effective explanation of voluntary compliance based on instinctive incentives and was therefore adopted to construct the research framework. The chapter additionally noted that the human action theory was also adopted due to its suitability to the quantification of individual choices towards contributing to the wider debate on the economic rationale for planning intervention. Incentives were explained to mean the positive difference between appreciation in property value from compliance with planning regime requirements and the cost of compliance with the requirements.

Chapter 6 discussed the SSA region's urban planning systems. The chapter established that some parts of SSA had their own planning arrangements based on local customs and practices. The tenets of these planning arrangements were strictly complied with due to their provision of security and economic incentives for the indigenous people. However, with the advent of Western Europe's colonisation of Africa these planning arrangements were truncated and ushered in formal colonial planning arrangement in SSA. The chapter also established that the colonial planning arrangement, which was transplanted from colonialists' countries, prescribed a modernist planning arrangement with the use of master plans underpinned by the land use segregation concept. This planning arrangement therefore required zoning; preparation and approval of a sub-division plan; and provision of infrastructure, architectural designs, titling and building permits, among other things, prior to development. The chapter established further that the health, political, and economic incentives – securing the health of colonial administrators, assuaging nationalistic reprisals from indigenes and maintaining law and order, and economic gains from exploitation of the region's resources by European entrepreneurs – impelled the institutionalisation of the colonial planning regime. It was also established that the colonial planning arrangements, in the main, are still in force due to their provision of incentives for control of land and its resources by the few rich and elite in society.

The chapter found that the received planning regimes in SSA are weak. A major link to this weakness was low compliance with planning regulations (requirements) by regulated entities: property owners/developers. Based on the analysis using the human action theoretic framework (Chapter 5), the chapter established that a major determinant of this low compliance with regulations is the planning regimes' inability to provide economic incentives for property owners/developers; the benefits of compliance with the planning regimes' requirements do not match with their costs. Connected to this is the general lack of awareness of regulations and the poor perception of the relevance of planning to socio-economic development needs of most urban dwellers as well as high levels of urban poverty.

Chapter 6 further noted that planning reforms are taking place in several countries in SSA as part of wider land tenure reforms. These planning reforms are being driven by neoliberal ideals and Western normative planning models particularly the collaborative planning model. The chapter additionally noted that although insights from the collaborative planning model may not be new to the people of SSA it is debatable whether these planning reforms alone by themselves will succeed given the socio-economic conditions in the region.

Chapter 7 demonstrated how incentives from the human action perspective have influenced urban planning practice, especially on the policy formulation front in the UK, Japan, and SSA. The chapter brought to the fore the major role incentives played and can play in urban planning policy formulation and that planning's role in ensuring sustainable, safe, inclusive, productive, and liveable urban centres may not materialise without the appropriate doses of incentives.

Chapter 8 prescribed the measurement framework to calculate the extent of incentives provided by planning systems, particularly those in the developing world, such as SSA from compliance with a planning regulations perspective. In so doing, the chapter argued that due to complexities associated with conventional economic impact methodologies and their requirement for huge volumes of organised data, which are difficult to come by in the developing world, a bespoke measurement framework was needed. Consequently, the chapter presented an economic impact calibration framework built from scratch and based on insights from the human action theoretic framework, the conventional methodologies, and data peculiarities in SSA.

Chapter 9 presented findings from an evaluation of a case study in Ghana based on the methodologies developed in Chapter 8. It was established that the cost of compliance with planning regime requirements per property in the case study was high, about 71.54% of the mean value of a planned three-bedroom residential development in addition to excessive time lag. The bulk of the entire cost, however, came from pipe-borne water connections and tarred roads and concrete drains costs, which cumulatively constituted almost 70% of the cost. The express legal requirements for development rights, approved sub-division planning, architectural design, a formalised title, and a building permit accounted for 13.83%, with excessive time lag. The formalised title cost constituted the bulk of this cost, which alone accounted for 8.6% of the entire cost with about 95% of the cost emanating from costs other than statutory (official) fees. Commuting cost was the highest, accounting for almost 25% of the entire title formalisation cost. This was followed by the cost of time lag, which accounted for 22%. On the benefit side, the chapter confirmed the extant literature particularly those of the welfare economics school of thought that planning generates benefits. In the case study area, it was established that the subject planning regime generates benefits for the specified property. However, apart from tarred roads and concrete drains, electricity, pipe-borne water, and formalised title, which had a consistently positive appreciation, others, such as a worship centre, had a negative value. The chapter established that compliance with the subject planning regime requirements generates benefits of almost 39.8% of the mean value of a typical standard three-bedroom planned residential development in the study area. More importantly, however, the chapter found that despite the benefit of the subject planning regime, it produces a prime disincentive of about 31.8% of the mean value of a typical standard three-bedroom planned residential development in the study area. This, together with findings from Chapters 5 and 6, support the argument that SSA planning regimes do not provide economic incentives for property owners (Chapter 6). Consequently, from a human action standpoint this quirk accounts for one of the main reasons for low compliance with SSA planning regulations in the region and by extension broken planning regimes in the region.

10.3 Conclusions

10.3.1 Conceptual position of SSA urban planning

The success of any planning system depends, among other things, on compliance with its regulations (Chapter 5). Applying insights from the human action theory, Chapter 2 conceptually explained that human action underpinned by incentives determines compliance with planning regulations and then showed its consequences. Further to Chapter 5, Chapter 6, based on insights from human action, demonstrated that planning regimes in SSA are weak and dysfunctional with low compliance with planning regulations partly due to their lack of incentives for property owners/developers or land users. Therefore, from the conceptual viewpoint this study concludes that human action is an overarching determinant of the success or otherwise of planning regimes in SSA.

More importantly, while the theory of human action has applications in several policy arenas particularly in the developed world, this is the first time it has been applied to the planning question in SSA. In its application to the region's planning regimes, the study initially conceptualised compliance with planning regulations as human action, which is impelled by incentives, and then traced its consequences. Based on this framework the book subsequently analysed the weakness of planning regimes in SSA and their outcome. The theory was also used to demonstrate the influence of planning practice on policy formulation in the UK, Japan, and SSA. The book makes two contributions to knowledge in this regard. First, it contributes to the extension of the literature that provides a conceptual understanding of weak planning regimes in SSA. Second, it provides an additional framework within which economic analysis of the region's planning regimes and other planning regimes can be undertaken. These two contributions undoubtedly could serve as food for thought for planning theory, planning policy formulation and practice, and academic discourse across the globe.

10.3.2 Economic impact calibration method

This book applied insights from economics to provide a conceptual understanding of the weakness of SSA planning regimes and evaluated in quantitative terms the economic incentives/disincentives provided by a case study. The book argued that quantitative economic calibration of planning policies in the developing world remains a challenge due to complexities associated with conventional methodologies and lack of organised data. In the developed world, such as the UK and the US, where there are comparatively huge volumes of organised data, knowledge of the extent and magnitude of the economic impact of planning policies is still scanty due to disagreements over findings from relevant studies borne out of these methodological complexities (Chapter 8).

There is therefore a need for a bespoke quantitative economic impact methodology to calibrate the economic incentives/disincentives of SSA planning regimes' requirements. More so, this is needed at a time when the evidence of impact of urban interventionist projects in the developing world is scanty, despite millions of US dollars of funding for such projects, due to data paucity and methodological challenges. Bespoke methodologies based on insights from the conceptual framework, the conventional methodologies, and data peculiarities in SSA were therefore formulated. These methodologies are flexible and could be manipulated where necessary for application in SSA and even across the entire developing world.

10.3.3 Compliance, awareness, and relevance

The literature discussion in Chapter 6 established that there is low compliance with planning regulations in SSA. This is a major contributory factor to the weakness of planning regimes in the region. Although some studies had previously linked factors such as lack of awareness of planning regulations and perceived irrelevance of planning policies to socio-economic development to the low compliance with regulation, the linkage was predominantly descriptive and devoid of analytical touch. However, based on the human action theoretic framework this book carefully analyses how the above factors contribute to the low compliance with planning regulations and ultimately the weakness of SSA planning systems.

10.3.4 Cost of planning regime

There is a dearth of quantitative studies on the cost of planning regimes in SSA. Few of such studies that exist also concentrate on a single or few aspects of the urban development process in the region. These few studies even assessed cost in terms of time lag or in both time lag and money terms. Moreover, most of these studies overlook indirect costs, such as unofficial fees, commuting cost, cost of time lag, and waiting time. However, this work establishes that the cost of SSA planning regimes must be assessed based on a planned development incorporating all the necessary indirect costs as possible.

Chapter 9 demonstrated that the cost of SSA planning regimes is a combination of sub-division plan preparation and approval, and infrastructure and amenities costs. The remainder is architectural design, title formalisation, and building permit acquisition costs and indirect costs, such as time lag and commuting costs, unofficial and professional fees for facilitating services on the planning regime requirements. This revelation, unlike previous studies, gives a much broader and deeper indication of the quantitative cost of complying with planning regime requirements in SSA, in broad terms.

The book also established that the cost of compliance with planning regime requirements in the case study in Ghana is huge relative to the socio-economic conditions of the majority of urban dwellers (Chapter 9). Indeed, it established that the cost of compliance with the subject planning regime requirements in the case study regarding a typical standard three-bedroom house on a 0.065-hectare land is about 71.54% of the value of a planned three-bedroom residential development of the same size of land in the area. This in monetary terms means that the cost of compliance with planning regime requirements in respect of a standard three-bedroom planned residential development in the study area is GH¢56,087.58 or US$37,391.72 in addition to the time lag. This raises a query as to how many people could bear the cost and enjoy the benefit of such a planned residential development in a country where urban poverty continues to rise.

The above finding therefore supports the literature (Chapter 6) that suggests that meeting the regulative requirements under SSA planning regimes is costly in light of the precarious socio-economic conditions of most of the people in the region. The finding further reinforces the question why some of the requirements of these planning regimes are still in operation. After all, the people in whose interest planning was supposedly instituted are not in a position to bear the cost of its requirements and hence the requirements themselves.

10.3.5 Benefit of a planning regime

The literature is replete with quantitative empirical studies on the benefits of planning policies in the developed world, although it is inconclusive. However, like quantitative cost studies, few of such studies exist on SSA planning regimes. Besides, these few studies focus on limited conventional planning factors, such as government zoning, roads, distance to the CBD or amenities, particularly school, or measure it from the location standpoint. This book, however, identified a wide range of SSA planning regime requirements based on which the benefit was assessed. The research reported in this book incorporated unconventional planning regime requirements, such as the sub-division planning scheme, the formalised title to property, architectural design, and building permit, among others. As applied to a case study in Ghana, the book was thus able to establish quantitative evidence of benefits of Ghana's planning regime.

It was established that Ghana's planning regime generates benefits in the case study area. It was noted that typically compliance with planning regime requirements in the study area with respect to a standard three-bedroom residential development on a 0.065-hectare land generates a benefit of approximately 39.8% of the mean value of a standard three-bedroom planned development in the study area. Stated in monetary terms, the benefit of compliance with the planning regime's requirements regarding a standard three-bedroom residential development in the study area is GH¢31,161.85 or US$20,774.57. Apart from a worship centre, which generated a negative value, all the requirements generated positive values, albeit in different magnitudes. However, tarred road and concrete drains, formalised title, electricity, and pipe-borne water generated most of the benefit. Benefits from these four planning regime requirements constituted 79.26% of the cumulative benefit of the entire individual planning regime requirements' benefits and 31.5% of the mean value of a typical standard three-bedroom planned residential development in the study area. Tarred road and concrete drains also generated most of the benefits among the four requirements, that is, about 38.67% of the benefits from the four requirements. This suggests that the subject planning regime should put in more effort towards addressing these requirements. This is very important because it can enable urban authorities not only in the case study country but across the developing world to mobilise revenues through land-based financing tools such as property tax to finance urban infrastructure development.

10.3.6 Economic incentives/disincentives of planning regimes (economic impact)

It was found that Ghana's planning regime generates economic disincentives in the study area. Chapter 9 noted that, although some planning regime requirements – approved sub-division planning scheme, electricity, and formalised title – generated marginal positive economic impact, Ghana's planning regime generates a huge economic disincentive in the study area. Based on empirical evidence, Chapter 9 demonstrates that the extent of the economic disincentive is approximately 31.8% of the value of a standard three-bedroom planned residential development in the study area, which is more than the benefit it generates. In monetary terms, this amounts to GH¢24,925.33 or US$16,616.89 in addition to the time lag it creates.

This finding undoubtedly runs contrary to the theoretical prescriptions of the human action-based economic framework, which underpins this book. The human action-based economic theoretic framework demonstrates that compliance with planning regulations and the manifestation of an efficient and effective planning regime is driven by incentives. However, contrary to this proposition, a major finding from the empirical evidence has established that Ghana's planning regime generates a huge disincentive to property owners/developers in the study area. This is because the cost of compliance with the requirements of the planning regime is far beyond its benefit apart from the fact that it may not be possible for most of the people in the country to afford it given their precarious socio-economic conditions.

The foregoing gives evidence that Ghana's planning regime with respect to the study area is not worthwhile from the standpoint of economics. Given this evidence and the volumes of literature discussion on the weakness of SSA planning regimes, the ongoing planning reforms are in the right direction (Chapter 6). However, the critical question that confronts these planning reforms occurring in SSA is in what direction should they be pursued?

10.4 Proposal for improvement

Based on its findings and conclusions, the book presents herewith recommendations for policy formulation and practice. Although most of these recommendations focus on the case study, they are useful for SSA planning systems.

10.4.1 Overall policy direction

Chapter 6 established that current planning regime revisions as part of larger land tenure reforms taking place in SSA are along the lines of neoliberal prescriptions premised on Western normative planning models particularly the collaborative planning model. These prescriptions, among others, profess that the state should take a back seat in urban planning and development as well as urban governance but facilitate public-private partnership in urban development. Insights from the findings based on the human action theory, however, have shown that the weak state of SSA planning regimes has partially resulted from its promotion of disincentives to property owners/developers. Conversely, the existing planning systems, which are weak and ineffective, provide incentives for the few elites. This suggests that any policy formulation towards improvement of SSA planning regimes should be guided by insights from human action. To this end, it is recommended that planning policies in the region should provide incentives for property owners/developers or land users. Thus, property owners/developers should be made aware of planning policies, and they should be made to establish the relevance of planning, and thus planning policies, to the attainment of their socio-economic needs. For example, it was noted from the literature discussion in Chapter 6 that planning policies in SSA operate a strict land use segregation concept across the board. Meanwhile a significant number of urban dwellers in the region, particularly those within low-income communities, want to put their homes into compatible multiple uses to earn additional incomes. This is compounded by the rise of the informal sector, which provides the source of livelihood for most of the urban dwellers in SSA. Yet planning in the region has not incorporated the sector. Additionally, due to their restrictive nature, planning regimes in the region do not provide developable lands for most urban residents. Indeed, it is estimated that about three-quarters of lands for new housing developments in the region's urban areas are supplied through informal channels. It is thus recommended that planning policies in the region should promote integration of compatible land uses, especially in low-income communities, and ensure an adequate supply of developable lands through forward planning and flexible requirements. More importantly, the benefits of compliance with planning policies should exceed the cost of their compliance, and such cost should be within the reach of land users.

10.4.2 Cost of planning regime requirements

The book established that the cost of compliance with planning regulations in SSA is high. For the case study, the cost of compliance with the subject planning regime requirements was very huge. Apart from its monetary cost exceeding that of its benefit, property owners/developers also incur a long period of time lag. Besides the cost of compliance with planning requirements, one other implication of the insights from the human action theory is that where resources are not available there will be a lack of incentives for property/developers to comply with planning requirements. That is, even if the benefit of compliance with planning regime requirements exceeds its cost, there will still not be compliance.

Based on these findings and dictates of the human action theory, it is recommended that the cost of compliance with the subject planning regime requirements should be made to come down as far as possible. The recommended strategies to address the cost of compliance with the subject planning regime requirements are discussed as follows:

10.4.2.1 Cost of infrastructure and amenities

Cost of infrastructure – tarred roads and drains, electricity, pipe-borne water, fixed line telephones, and community parks – accounted for a substantial part of the planning regime requirements' cost for the case study. Cost of these items accounted for 86% of the entire planning regime cost. Pipe-borne water cost alone was almost half of this cost. While it is acknowledged that the case study area had a peculiar situation, hence the huge cost implication, it is recommended that community water projects and construction of bole holes and water wells in individual homes should be promoted. However, high constructional standards for bole holes and water wells should be ensured to avoid contamination.

For tarred roads and concrete drains, which was the next item with huge cost incidence and reflects the situation in SSA, several type of road designs can be introduced which are comparatively up to standard and yet less expensive. For example, unpaved road types, such as gravel and earthwork roads, can be earmarked for low- and middle-income communities. Besides, cost overruns other than delays in road and drain contract executions, such as the deliberate inflation of contract sums to satisfy interest groups, must be checked. The cost of electricity can be reduced through effective and efficient practices. Indeed, during discussions with experts from Electricity Company of Ghana (ECG) in relation to the case study, it came to the fore that the practice of connecting electric power to unplanned settlements is quite expensive. Consequently, it is proposed that, to further reduce the cost of an electric power connection, there should be continuous effort to ensure the timely planning of settlements and the avoidance of undue inflation of contract sums.

Extension of fixed line telephone facility to a residential neighbourhood was found to generate little benefit at least compared to its cost in respect of the case study. The possible reason as noted in the earlier discussions may be due to proliferation of the mobile phone facility. However, it emerged from discussions with relevant officials from VGL (case study) that with the deregulation of the telecom sector, which is the situation in most SSA countries, telecommunication services are extended to settlements on a demand-driven basis. This is to ensure that telecommunication network operators do not run at a loss. It is therefore recommended that while this demand-driven approach may be suitable for prime communities, a strategic corporate responsibility arrangement should be encouraged to reduce the cost of extending the facility to middle- and low-income areas. Alternatively, the facility should not be part of planning requirements whether express or implied.

Community parks in the case study country have various purposes including religious and recreation. However, given that this land use is not in high demand in the case study country, one way of dealing with its cost is to promote the amenity on a demand driven basis, acknowledging that affluent communities usually prefer the amenity. Alternatively, community parks should be earmarked at vantage points that can be accessed by several communities and run along business lines. Under such circumstances, business-oriented people will pay for the cost of the development of the amenity and charge people who patronise it.

Given that the cost of infrastructure and amenities is so huge, it is further recommended that the central government play a fundamental role in the provision of these facilities through collaboration with traditional landowners and under strong and good governance practices. For example, under strong and good governance practices government can enter into some arrangement with traditional land owing groups to provide basic infrastructure and take payments in the form of serviced lands, sell them, and replicate the idea. Thus, in the case study country institutions such as the Lands Commission (LC) in collaboration with planning authorities and other relevant government agencies with funds from public lands revenue can enter into an arrangement with a land-owning group to provide the basic infrastructure. The LC will then take payment by way of serviced lands, which it will manage or sell to generate revenue to provide similar services to other land-owning groups.

10.4.2.2 Architectural design, title formalisation, and building permit cost

Apart from title formalisation, which was found to have a marginal positive economic impact, the other requirements generated an adverse economic impact. Even so, the cost of title formalisation was established to be too high: 8.6% of the entire planning regime requirements' cost. About 95% of the costs were costs other than statutory fees paid at public agencies for title formalisation. These include commuting cost, unofficial fees, and professional fees for facilitation of formalisation activities. This means that a drastic reduction in these incidental costs will make compliance with title formalisation requirement more beneficial to property owners. Similarly, the incidental costs to building permit and architectural design requirements were substantial. Therefore, it is recommended that incidental costs to these planning regime requirements cost should be reduced to the barest minimum.

On the above score, this book recommends that satellite offices for public agencies involved in title formalisation and building permit acquisition activities should be set up at vantage points across urban areas to reduce commuting cost. Further, this book notes that unofficial fees go to private pockets for works, which under normal circumstance should be undertaken by beneficiaries of these fees. In fact, such fees can be used to improve service delivery at these public agencies. It is therefore proposed that, to eliminate this syndrome of unofficial fees or reduce it to the barest minimum, there is a need to introduce different grades of services, such as ordinary and premium services. The premium service, for example, can be made expeditious at a slightly higher fee in which case portion of the monies paid as unofficial fees could be directed to. Similarly, professionals through their professional bodies should be encouraged to minimise their fees especially when dealing with low- and middle-income groups.

10.4.2.3 Cost of time lag

Despite the preceding section, it was noted that the cost of time lag for the case study contributed substantially to the planning regime requirements' compliance cost. It is therefore recommended that contracts particularly for the execution of infrastructural and amenities projects should be undertaken under strict good governance checks and practices.

10.4.2.4 Economic empowerment

The literature discussions established that poverty is rife in urban Ghana and, indeed, SSA. To the extent that poverty levels are growing, it can be expected that the levels of compliance with planning regulations particularly within poor neighbourhoods may fall as people within these neigbourhoods may simply not have the resources to comply with the regulations. Consequently, any effort to reduce the planning regime requirements' compliance cost needs to be complemented by strategies to economically empower most urban dwellers so that they can have the resources to meet the cost of compliance with these requirements. As noted in the extant literature, most urban dwellers in the developing world earn their living from the informal sector. This means that the sector, when properly managed, holds the key to empowering most urban dwellers in SSA economically. As such, it is proposed that governments of SSA countries should institutionalise and support the sector.

10.5 Assumptions and limitations

There is no doubt that there are variations in SSA. Therefore, any analysis that tends to treat the region as a single unit risks the likelihood of making an overgeneralisation. However, there are equally similar political and socio-economic structures, such as the planning systems bequeathed to constituent economies by colonialism, which, except for Republic of South Africa, makes it suitable to analyse the region as a single unit (Mamdani, 1996). Even so, despite the steps that were taken to ensure a high standard of reliability and validity, the sole focus on Accra, Ghana (case study empirical analysis), makes the geographical sample for this book inadequate for generalisation of its findings across the region. That said, as adequately stated elsewhere in this chapter useful insights and lessons could be drawn from the findings in this book for application across the region.

The book presumed a planned residential area where residential property owners/developers are responsible for the cost of an approved sub-division planning scheme, infrastructure, and amenities. The economic appraisal focussed on a standard three-bedroom house with a floor area of 254 m^2 on a 0.065-hectare leasehold land with a term of 50 years or more. Besides, all the infrastructural cost assessments other than roads and concrete drains were based on their connection from public mains at the shortest possible distance while land uses, such as worship centre, school, and convenience shop, were assumed to be privately owned and managed. There is a possibility that changes in these assumptions will result in variations in the outcome of the economic appraisal. However, it was not possible to use alternative assumptions to ascertain the probable variations given the time and resource constraints. That notwithstanding, these assumptions are not envisaged to affect the credibility of the findings from the empirical analysis of this book since they were adopted based on the requirements of the extant planning regime at the relevant time and the usual practices in the case study country.

The CVM used as part of the assessment of the subject planning regime requirements' compliance benefits relied on opinions of real estate valuers and agents on professional valuation instead of individual property owners/developers in accordance with insights from the conceptual framework. The adoption of this approach was premised on data peculiarities in the case study country and SSA in general, and the fact that these professionals were comparatively better placed to submit opinions of value on the requirements due to their training and experience.

Due to time and resource constraints the economic analysis based on empirical data could not be extended to planning institutions and the effect of planning beyond its area of influence. Also, other forms of land ownership were not considered. In other words, the work was limited to family and private lands. However, while the variation that can arise from other types of land may not be much, and findings from the work are legitimate for all the categories of land holdings in the case study country, extracting the impact of planning beyond the legitimate area of influence of planning institutions may require a long period of methodological research. For the economic impact of planning institutions, an extension of this work to that effect has been recommended.

This work relied on the information provided by experts and informants among others. Although measures were taken to ensure validity, the responses obtained from them were believed to be true and accurate. This is a possible limitation to this work.

10.6 Prescriptions for further research & discussions

Several areas have been identified for extension of this work. These are:

1 The conceptual framework devised in Chapter 5 acknowledged the prime incentive/disincentive as the main driver of compliance or otherwise with planning regime requirements. The empirical part of this work, however, concentrated, among other things, on the quantitative determination of the extent of the prime incentive/disincentive under the case study planning regime. This means that the relationship between the SSA planning regime's prime incentive/disincentive and compliance with their requirements still begs an empirical question. Therefore, a study to that effect will be imperative.
2 Further, insights of the human action theory were used based on empirical data to examine the SSA planning question, primarily from the viewpoint of individual property owners/developers. It will therefore be useful for another work to apply the insights to SSA planning institutions and empirically provide a quantitative notion of their extent of economic cost and benefit.
3 Additionally, this work due to its exigencies used real estate valuers and agents as proxies to actual property owners/developers to elicit benefits of the planning regime requirements of the case study. A study to obtain the benefits of the requirements from actual property owners/developers will therefore be essential to complement findings from this work.
4 Finally, the empirical part of this work concentrated on Ghana as the case study country. Consequently, the findings from the work are technically restricted to Ghana. There is therefore a need for similar studies in other countries in the SSA region to inform policy direction on extant planning regimes region.

Glossary

Sub-division Planning Scheme: A plan that divides raw land into parts, governs its development for residential or other purposes, and prescribes standards for lot sizes, layout, and procedures for dedicating private land for public purposes, among others (GoG, 1990; Farcquave and McAuslan, 1992).

Sub-Saharan Africa: According to the World Bank (2009), Sub-Saharan Africa refers to countries within Africa which lie south of the Sahara Desert and therefore excludes North Africa. Thus, as per the World Bank designation Sub-Saharan Africa excludes Egypt, Libya, Tunisia, Algeria, and Western Sahara, and is made of 48 countries inclusive of the offshore islands. The geographical location of the region is shown by Figure 1.3, and its 48 constituent countries are Botswana, Gambia, Ghana, Kenya, Lesotho, Liberia, Mauritius, Namibia, Nigeria, Sierra Leone, South Africa, Uganda, Zambia, and Zimbabwe, known as Anglophone countries; Benin, Burkina Faso, Congo, Cote D'Ivoire (Ivory Coast), the Democratic Republic of Congo, Gabon, Guinea, Mali, Niger, Senegal, and Togo, commonly referred to as Francophone countries; Cameroun and Seychelles, referred to as Anglo-Francophone countries; Angola, Cape Verde, Guinea Bissau, Mozambique, and Sao Tome and Principe, referred to as Lusophone countries; and Burundi, the Central African Republic, Chad, Djibouti and Comoros, Equatorial Guinea, Ethiopia, Eritrea, Madagascar, Mauritania, Rwanda, Somalia, Sudan, Swaziland, and Tanzania, also called residual countries.

Urban Planning System: The collection of agencies, procedures, instruments, and protocols that are often sanctioned by the formal state, backed by formal law, and linked especially to rights to develop and use housing, land, and property (UN-Habitat, 2009). Urban planning system is, however, used interchangeably with urban planning regime.

Zoning: The division of a community into districts or development zones in which certain activities are prohibited while others are permitted (GoG, 1990).

References

Abdulai, R.T. (2007). *The Operation of Traditional Landholding Institutions in Sub-Saharan Africa: A Case Study of Ghana*. PhD Thesis, University of Wolverhampton, UK.

Abdulai, R.T. (2010). *Traditional Landholding Institutions in Sub-Saharan Africa – The Operation of Traditional Landholding Institutions in Sub-Saharan Africa: A Case Study of Ghana*. Saarbrücken: Lambert Academic Publishing AG & CO KG.

Abeka, F.A. (2005). *The Effects of Housing Environment on the Health Status of the Urban Poor in the Accra Metropolitan Area*. Unpublished Mphil Thesis, University of Ghana, Accra, Ghana.

Abubakar, I.R. and Doan, P.L. (2017). Building New Capital Cities in Africa: Lessons for New Satellite Towns in Developing Countries. *African Studies*, 76(4): 546–565.

Abukhater, A.B. (2009). Rethinking Planning Theory and Practice: A Glimmer of Light for Prospects of Integrated Planning to Combat Complex Urban Realities. *Theoretical and Empirical Researches in Urban Management*, 2(11), 64–79.

Acquaah-Harrison, R. (2003). The Restructuring of the Town and Country Planning Department. Paper presented at a Town and Country Planning Department Seminar held at Little Acre Hotel, Aburi, Ghana, February 12–13.

Adamowicz, W.L. (2004). What's It Worth? An Examination of Historical Trends and Future Directions in Environmental Valuation. *Australian Journal of Agricultural and Resource Economics*, 48(30), 419–443.

Adams, D., Watkins, C. and White, M. (2005). Examining Public Policy and Property Markets. In: Adams, D., Watkins, C. and White, M. (Eds.) *Planning, Public Policy and Property Markets*. Oxford: Blackwell Publishing Ltd.

Adams, D. (2008). Mapping out the Regulatory Environment and Its Interaction with Land and Property Markets. *Energy Policy*, 36, 4570–4574.

Adler, M.D. and Posner, E.A. (1999). Rethinking Cost – Benefit Analysis. *The Yale Law Journal*, 109, 165–247.

Afrane, S.K. (1993). *The Integration of Housing and Economic Activities: A Case Study of Low-Income Settlements in Kumasi, Ghana*. Unpublished PhD Thesis, University of British Columbia, Canada.

Africa Rising 21st Century. (2010). Africa's Infrastructure Challenge. [Online], Available at: htpp://africarising2010.blogspot.co.uk/2010/06/africas-infrastructure-challenge.html [Accessed March 1, 2010].

African Development Bank (AFDB). (2013). *An Integrated Approach to Provision of Infrastructure in Africa.* Abidjan: AfDB.

Agger, A. and Lofgren, K. (2008). Democratic Assessment of Collaborative Planning Processes. *Planning Theory*, 7(2), 145–164.

Akwansivie, G.A., Iddi, N.K. and Dayuo, A. (2010). Contingent Valuation Method (CVM) in Water Quality Management: Studies on the Odaw and Subin Rivers in Ghana. *The Journal of Business and Estate Management Research*, 2(1), 83–95.

Alberini, A., Kanninen, B. and Carson, R.T. (1997). Modelling Response Incentive Effects in Dichotomous Choice Contingent Valuation Data. *Land Economics*, 73(3), 309–324.

Albrechts, L. (2006). Shifts in Strategic Spatial Planning? Some Evidence from Europe and Australia. *Environment and Planning*, 38, 1149–1170.

Alchian, A.A. and Demsetz, H. (1973). The Property Rights Paradigm. *Journal of Economic History*, 33(1), 16–27.

Alexander, E.R. (1992). A Transaction Cost Theory of Planning. *Journal of the American Planning Association*, 58(2), 190–200.

Alexander, E.R. (2006). Evaluation and Status; Where Is Planning Evaluation Today and How Did It Get There? In: Alexander, E.R. (Ed.) *Evaluation in Planning: Evolution and Prospects, Contributions in Honour of Nathaniel Lichfield.* London: Ashgate Publishing Ltd.

Allmendinger, P. (2002). Towards a Post-Positivist Typology of Planning Theory. *Planning Theory*, 1(1), 77–99.

Allmendinger, P. and Haughton, G. (2012). Post-Political Spatial Planning in England: A Crisis of Consensus. *Transactions of the Institute of British Geographers*, 37(1), 89–103.

Amaro, S. (2020). EU Predicts Region will Contract 7.4% this Year in Worst Economic Shock since 1930s, CNBC News. [Online], Available at: https://www.cnbc.com/2020/05/06/coronavirus-european-union-to-contract-7point5percent-due-to-the-pandemic.html [Accessed June 1, 2020].

Amin, S. (1972). Underdevelopment and Dependence in Black Africa – Origins and Contemporary Forms. *Journal of Modern African Studies*, 10, 503–524.

Amissah, S.B. (1979). *Guidelines for the Formulation of Land Policies and Title Registration in Ghana: A Documentation.* Kumasi: Land Administration Research Centre, University of Science & Technology.

Anderson, J. (1990). The New Right, Enterprise Zones and Urban Development Corporations. *International Journal of Urban & Regional Research*, 14(3), 468–489.

Anim-Odame, W.K., Key, T. and Stevenson, S. (2006). Measures of Real Estate Values from Land Registration and Valuation Systems in Emerging Economies: The Case of Ghana. Paper presented at 23rd FIG Congress held in Munich, Germany, October 8–13.

Anim-Odame, W.K. (2008). *Residential Real Estate Investment in Emerging Economies: The Case of Ghana.* Unpublished PhD Thesis, City University, London, UK.

Antwi, A.Y. (2000). *Urban Land Markets in Sub Saharan Africa: A Quantitative Study of Accra, Ghana.* Unpublished PhD Thesis, Napier University, Edinburgh, UK.

Aribigbola, A. (2007). Urban Land Use Planning, Policies and Management in Sub Saharan African Countries: Empirical Evidence from Akure, Nigeria. Paper presented at the 4th World Bank Urban Research Symposium, Washington, DC, June.

Arimah, B.C. (1992). Hedonic Prices and the Demand for Housing Attributes in a Third World City: The Case of Ibadan, Nigeria. *Urban Studies*, 29(5), 639–651.

Arimah, B.C. and Adeagbo, D. (2000). Compliance with Urban Development and Planning Regulations in Ibadan, Nigeria. *Habitat International*, 24, 279–294.

Arku, G. (2006). Housing and Development Strategies in Ghana, 1945–2000. *IDPR*, 28(3), 333–358.

Armstrong, H. and Taylor, J. (1985). *Regional Economics and Policy*. Oxford: Philip Alan Publishers Ltd.

ARUP and Cities Alliance. (2016). Future Proofing Cities: *Ghana – Metropolitan Cities*. London: ARUP.

Asabere, P.K. (1981). The Determinants of Land Values in an African City: The Case of Accra, Ghana. *Land Economics*, 57(3), 385–397.

Atwood, D.A. (1990). Land Registration in Africa: The Impact on Agricultural Production. *World Development*, 18(5), 659–671.

Babbie, E. (1990). *Survey Research Methods* (2nd Edn.). Belmont, CA: Wadsworth Publishing Company.

Babbie, E. (2001). *The Practice of Social Science Research*. Belmont, CA: Wadsworth.

Baffour Awuah, K.G., Hammond, F., Bloch, R., Proverbs, D., Booth, C. and Lamond, J. (2010). Sub Saharan Urban Land Use Planning Systems: The Need for an Economic Appraisal. Paper presented at Royal Institute of Chartered Surveyors – Construction and Built Environment Conference, 2–3 September, Dauphine University, Paris.

Baffour Awuah, K.G., Hammond, F., Booth, C. and Lamond, J. (2011a). Improving the Performance of the Construction Industry: The Urban Land Use Planning Factor. Paper submitted at the ARCOM and LCI, UK Doctoral Workshop, 2 March, School of the Built Environment, University of Northumbria, Newcastle, UK.

Baffour Awuah, K.G., Hammond, F., Booth, C. and Lamond, J. (2011b). Urban Land Use Planning in Ghana: A Policy Input Discussion. Paper presented at the West Africa Built Environment Research (WABER) Conference, 19–21 July, British Council, Accra, Ghana.

Baffour Awuah, K.G., Hammond, F., Booth, C., Lamond, J., Proverbs, D. and Bloch, R. (2011c). Conceptual Analysis of the Role of Human Action Theory in Sub Saharan Africa Urban Land Use Planning. *Journal of International Real Estate and Construction Studies*, 1(2), 147–165.

Baffour Awuah, K.G. and Hammond F.N. (2014). Determinants of Low Land use Planning Regulation Compliance Rate in Ghana. *Habitat International*, 41, 17–23.

Baffour Awuah, K.G., Hammond, F.N., Lamond, J.E. and Booth, C.A. (2014). Benefits of Land Use Planning in Ghana. *Geoforum*, 51, 37–46.

Baffour Awuah, K.G. (2016). Leveraging Rising Land Values to Finance Urban Infrastructure Development in Ghana: A Case Study of Accra. Final Report: UWE/GLGS.

Baffour Awuah, K.G. and Gyamfi-Yeboah, F. (2017). The Role of Task Complexity in Valuation Errors Analysis in a Developing Real Estate Market. *Journal of Property Research*, 34(1), 54–76.

Baffour Awuah, K.G. (2018). The Role of Urban Planning in Sub-Saharan Africa Urban Pollution Management. In: Charlesworth, S.M. and Booth, C.A. (Eds.) *Urban Pollution: Science and Management*. London: John Wiley and Sons Ltd.

Baird, C.W. (1998). Profit and Loss. In: J. Boettke (Ed.) *The Elgar Companion to Austrian Economics*. Cheltenham: Edward Elgar Publishing Inc.

Barbot, J. (1732). *A Description of the Coasts of North and South Guinea*. London: Churchill's Collection of Voyages and Travels.

Barnett, R.E. (1997). Toward a Theory of Legal Naturalism. *Journal of Libertarian Studies*, 2(2), 97–107.

Barone, T.E. (1992). On the Demise of Subjectivity in Education Inquiry. *Curriculum Inquiry*, 22, 25–38.

Bart, I.L. (2010). Urban Sprawl and Climate Change: A Statistical Exploration of Cause and Effect with Policy Options for the EU. *Land Use Policy*, 27(2), 283–292.

Barton, H. (2009). Land Use Planning and Health and Well-Being. *Land Use Policy*, 26, S115–S123.

Bergstrom, J.C., Cordell, H.K., Watson, A.E. and Ashley, G.A. (1990). Economic Impacts of State Parks on State Economies in the South. *Southern Journal of Agricultural Economics*, 22, 69–77.

Bertaud, A. and Malpezzi, S. (2001). Measuring the Costs and Benefits of Urban Land Use Regulation: A Simple Model with an Application to Malaysia. *Journal of Housing Economics*, 10, 393–418.

Blocher, J. (2006). Building on Custom: Land Tenure Policy and Economic Development in Ghana. *Yale Human Rights and Development L.J.*, 9, 166–202.

Boamah, N.A., Gyimah, C. and Nelson, J.K.B. (2012). Challenges to the Enforcement of Development Control in the Wa Municipality. *Habitat International*, 36, 136–142.

Boelens, L. (2006). Beyond the Plan: Towards a New Kind of Planning. *disP – The Planning Review*, 42(167), 25–40.

Bogdan, R.C. and Biklen, S.K. (1998). *Qualitative Research in Education: An Introduction to Theory and Methods* (3rd Edn.). Needham Heights, MA: Allyn and Bacon.

Bolay, J.C. (2015). Urban Planning in Africa: Which Alternative for Poor Cities? The Case of Koudougou in Burkina Faso. *Current Urban Studies*, 3, 413–431.

Booth, C.A., Hammond, F.N., Lamond, J. and Proverbs, D.G. (Eds.) (2012). *Conclusions. Solutions to Climate Change Challenges in the Built Environment*. Chichester: Wiley-Blackwell.

Borras Jr., S.M. and Franco, J.C. (2008). Contemporary Discourses and Contestations around Pro-Poor Land Policies and Land Governance. *Journal of Agrarian Change*, 10(1), 1–32.

Boyd, R. (1991). Confirmation, Semantics and the Interpretation of Scientific Theories. In: Boyd, R., Gasper, P. and Trout, J.D. (Eds.) *The Philosophy of Science*. Cambridge, MA: The MIT Press.

Brachinger, H.W. (2002). Statistical Theory of Hedonic Price Indices. Department of Quantitative Economics, University of Freiburg, DQE Working Papers No. 1.

Braimah, I., Amponsah, O. and Asibey, M.O. (2016). The Effectiveness of the Local Management Systems of Rural Water Facilities for Sustainable Service Delivery: A Case Study of the Sekyere East 426 District, Ghana. *Sustainable Water Resources Management*, 2(4), 405–418.

Bramley, G. and Watkins, C. (1996). The Cutting Edge 1996: Modelling the Relationship between Land Use Planning and New Housing Supply in a System of Local Housing Markets. *RICS Research Paper*, 930–935.

Bramley, G. and Leishman, C. (2005). Modelling Local Housing Market Adjustment in England. In: Adams, D., Watkins, C. and White, M. (Eds.) *Planning, Public Policy and Property Markets*, Oxford: Blackwell Publishing Ltd.

Bratland, J. (2000). Human Action and Socially Optimal Conservation: A Mises Inquiry into the Hotelling Principle. *The Quarterly Journal of Austrian Economics*, 3(1), 3–26.

Bravi, M. and Curto, R. (1997). Valuing Public Goods with Contingent Valuation Methods: User Purposes and Values. In: Brandon, P.S., Lombardi, P.L. and Bentivegna, V. (Eds.) *Evaluation of the Built Environment for Sustainability*. London: E & FN Spon.

Brookshire, D.S., Thayer, M.A., Schulze, W.D. and D'Arge, R.C. (1982). Valuing Public Goods: A Comparison of Survey and Hedonic Approaches. *The American Economic Review*, 72(1), 165–177.

Brown, A. (2012). Challenges of Development and Underdevelopment in a Globalising World. In: Campagna, M., De Montis, A., Isola, F., Lai, S., Pira, C. and Zoppi, C. (Eds.) *Planning Support Tools: Policy Analysis, Implementation and Evaluation*. Proceedings of the Seventh International Conference on Informatics and Urban and Regional Planning INPUT 2012. Milan: Franco Angeli.

Brown, A. and Sherrard, H. (1951). *Town and Country Planning*. Carlton: Melbourne University Press.

Brueckner, J.K. (2007). Government Land – Use Interventions: An Economic Analysis. A Paper presented at the Fourth World Bank Urban Research symposium held at Washington, DC. [Online], Available at: http://www.worldbank.org [Accessed December 1, 2009].

Buitelaar, E. (2004). A Transaction Cost Analysis of the Land Development Process. *Urban Studies*, 41(13), 2539–2553.

Buitelaar, E., Galle, M. and Sorel, N. (2011). Plan-Led Planning System in Development-Led Practices: An Empirical Analysis into the (Lack of) Institutionalisation of Planning Law. *Environment and Planning A*, 43, 928–941.

Burton, L.J. and Mazerolle, S.M. (2011). Survey Instrument Validity Part I: Principles of Survey Instrument Development and Validation in Athletic Training Education Research. *Athletic Training Educational Journal*, 6(1), 27–35.

Calderon, C. and Serven, L. (2008). *Infrastructure and Economic Development in Sub-Saharan Africa*. Policy Research Working Paper No. 4712, The World Bank, Development Research Group, Macroeconomics and Growth Team.

Calia, P. and Strazzera, E. (1998). Bias and Efficiency of Single vs. Double Bound Models for Contingent Valuation Studies: A Monte Carlo Analysis. [Online], Available at: http://veprints.unica.it/331/1/98 -1.pdf [Accessed June 4, 2010].

Campbell, D.T. and Stanley, J.C. (1963). *Experimental and Quasi-Experimental Designs for Research*. Chicago, IL: Rand McNally and Company.

Campbell, H. and Marshall, R. (2002). Utilitarianism's Bad Breath? A Re-evaluation of the Public Interest Justification for Planning. *Planning Theory*, 1(2), 163–187.

Campbell, S. and Fainstein, S.S. (2003). Introduction: The Structure and Debates of Planning Theory. In: Campbell, S. and Fainstein, S.S. (Eds.) *Readings in Planning Theory* (2nd Edn.). Berlin: Blackwell.

Car, E.R. (2008). The Millennium Village Project and African Development Problems and Potentials. *Progress in Development Studies*, 8, 333–344.

Carnis, L.A.H. (2009). The Economic Theory of Bureaucracy: Insights from the Niskanian Model and the Misesian Approach. *The Quarterly Journal of Australian Economics*, 12(3), 57–78.

Centre for Affordable Housing Finance in Africa. (2010). *Housing Finance in Africa: A Review of Some Africa's Housing Finance Markets*. Parkview: Centre for Affordable Housing Finance in Africa.

Centre for Strategic International Studies (CSIS). (2018). Urbanisation in Sub-Saharan Africa Meeting Challenges by Bridging Stakeholders. [Online], Available from www.csis.org [Accessed September 10, 2019].

Chambers, D.E., Wedel, K.R. and Rodwell, M.K. (1992). *Evaluating Social Programs*. Boston, MA: Allyn and Bacon.

Cheah, B.C. (2009). Clustering Standard Errors or Modelling Multi-level Data. [Online], Available at: http://andrewgelman.com/moveabletype/mlm/RevisitMoulton_2pdf. [Accessed November 2, 2011].

Cheshire, P. and Sheppard, S. (2002). The Welfare Economics of Land Use Planning. *Journal of Urban Economics*, 52, 242–269.

Cheshire, P. and Sheppard, S. (2004). Land Markets and Land Market Regulation: Progress towards Understanding. *Regional Science and Urban Economics*, 34, 619–637.

Cheshire, P. (2008). Introduction of Price Signals into Land use Planning: Are they Applicable in China. In: Song, Yang and Ding, Chengri (Eds.) *Urbanisation in China: Critical Issues in an Era of Rapid Growth*. Cambridge, MA: Lincoln Institute of Land Policy.

Cheshire, P. and Vermeulen, W. (2008). *Land Markets and their Regulation: The Welfare Economics of Planning*. [Online], Available at: http://www.cpb.nl/nl/org/homepages/wvm/welfare_economics_ofplanning.pdf [Accessed January 4, 2010].

Ciriacy-Wantrup, S.V. (1938). Soil Conservation in European Farm management. *Journal of Farm Economics*, 20(1), 86–101.

Clarke, A. and Dawson, R. (1999). *Evaluation Research: An Introduction to Principles, Methods and Practice*. London: Sage Publications Ltd.

Coase, R.H. (1960). The Problem of Social Cost. *Journal of Law and Economics*, 3, 1–44.

Cobbinah, P.B., Erdiaw-Kwasie, M.O. and Amoateng, P. (2015). Africa's Urbanisation: Implications for Sustainable Development. *Cities*, 47, 62–72.

Conyers, D. and Hills, P. (1984). *An Introduction to Development Planning in the Third World*. New York: John Wiley & Sons.

Corkindale, J. (2004). *The Land Use Planning System: Evaluating Options for Reform*. London: The Institute of Economic Affairs.

Cousey, D.L., Hovis, J.J. and Schulze, W.D. (1987). On Supposing Disparity between Willingness to Accept and Willingness to Pay for Measures of Value. *Quarterly Journal of Economics*, 102, 679 – 690.

Creswell, J.W. (2003). *Research Design, Qualitative, Quantitative and Mixed Methods Approaches* (2nd Edn.). London: Sage Publications.

Creswell, J.W. (2007). *Qualitative Inquiry & Research Design, Choosing Among Five Approaches* (2nd Edn.). London: Sage Publications.

Creswell, J.W. (2009). *Research Design Qualitative, Quantitative and Mixed Methods Approaches*, (3rd Edn.). London: Sage Publications.

Crompton, J.L. (1995). Economic Impact Analysis of Sports Facilities and Events: Eleven Sources of Misapplication. *Journal of Sport* Management, 9, 14–35.

Cummings, R.G., Brookshire, D. and Schulze, W.D. (1986). *Valuing Environmental Goods: An Assessment of the Contingent Valuation Method.* Totowa, NJ: Rowmand and Allanheld.

Czaja, R. and Blair, J. (1996). *Designing Surveys a Guide to Decisions and Procedures.* London: Pine Forge Press.

Dale, P. and McLaughlin, J. (1999). *Land Administration.* New York: Oxford University Press Inc.

Davis, R. (1963). Recreation Planning as an Economic Problem. *Natural Resources Journal*, 3, 239–249.

del Saz-Salazar, S. and Garcia – Menéndez, L. (2005). Public Provision versus Private Provision of Industrial Land: A Hedonic Approach. *Land Use Policy*, 22, 215–223.

Demsetz, H. (1967). Towards a Theory of Property Rights. *American Economic Review*, 57(2), 347–359.

Denzin, N.K. and Lincoln, Y.S. (1998). *Collecting and Interpreting Qualitative Materials.* London: Sage.

Denzin, N.K. and Lincoln, Y.S. (Eds.) (2005). *The Handbook of Qualitative Research* (3rd Edn.). Thousand Oaks, CA: Sage.

Department of the Environment, Transport and the Regions (DETR) (2000). *Urban Design in the Planning System: Towards Better Practice.* London: DETR.

Domfeh, S.N. (2001). *Town and Country Planning in Brief.* Accra, Ghana: Town Country Planning Department.

Donnelly, M.P., Vaske, J.J., DeRuiter, D.S. and Loomis, J.B. (1998). Economic Impacts of State Parks: Effect of Park Visitation, Park Facilities, and County Economic Diversification. *Journal of Park and Recreation Administration*, 16(4), 57–72.

Dowall, D.E. and Clark, G. (1996). *Urban Management Programme – A Framework for Reforming Urban Land Policies in Developing Countries.* Washington, DC: The World Bank.

Du Pisani, J.A. (2006). Sustainable Development – Historical Roots of the Concept. *Environmental Sciences*, 3(2), 83–96.

ECDPC. (2020). COVID-19 Situation update Worldwide, as of 19 May 2020. [Online], Available at: https://www.ecdc.europa.eu/en/geographical-distribution-2019-ncov-cases [Accessed June 5, 2020].

Effah-Gyamfi, K. (1975). *Traditional History of the Bono State: An Archaeological Approach.* Legon: Institute of African Studies, University of Ghana.

Egbu, A.U. (2007). *Impact of Land Use Planning on Urban Housing Development in Nigeria.* Unpublished PhD Thesis, University of Wolverhampton, UK.

Egbu, A.U., Olomolaiye, P. and Gameson, R. (2007). A Quantitative Model for assessing the Impact of Land Use Planning on Urban Housing Development in Nigeria. *International Development Planning Review*, 29(2), 215–239.

Egbu, A.U., Olomolaiye, P. and Gameson, R. (2008). A Neo-Institutional Economic Critique of the System for Allocating Urban Land and Development Rights in Nigeria. *Habitat International*, 32,121–135.

El-Khole, A.O. (2018). Development of Planning Theory and Profession: Implications for Planning Education and Practice in Arab States. *International Journal of Architectural Research*, 12(1), 182–208.

Ellis, L.B. and Crookes, P.A. (2006). Philosophical and Theoretical Underpinnings of Research. In: Crookes, P.A. and Davies, S. (Eds.) *Research into Practice; Essential Skills for Reading and Applying Research in Nursing and Health Care* (2nd Edn.). London: Bailiere Tindall.

Evans, A. (1996). The Impact of Land Use Planning and Tax Subsidies on the Supply and Price of Housing in Britain: A Comment. *Urban Studies*, 33(3), 581–585.

Evans, N. (2001). Discourses of Urban Community and Community Planning: A Comparison between Britain and Japan. Available at: http://www.shef.ac.uk [Accessed November 4, 2012].

Evans, N. (2002). Machi-zukuri as a New Paradigm in Japanese Urban Planning: Reality or Myth? *Japan Forum*, 14(3), 443–464.

Evans, A. (2003). Shouting Very Loudly Economics, Planning and Politics. *Town Planning Review*, 74(2), 195–211.

Facchini, F. (2007). Apriorism, Introspection, and the Axiom of Action: A Realist Solution. *The Quarterly Journal of Austrian Economics*, 10, 234–249.

Fainstein, S.S. (2003). New Directions in Planning Theory. In: Campbell, S. and Fainstein, S.S. (Eds.) *Readings in Planning Theory* (2nd Edn.). Berlin: Blackwell.

Faludi, A. (1994). Coalition Building and Planning for Dutch Growth Management: The Role of the Randstad Concept. *Urban Studies*, 31(3), 485–507.

Farrar, T. (1996). *Building Technology and Settlement Planning in West Africa Civilization: Precolonial Akan Cities*. Cambridge, MA: Edwin Mellen Press.

Farvacque, C. and McAuslan, P. (1992). *Urban Management Programme: Reforming Urban Land Policies and Institutions in Developing Countries*. Washington, DC: The International Bank for Reconstruction and Development (The World Bank).

Field, A. (2005). *Discovering Statistics Using SPSS* (2nd Edn.). London: Sage Publications.

Filion, P. and McSuperren, K. (2007). Smart Growth and Development Reality: The Difficult Co-ordination of Land Use and Transport Objectives. *Urban Studies*, 44(3), 501–523.

Fischel, W.A. (1990). Introduction: Four Maxims for Research on Land-Use Controls. *Land Economics*, 66(3), 229–236.

Foley, P. (1992). Local Economic Policy and Job Creation: A Review of Evaluation Studies. *Urban Studies*, 29(3/4), 557–598.

Forss, K., Rebien, C.C. and Carlsson, J. (2002). Process Use of Evaluation, Types of Use that Precede Learned and Feedback. *Evaluation*, 8(1), 29–45.

Francis, J., Laford, R., Olsson, P. and Schipper, K. (2007). Information Uncertainty and Post-Earnings Announcement Drift. *Journal of Business Finance and Accounting*, 34(3&4), 403–433.

Friedmann, J. (2005). Globalisation and the Emerging Culture of Planning. *Progress in Planning*, 64, 183–234.

Friedman, M. (1962). *Capitalism and Freedom*. Chicago, IL: University of Chicago Press.

Gage, N. (1989). The Paradigm Wars and their Aftermath. *Educational Researcher*, 18, 85–102.

Gambrah, A. (1994). *Regulation of Housing and Services for the Urban Poor: A Case Study of Accra, Ghana*. Unpublished MSc Thesis, University of British Columbia, Canada.

Gandy, M., (2005). Learning from Lagos. *New Left Review*, 33, 36–52.

Garber, A.M., Wienstein, M.C., Torrance, G.W. and Kamlet, M.S. (1996). Theoretical Foundations of Cost-Effective Analysis. In: Gold, M.R., Siegel, J.E., Russell, L.B., & Wienstein, M.C. *Cost-Effectiveness in Health and Medicine*. New York: Oxford University Press.

Gelan, A. (2003). Local Economic Impacts: The British Open. *Annals of Tourism Research*, 30(2), 406–425.

Gilbert, A. (2014). Free Housing for the Poor: An Effective Way to Address Poverty? *Habitat International*, 41, 253–261.

Glaeser, E.L. (2004). Psychology and the Market. *American Economic Review*, 94, 408–413.

Glaeser, E.L. and Ward, B.A. (2009). The Causes and Consequences of Land Use Regulation: Evidence from Greater Boston. *Journal of Urban Economics*, 65, 265–278.

Gleeson, B. and Low, N. (2000). *Australian Urban Planning: New Challenges, New Agendas*, Sydney: BPA Print Group.

Glesne, C. and Peshkin, P. (1992). *Becoming Qualitative Researches: An Introduction*, New York: Longman.

Godschalk, D.R. (2004). Land Use Planning Challenges: Coping with Conflicts in Visions of Sustainable Development and Liveable cCmmunities. *Journal of the American Planning Association*, 70(1), 5–13.

Government of Ghana (GoG). (1990). *Accra Planning and Development Programme Planning Standards and Development Guild Lines*. Accra: Ministry of Local Government/Town and Country Planning Department.

Government of Ghana. (1992). *The Fourth Republican Constitution of Ghana*. Accra: Ghana Publishing Corporation (Assembly Press).

Government of Ghana. (1993). *The Local Government Act (Act 462)*. Accra: Ghana Publishing Corporation (Assembly Press).

Government of Ghana. (1996a). *National Building Regulations (LI1630)*. Accra: Ghana Publishing Corporation (Assembly Press).

Government of Ghana. (1996b). *Ghana – The New Local Government System*. Accra: Ministry of Local Government and Rural Development.

Government of Ghana. (2009). *Human Settlements and Land Use Policy and Planning in Ghana: A Policy Study*. Accra: Land Use Planning and Management Project, Town and Country Planning Department, Ghana.

Government of Ghana. (2012). *Ghana National Urban Policy*. Accra: Assembly Press.

Grant, R. and Yankson, P. (2003). City Profile: Accra. *Cities*, 20(1), 65–74.

Greaves, B.B. (1949). An Abridgement of Human Action a Treatise on Economics. [Online], Available at: http://www.samassavcneessa.info/kasso/pdf/HumanActiononEconomics.pdf [Accessed December 4, 2009].

Green, P.E., Krieger, A.M. and Wind, Y.J. (2001). Thirty Years of Conjoint Analysis: Reflections and Prospects. *Interfaces*, 31(3), 556–573.

Griliches, Z. (1961). The Demand for Fertilizer: An Econometric Reinterpretation of a Technical Change. *Journal of Farm Economics*, 40, 591–606.

GSS. (1984). *Population and Housing Census*. Accra: Ghana Statistical Service.

GSS. (2007). *Pattern and Trends of Poverty in Ghana 1991–2006*. Accra: Ghana Statistical Service.

Guba, E.G. and Lincoln, Y.S. (1981). *Effective Evaluation: Improving the Usefulness of Evaluation Results through Responsive and Naturalistic Approaches*. San Francisco: Jossey-Bass.

Guba, E.G. (Ed.) (1990). *The Paradigm Dialog*. London: Sage Publications.

Gümüs, E. (2007). The Social Cost of Monopoly: A Survey and an Evaluation. *Akdeniz I. I. B. F. Dergisi*, 13, 149–164.

Guo, J.Y. and Gandavarapu, S. (2010). An Economic Evaluation of Health-Promotive Built Environment Changes. *Preventive Medicine*, 50, 544–549.

Gurran, N., Ruming, K., Randolph, B. and Quintal, D. (2008). *Planning, Government Charges, and the Costs of Land and Housing*. AHURI Positioning Paper No. 109, Australian Housing and Urban Research Institute, UNSW – UWS Research Centre, Sydney Research Centre.

Gutman, J., Sy, A. and Chattopadhyay, S. (2015). *Financing African Infrastructure: Can the World deliver*? Brookings: Global Economy and Development.

Hall, P. (2002). *Urban and Regional Planning* (4th Edn.). London: Routledge.

Hammond, F.N. (2006). *The Economic Impacts of Sub-Saharan Africa Urban Real Estate Policies*. Unpublished PhD Thesis, University of Wolverhampton, UK.

Hammond, F.N., Antwi, A. and Proverbs, D. (2006). The Political Economy of Sub-Saharan Africa Land Policies. *American Review of Political Economy*, 4(1/2), 19–35.

Hammond, F.N. and Antwi, Y.A. (2010). *Economic Analysis of Sub-Saharan Africa Real Estate Policies*. London: Palgrave Macmillan.

Hammond, F.N., Baffour Awuah, K.G. and Adiaba, S. (2012). Urbanisation and Climate Change. In: Booth, C.A., Hammond, F.N., Lamond, J.E. and Proverbs, D.G. (Eds.) *Solutions to Climate Change Challenges for the Built Environment*. Oxford: Wiley Black Wells.

Harberger, A.C. (1954). Monopoly and Resource Allocation. *American Economic Review*, 44(2), 77–87.

Harberger, A.C. (1971). Three Basic Postulates for Applied Welfare Economics: An Interpretive Essay. *Journal of Economic Literature*, 9(3), 784–797.

Harris, N. (2010). Discretion and Expediency in Enforcement of Planning Controls. *Town Planning Review*, 81, 675–700.

Harrison, A.J. (1977). *Economics and Land Use Planning*. London: Croom Helm Ltd.

Harrison, P. (2006). On the Edge of Reason: Planning and Urban Futures in Africa. *Urban Studies*, 43(2), 319–335.

Hayek, F.A. (1944). *The Road to Serfdom*. London: Routledge.

Hayek, F.A. (1945). The Use of Knowledge in Society. *The American Economic Review*, 35(4), 519–530.

Hayek, F.A. (1976). *The Constitution of Liberty*. Thetford: Lowe & Brydone Printers Ltd.

Hayek, F.A. (1983). *Knowledge, Evolution, and Society*. London: Adam Smith Institute.

Healey, P. (1997). *Collaborative Planning: Shaping Places in Fragmented Societies*. London: Macmillan.

Healey, P. (2003). Collaborative Planning in Perspective. *Planning Theory*, 2(2), 101–123.

Healey, P. (2004). The Treatment of Space and Place in the New Strategic Spatial Planning in Europe. *International Journal of Urban and Regional Research*, 28(1), 45–67.

Heikkila, E.J. (2000). *The Economics of Planning*. New Brunswick: New Jersey Centre for Urban Policy Research.

Herath, S. and Maier, G. (2010). *The Hedonic Price Method in Real Estate and Housing Market Research: A Literature Review*. WU Vienna University of Economics and Business, Vienna: Discussion Paper 2010/03.

Hertsgaard, T.A., Leistritz, F.L., Leholm, A.G. and Coon, C. (1984). The North Dakota Input – Output model: A Tool for Measuring Economic Linkages. [Online], Available at: http://www.library.ndusu.edu/respsitory/bitstream/handle/1. [Accessed November 15, 2010).

Home, R.K. (1990). Town Planning and Garden Cities in the British Colonial Empire 1910–1940. *Planning Perspectives*, 5(1), 23–37.

Home, R. (2012). Towards a Pro-Poor Land Law in Sub-Saharan Africa. In: Home, R. (Ed.) *Essays in African Land Law*. Pretoria: Pretoria University Law Press.

Hopkins, L.D. (2001). *Urban Development*, the Logic of Making Plans. Washington, DC: Island Press.

Hoppe, H. (1989). *The Theory of Socialism and Capitalism*. Boston: Kluwer Academic Publishers.

Hoppe, H. (1995). *Economic Science and Austrian Method*. Auburn, AL: Ludwig von Mises Institute.

Huang, C., Wang, Y., Li, X., Ren, L., Zhao, J., Hu, Y., et al. (2020). Clinical Features of Patients infected with 2019 Novel Coronavirus in Wuhan, China. *Lancet*; 395(10223), 497–506. Hughes, D.W. (2003). Policy Uses of Economic Multiplier and Impact Analysis. *Choices*, 18, 25–29.

Huxley, M. and Yiftachel, O. (2000). New Paradigm or Old Myopia? Unsetting the Communicative Turn in Planning Theory. *Journal of Planning Education and Research*, 19(4), 333–342.

Hülsmann, J.G. (2004). The a Priori Foundations of Property Economics. *The Quarterly Journal of Austrian Economics*, 7(4), 41–68.

Ihlanfeldt, K.R. (2007). The Effect of Land Use Regulation on Housing and Land Prices. *Journal of Urban Economics*, 61(3), 420–435.

Ihlanfeldt, K.R. (2009). Does Comprehensive Land Use Planning Improve Cities? *Land Economics*, 85, 74–86.

IIED. (2016). Why Is Water Still Unaffordable for Sub-Saharan Africa's Urban Poor? *Briefing*. Available at: https://pubs.iied.org/17353IIED/ [Accessed September 4, 2020].

Jevons, W.S. (1871). *The Theory of Political Economy*. London: Macmillan & Co.

JICA Research Institute. (2013). Development Challenges in Africa. Towards 2050. [Online], Available at: https://www.jica.go.jp/jica-ri/publication/booksandreports/development_challenges_in_africa_towards_2050.html [Accessed February 14, 2018].

Johnson, R.B. and Onwuegbuzie, A.J. (2004). Mixed Methods Research: A Research Paradigm Whose Time Has Come. *Educational Research Association*, 33(7), 14–26.

Keeble, L. (1959). *Principles and Practice of Town and Country Planning* (2nd Edn.). London: The Estate Gazette.

Keeton, R. and Nijhuis, S. (2019). Spatial Challenges in Contemporary African New Towns and Potentials for Alternative Planning Strategies. *International Planning Studies*, 24(3–4), 218–234.

Keeton, R. and Provoost, M. (Eds.) (2019). *To Build a City in Africa: A History and a Manual.* Rotterdam: Nai010.

Keith, L.C. and Ogundele, A. (2007). Legal Systems and Constitutionalism in Sub-Saharan Africa: Empirical Examination of Colonial Influence on Human Rights. *Human Rights Quarterly*, 29, 1065–1097.

Keogh, G. and Evans, A.W. (1992). The Private and Social Costs of Planning Delay. *Urban Studies*, 29(5), 687–699.

Kerlinger, F.N. and Lee, H.B. (2000). *Foundations of Behavioural Research* (4th Edn.). Philadelphia, PA: Harcourt College Publishers.

Khakee, A. (2003). The Emerging Gap between Evaluation Research and Practice. *Evaluation*, 9, 340–352.

Kim, J. (2009a). Linking Land Use Planning and Regulation to Economic Development: A Literature Review. [Online], Available at: http://www.real.illinois.edu [Accessed December 15, 2009].

Kim, Y. (2009b). Validation of Psychometric Research Instruments: The Case of Information Science. *Journal of the American Society for Information Science and Technology*, 60(6), 1178–1191.

Kinsella, N.S. and Tinsley, P. (2004). Causation and Aggression. *The Quarterly Journal of Austrian Economics*, 7(4), 97–112.

Kironde, J.M.L. (2006). The Regulatory Framework, Unplanned Development and Urban Poverty: Findings from Dar es Salaam, Tanzania. *Land Use Policy*, 23, 460–472.

Klosterman, R.E. (1997). "Planning Support Systems: A New Perspective on Computer-aided Planning." *Journal of Planning Education and Research*, 17(1), 45–54.

Klosterman, R.E. (2003). Argument for and against Planning. In: Campbell, S. and Fainstein, S.S. (Eds.) *Readings in Planning Theory* (2nd Ed.). Berlin: Blackwell.

Kombe, W.J. (2005). Land Use Dynamics in Peri-Urban Areas and Their Implications on the Urban Growth and Form: The Case of Dar-es-Salaam, Tanzania. *Habitat International,* 29, 113–135.

Konadu-Agyemang, K. (1998). *The Political Economy of Housing and Urban Development in Africa: Ghana's Experience from Colonial Times to 1998.* Westport: Praeger Publishers.

Konadu-Agyemang, K. (2000). The Best of Times and the Worst of Times: Structural Adjustment Programs and Uneven Development in Africa. *Professional Geographer*, 53(3), 469–483.

Konadu-Agyemang, K. (2001). Structural Adjustment Programs and Housing Affordability in Accra, Ghana. *The Canadian Geographer*, 45, 528–544.

Kotey, N.A., Dowuona-Hammond, C. and Atuguba, R. (2004). *Ghana Land Administration Project Legislative and Judicial Review, Draft Final Report.* Accra: Ministry of Lands and Forestry.

Kuhn, T. (1970). *The Structure of Scientific Revolutions.* Chicago, IL: University of Chicago Press.

Kula, K. (1997). *Economics of Natural Resources, the Environment and Policies,* (2nd Edn.). London: Chapman and Hall.

Lai, W.L. (2005). Neo-Institutional Economics and Planning Theory. *Planning Theory*, 4(1), 7–19.

Lai, W.L., Yung, P., Li, R.Y. and Ho, D.C. (2007). The Private Supply of and Public Demand for Planning Conditions in the Absence of Direct Statutory Enforcement Measures. *Planning Practice and Research*, 22(4), 535–557.

Lall, S.V., Henderson, J.V. and Venables, A.J. (2017). *Africa's Cities: Opening Doors to the World*. Washington, DC: World Bank.

Lamond, J., Baffour Awuah, K.G., Bloch, R., Lewis, E. and Falade, J. (2015). Baseline Study on Urban Land, Planning and Governance in Nigerian Cities. Final Report Submitted to DFID.

Lancaster, K. J. (1966). A New Approach to Consumer Theory. *Journal of Political Economy*, 74, 132–157.

Larbi, W.O (1994). *Urban Land Policies and Delivery of Developable Land in Ghana*. PhD Thesis, Department of Land Management and Development, University of Reading, UK.

Larbi, W.O. (1996). Spatial Planning and Urban Fragmentation in Accra. *Third World Planning Review*, 18(2), 193–215.

Larbi, W.O, Antwi, A. and Olomolaiye, P. (2004). Compulsory Land Acquisition in Ghana – Policy and Praxis. *Land Use Policy*, 21, 115–127.

Lavoie, D. (1985). *National Economic Planning: What Is Left?* Cambridge, MA: Ballinger Publishing Company.

Lee, C. and Taylor, T. (2005). Critical Reflections on the Economic Impact Assessment of a Mega-Event: The Case of 2002 FIFA World Cup. *Tourism Management*, 26, 595–603.

Leontief, W. (1966). *Input-Output Economics*. New York: Oxford University Press.

Lichfield, N. (1966). Cost-Benefit Analysis and Town Planning a Case Study: Swanley. *Urban Studies*, 3, 215–249.

Lichfield, N. (1996). *Community Impact Evaluation*. London: UCL Press.

Lichfield, N., Adams, D., Needham, B., Teitz, M. and Wenban-Smith, A. (2003). The Concept of Planned Development: A Presentation and Commentaries on the Contribution of Nathaniel Licfield. *Planning Theory and Practice*, 4(1), 45–71.

List, J.A. and Gallet, C.A. (2001). What Experimental Protocol Influence Disparities between Actual and Hypothetical Stated Values? *Environmental and Resource Economics*, 20(3), 241–254.

Little, J.M. and Berrens, R. (2004). Explaining Disparities between Actual and Hypothetical Stated Values: Further Investigation Using Meta-Analysis. *Economics Bulletin*, 3(6), 1–12.

Lovering, J. (2009). The Recession and the End of Planning as We Have Known It. *International Planning Studies*, 14(1), 1–6.

Lusk, J.L. and Norwood, F.B. (2009). An Inferred Valuation Method. *Land Economics*, 85(3), 500–514.

Mabogunje, A.L. (1968). *Urbanisation in Nigeria*. London: University of London Press.

Mabogunje, A.L. (1990). Urban Planning and the Post-Colonial State in Africa: A Research Overview. *African Studies Review*, 33(2), 121–203.

Malpass, P. (2000). The Discontinuous History of Housing Association in England. *Housing Studies*, 15(2), 195–212.

Malpezzi, S. and Mayo, S.K. (1997). Getting Housing Incentives Right: A Case Study of the Effects of Regulation, Taxes, and Subsidies on Housing Supply in Malaysia. *Land Economics*, 73(3), 372–391.

Mamdani, M. (1996). *Citizen and Subject. Contemporary Africa and the Legacy of Late Colonialism.* Princeton, NJ: Princeton University Press.

Mankiw, N.G. (2011). *Principles of Economics* (6th Edn.). Mason, IA: South-Western Cengage Learning.

Mark, M.M. and Cook, T.D. (1984). Design of Randomised Experiments and Quasi-Experiments. In: Rutman, L. (Ed.) *Evaluation Research Methods: A Basic Guide* (2nd Edn.). Beverly Hills, CA: Sage.

Marshall, T. (2009). Planning and the New Labour in the UK. *Planning Practice & Research*, 24(1), 1–9.

Mayer, C.J. and Somerville, C.T. (2000). Land Use Regulation and New Construction. *Regional Science and Urban Economics*, 30, 639–662.

McGranaham, G., Jacobi, P., Songsore, J., Surdjadi, C. and Kjellen, M. (2001). *The Citizens at Risk: From Urban Sanitation to Sustainable Cities.* London: Earthscan.

Mckay, S. (2003). Sheriffs and Outlaws: In Pursuit of Effective Enforcement. *Town Planning Review*, 74(4), 423–443.

Mckay, S., Berry, J. and McGreal, S. (2003). Planning Enforcement: Lessons for Practice and Procedure. *Planning Theory and Practice*, 4(3), 325–344.

Mckay, S. (2007). Contravention and Conformity in EIA: An Investigation into Regulatory Compliance in Northern Ireland. *European Planning Studies*, 15(1), 87–105.

McConnell, V. and Walls, M. (2005). The Value of Open Space: Evidence from Studies of Non-market Benefits. [Online], Available at: http://www.rff.org/Documents/REF-REPORT-open/.20Spaces.pdf [Accessed November 20, 2010].

Mckinsey Global Institute. (2012). Urban World: Cities and the Rise of the Consuming Class. Available at: http://www.mckinsey.com/mgl [Accessed August 13, 2012].

Menger, C. (1871). *Principles of Economics,* (2007 Edn.) [Online], Available at: http://www.mises.org/books/mengerprinciples.pdf [Accessed September 8, 2011].

Mensah, C.A. (2010). *Causes and Consequences of Informal Settlement Planning in Ghana: A Case Study of Aboabo, a Suburb of Kumasi Metropolis.* Mphil Thesis, University of Cape-Coast, Ghana.

Miernyk, W.H. (1982). *Regional Analysis and Regional Policy.* Cambridge, MA: Gunn & Hain, Publishers, Inc.

Mises, L.V. (1949). *Human Action: A Treatise on Economics* (Scholar's Edn.). Auburn, AL: Ludwig von Mises Institute.

Monk, S. and Whitehead, C.M.E. (1999). Evaluating the Economic Impact of Planning Controls in the United Kingdom: Some Implications for Housing. *Land Economics*, 75(1), 74–93.

Morgan, D. (2007). Paradigms Lost and Pragmatism Regained: Methodological Implications of Combining Qualitative and Quantitative Methods. *Journal of Mixed Methods Research*, 1(1), 48–76.

Mulherin, J.H. (2007). Measuring Cost and Benefits of Regulation: Conceptual Issues in Securities Markets. *Journal of Corporate Finance*, 13(2–3), 421–437.

Mullins, D. and Murie, A. (2006). *Housing Policy in the UK*. London: Palgrave Macmillan.

Mundell, R. (1968). *Man and Economics*. New York: McGraw Hill.

Murphy, J., Allen, P.G., Stevens, T.H. and Whitehead, D. (2005). A Meta-Analysis of Hypothetical Bias in Stated Preference Valuation. *Environmental and Resource Economics*, 30(3), 313–325.

Murray, M. (2017). Frictionless Utopias for the Contemporary Urban Age: Large-Scale, Master-Planned Redevelopment Projects in Urbanising Africa. In: Datta, A. and Shaban, A. (Eds.) *Mega-Urbanisation in the Global South: Fast Cities and New Urban Utopias of the Postcolonial State*, 31–53. New York: Routledge.

Musandu-Nyamayaro, O. (2008). The Case for Modernisation of Local Planning Authority Frameworks in Southern and Eastern Africa: A Radical Initiative for Zimbabwe. *Habitat International*, 32, 15–27.

Musole, M. (2009). Property Rights, Transaction Costs and Institutional Change: Conceptual Framework and Literature Review. *Progress in Planning*, 71, 43–85.

Mutikani, L. (2020). Coronavirus Savages US Economy in First Quarter; Bigger Hit Still to Come, Reuters. [Online], Available at: https://uk.reuters.com/article/us-usa-economy/coronavirus-savages-u-s-economy-in-first-quarter-bigger-hit-still-to-come-idUKKCN22B0A1 [Accessed June 1, 2020].

Mutuku, B., Boerboom, L. and Madureira, A.M. (2019.) The Role of Planning Support Systems in National Policy Transfer and Policy Translation in Secondary Cities. *International Planning Studies*, 24(3–4), 293–307.

Mwimba, C. (2002). The Colonial Legacy of Town Planning in Zambia. Paper presented at South African Planning Institute International Conference on Planning Africa, 18–20 September, Durban, South Africa.

Nachmias-Frankfurt, C. and Nachmias, D. (1996). *Research Methods in Social Science* (5th Edn.). London: Arnold.

Nadin, V. (2007). The Emergence of the Spatial Planning Approach in England. *Planning, Practice & Research*, 22, 43–62.

Nadin, V. and Stead, D. (2008). European Spatial Planning Systems, Social Models and Learning. *disP – The Planning Review*, 172, 35–47.

Naess, P. (2001). Urban Planning and Sustainable Development. *European Planning Studies*, 9(4), 503–524.

Namangaya, A.H. (2014). Urban Spatial Planning and Local Economic Development: Comparative Assessment of Practice in Tanzanian Cities. *International Journal of Business, Humanities and Technology*, 4(6), 20–31.

Newman, P. and Thornley, A. (1996). *Urban Planning in Europe: International Competition, National Systems and Planning Projects*. London: Routledge.

Niskanen, W.N. (1994). *Bureaucracy and Public Economics*. Fairfax, VA: The Lock Institute.

Njoh, A.J. (1997). Colonial Spatial Development Policies, Economic Instability, and Urban Public Transportation in Cameroon. *Cities*, 14(3), 133–143.

Njoh, A.J. (2003). Planning in Contemporary Africa: The State, Town Planning and Society in Cameroon. *Habitat International*, 29, 367–374.

Njoh, A.J. (2004). The Experience and Legacy of French Colonial Urban Planning in Sub-Saharan Africa. *Planning Perspectives*, 19, 435–454.

Njoh, A.J. (2009). Urban Planning as a Tool of Power and Social Control in Colonial Africa. *Planning Perspectives*, 24(3), 301–317.

Nkrumah, K. (1970). *Africa Must Unite*. New York: International Publishers.

Nkum and Associates. (2001). *Towards a Concept for Participatory Urban Planning in District Towns. Final Report for Promotion of District Capitals II submitted to Programme Co-ordination Office PRODICAP II.* Accra: GTZ and Ministry of Local Government and Rural Development.

North, D.C. (1995). The New Institutional Economics and the Third World Development. In: J. Harriss, J. Hunter and C.M. Lewis (Eds.) *The New Institutional Economics and The Third World Development.* London: Routledge.

Nozick, R. (1974). *Anarchy, State and Utopia.* Oxford: Blackwell.

Oduro, C.Y. (2010). *Effects of Rapid Urbanisation on Livelihoods in the Peri-Urban Areas of Accra, Ghana.* Unpublished PhD Thesis, Florida State University, USA.

Organisation for Economic Co-operation and Development (OECD). (2020). COVID-19 and Africa: Socio-economic Implications and Policy Responses. [Online], Available at: http://www.oecd.org/coronavirus/policy-responses/covid-19-and-africa-socio-economic-implications-and-policy-responses-96e1b282/ [Accessed July 10, 2020].

Okoth-Ogendo, H.W.O. (2000). Legislative Approaches to Customary Tenure and Tenure Reform in East Africa. In: Toulmin, C., Quan, J.F. (Eds.) *Evolving Land Rights, Policy and Tenure in Africa.* London: DFID/IIED/INR.

O'Sullivan, S. and Sheffrin, M. (2007). *Economics Principles* (California Edn.). Upper Saddle River, NJ: Prentice Hall.

Owusu, G. (2008). Indigenes' and Migrants' Access to Land in Peri-Urban Areas of Accra, Ghana. *International Development Planning Review*, 30(2), 177–197.

Owusu, J.H. (2001). Spatial Integration, Adjustment and Structural Transformation in Sub-Saharan Africa: Some Linkage Pattern Changes in Ghana. *Professional Geographer*, 53(2), 230–247.

Oyugi, O.M. and K'Akumu, O.A. (2007). Land Use Management Challenges for the City of Nairobi. *Urban Forum*, 18(1), 94–112.

Panagopoulos, T., Duque, J.A.G. and Dan, M.B. (2016). Urban Planning with Respect to Environmental Quality and Human Well-Being. *Environmental Pollution*, 208, 137–144.

Pansiri, J. (2009). Evolution of Doctoral Thesis Research Topic and Methodology: A Personal Experience. *Tourism Management*, 30, 83–89.

Parker, J. (2000). *Making the Town: GA State and Society in Early Colonial Accra.* Portsmouth, NH: Heinemann.

Pasour, Jr., E.C. (1983). Land-Use Planning Implication of the Economic Calculations Debate. *The Journal of Liberiterian Studies*, 7(1), 126–139.

Paton, M.Q. (2002). *Qualitative Research and Evaluation Methods* (3rd Edn.). Thousand Oaks, CA: Sage.

Payne, G. and Majale, M. (2004). *The Urban Housing Manual: Making Regulatory Frameworks Work for the Poor.* London: Earthscan.

Pejovich, S. (1999). The Effects of the Interaction of Formal and Informal Institutions on Social Stability and Economic Development. *Journal of Markets and Morality*, 2, 164–181.

Pena, S. (2002). Land Use Planning on the U.S. – Mexico Border: A Comparison of the Legal Framework. *Journal of Borderlands Studies,* 17(1), 1–20.

Pennington, M. (2000). *Liberating the Land. The Case for Private Land Use Planning.* London: The Institute of Economic Affairs.

Perera, N.G.R. and Emmanuel, R. (2016). A 'Local Climate Zone' Based Approach to Urban Planning in Colombo, Sri Lanka. *Urban Climate*, 23, 1–16.

Petersen, M.A. (2008). Estimating Standard Errors in Finance Panel Data Sets: Comparing Approaches. *Review of Financial Studies*, 22(1), 435–480.

Philipps, D.C. and Burbules, N.C. (2000). *Postpositivism and Educational Research*. Lanham, NY: Rowman and Littlefield.

Pigou, A.C. (1932). *The Economics of Welfare*. London: Macmillan.

Pinkerton, S.D., Johnson-Masotti, A.P., Derse, A. and Layde, P.M. (2002). Ethical Issues in Cost-Effectiveness Analysis. *Evaluation and Program Planning*, 25, 71–83.

Platteau, J.P. (1992). Land Reform and Structural Adjustment in Sub-Saharan Africa: Controversies and Guidelines, FAO Economic and Social Development Paper, No. 107, FAO, Rome.

Platteau, J.P. (2009). Institutional Obstacles to African Economic Development: State, Ethnicity and Custom. *Journal of Economic Behaviour and Organization*, 71, 669–689.

Pogodzinski, J.M. and Sass, T.R. (1990). The Economic Theory of Zoning: A Critical Review. *Land Economics*, 66(3), 295–314.

Pollakowski, H.O. and Wachter, S.M. (1990). The Effects of Land-Use Constraints on Housing Prices. *Land Economics*, 66(3), 315–324.

Popper, K. (1945). *The Open Society and its Enemies Vol. 2 Hegel and Marx*. London: Routledge.

Posner, R.A. (1975). Theories of Economic Regulation. *The Bell Journal of Economics and Management Science*, 5(2), 334–358.

Price, S.M., Gatzlaff, D.H. and Sirmans, C.F. (2010). Information Uncertainty and the Post-Earnings-Announcement Drift Anomaly: Insights from REITs. *Journal of Real Estate Finance Economics*, 44(1–2), 250–274.

Purcell, M. (2009). Resisting Neoliberalisation: Communicative Planning or Counter-Hegemonic Movements? *Planning Theory*, 8(2), 140–165.

Pyle, K.B. (1973). The Technology of Japanese Nationalism: Local Improvement Movement, 1900–1918. *The Journal of Asian Studies*, 31(1), 51–65.

Qian, Z. (2010). Without Zoning: Urban Development and Land Use Controls in Houston. *Cities*, 27(1), 31–41.

Quigley, J.M. and Rosenthal, L.A. (2005). The Effects of Land Use Regulations on the Price of Housing: What Do We Know? What Can We Learn? *Cityscape*, 8(1), 69–137.

Quigley, J.M. and Raphael, S. (2006). Regulation and the High Cost of Housing in California. [Online], Available at: http://www.escholarship.org/uc/item/3hh7s35m [Accessed August 13, 2010].

Quigley, J.M. (2007). Regulation and Property Values in the United States: The High Cost of Monopoly. [Online], Available at: http://www.escholarship.org/uc/item/5692w323 [Accessed August 13, 2010].

Rakodi, C. (1990). Policies and Preoccupations in Rural and Regional Development Planning in Tanzania, Zambia and Zimbabwe. In: David Simons (Ed.) *Third World Regional Development*. London: Paul Chapman Publishing Ltd.

Rakodi, C. (1998). Globalization Trends and Sub-Saharan African Cities. In: Lo, F.C. and Yeung, Y.M. (Eds.) *Globalization and the World of Large Cities*. New York: United Nations University Press.

Rakodi, C. (2001). Forget Planning: Put Politics First? Priorities for Urban Management in Developing Countries. *The International Journal of Applied Earth Observation and Geoinformation (JAG)*, 3(3), 209–223.

Rakodi, C. (2006a). Relationships of Power and Place: The Social Construction of African Cities (Editorial). *Geoforum*, 37, 312–317.

Rakodi, C. (2006b). State-Society Relations in Land Delivery Processes in Five African Cities: An Editorial Introduction. *International Development Planning Review*, 28(2), 127–136.

Rakodi, C. (2006c). Social Agency and State Authority in Land Delivery Processes in African Cities. Compliance, Conflict and Cooperation. *International Development Planning Review*, 28(2), 263–285.

Ratcliff, R.U. (1949). *Urban Land Economics*. New York: McGraw-Hill Book Company.

Ratcliffe, J. (1983). *An Introduction to Town and Country Planning*. London: Hutchinson.

Refuge. (2020). 25% Increase in Calls to National Domestic Abuse Helpline Since Lockdown Measures Began, Refuge, Press Release. [Online], Available at: https://www.refuge.org.uk/25-increase-in-calls-to-national-domestic-abuse-helpline-since-lockdown-measures-began/ [Accessed June 2, 2020].

Reichardt, C.S. and Gollob, H.F. (1989). Ruling Out Threats to Validity. *Evaluation Review*, 13, 3–17.

Robinson, F. and Shaw, K. (1994). Urban Policy under the Conservatives: In Search of the Big Idea? *Local Economy*, 9(3), 224–235.

Rodney, W. (1972). *How Europe Underdeveloped Africa*. London: Bogle L'Ouverture Publishing Co.

Roe, B., Boyle, K.J. and Teisl, M.F. (1996). Using Conjoint Analysis to Derive Estimates of Compensating Variation. *Journal of Environmental Economics and Management*, 31, 145–159.

Rosalía, P., Julio Roldán, J., Gago, E.J. and Ordó˜nez, J. (2017). Assessing the Relationship between Urban Planning Options and Carbon Emissions at the Use Stage of New Urbanised Areas: A Case Study in a Warm Climate Location. *Energy and Buildings*, 136, 73–85.

Rosen, S. (1974). Hedonic Prices and Implicit Markets: Product Differentiation in Pure Competition. *Journal of Political Economy*, 82(1), 34–55.

Rothbard, M.N. (2004). *Man, Economy and State* (Scholar's Edn.). Alabama: Ludwig Von Mises Institute.

Roy, M. (2009). Planning for Sustainable Urbanisation in Fast Growing Cities: Mitigation and Adaption Issues Addressed in Dhaka, Bangladesh. *Habitat International*, 33, 276–286.

Ruben, A. and Babbie, E.R. (2009). *Essential Research Methods for Social Work* (2nd Edn.). Belmont, CA: Brooks.

Ryan, A. (1987). *John Stuart Mills and Jeremy Bentham: Utilitarianism and Other Essays*, New York: Penguin Books.

Saadat, S., Rawtani, D. and Hussain, C.M. (2020). Environmental Perspective of COVID-19. *Science of the Total Environment*, 728. [Online]. Available at: https://www.sciencedirect.com/science/article/pii/S0048969720323871 [Accessed June 2, 2020].

Salas-Zapata, W.A. and Ortiz-Muñoz, S.M. (2019). Analysis of Meanings of the Concept of Sustainability. *Sustainable Development*, 27, 153–161.

Satterthwaite, D. (1996). *The Scale and Nature of Urban Change in the South*. London: IIED, Human Settlements Programme.

Sawyer, L. (2014). Piecemeal Urbanisation at the Peripheries of Lagos. *African Studies*, 73(2), 271–289.

Schmidt, S. and Buehler, R. (2007). The Planning Process in the US and Germany: A Comparative Analysis. *International Planning Studies*, 12, 55–75.

Scholz, J.T. (1997). Enforcement Policy and Corporate Misconduct: The Changing Perspective of Deterrence Theory. *American Journal of Political Economy*, 693–717.

Shapiro, E., Davies, K. and Mackmin, D. (2009). *Modern Methods of Valuation* (10th Edn.). London: Estates Gazette.

Shaw, D. and Lord, A. (2007). The Cultural Turn? Culture Change and What It Means for Spatial Planning in England. *Planning, Practice and Research*, 22, 63–78.

Shaw, D. and Lord, A. (2009). From Land-use to 'Spatial Planning' Reflections on the Reform of the English Planning System. *Town Planning Review*, 80(4–5), 415–435.

Shibata, K. (2008a). The Origins of Japanese Planning Culture: Building a Nation-state 1868–1945. [Online], Available at: http://eprints.lse.ac.uk/21682/ [Accessed February 2, 2010].

Shibata, K. (2008b). Neoliberalism, Risk, and Spatial Governance in the Developmental State: Japanese Planning in the Global Economy. *Critical Planning*, 15, 92–118.

Shrader-Frechette, K. (1994). *Ethics of Scientific Research*. New York: Rowman and Littlefield.

Silva, C.N. (Ed.) (2015). *Urban Planning in Sub-Saharan Africa: Colonial and Post-colonial Planning Cultures*. New York: Routledge.

Simpson, M., Hardy, D. and Ward, S. (1989). *British Planning History 1900–1952*. [Online], Available at: http://www.st-andrews.ac.uk [Accessed April 13, 2013].

Sirmans, G.S., Macpherson, D.A. and Zietz, E.N. (2005). The Composition of Hedonic Pricing Models. *Journal of Real Estate Literature*, 13(1), 3–43.

Smith, A. (1776). *An Inquiry into the Nature and Causes of the Wealth of Nations*, (1976 Edn.). Chicago, IL: University of Chicago.

Sorensen, A. (2000). Conflict, Consensus or Consent: Implications of Japanese Land Readjustment Practice for Developing Countries. *Habitat International*, 24(1), 51–73.

Sorensen, A. (2002). *The Making of Urban Japan: Cities and Planning from Edo to the 21st century*. London: Nissan Institute/Routledge.

Splinter, E. and Leynseele, Y.N. (2019). The Conditional City: Emerging Properties of Kenya's Satellite Cities. *International Planning Studies*, 24(3–4), 308–324.

Staley, S.R. (2004). Urban Planning, Smart Growth, and Economic Calculation: An Austrian Critique and Extension. *The Review of Austrian Economics*, 17(2/3), 265–283.

Stevens, A. (2004). Economic Impacts of Intelligent Transportation Systems: Innovations and Case Studies. *Research in Transportation Economics*, 8, 91–111.

Stigler, J.G. (1956). The Statistics of Monopoly and Mergers. *Journal of Political Economy*, 68(6), 33–40.

Stigler, J.G. (1971). The Theory of Economic Regulation. *Bell Journal of Economics and Management Science*, 2(1), 3–21.

Stigler, J.G. (1974). Free Riders and Collective Action: An Appendix to Theories of Economic Regulation. *Bell Journal of Economics*, 5(2), 359–365.

Sutinen, J.G. and Kuperan, K. (1999). A Socio-Economic Theory of Regulatory Compliance. *International Journal of Social Economics*, 26(1/2/3), 174–193.

Tallberg, J. (2002). Paths to Compliance Enforcement, Management, and the European Union. *International Organisation*, 56(3), 609–643.

Te Brömmelstroet, M. (2013). Performance of Planning Support Systems. *Computers, Environment and Urban Systems*, 41, 299–308.

Teddlie, C. and Yu, F. (2007). Mixed Methods Sampling: A Typology with Examples. *Journal of Mixed Methods Research*, 1(1), 77–100.

Tewdwr-Jones, M., Gallent, N. and Morphet, J. (2010). An Anatomy of Spatial Planning: Coming to terms with the Spatial Element of UK Planning. *European Planning Studies*, 18(2), 239–257.

Thompson, S. (2007). What Is Planning?' In: Thompson, S. (Ed.) *Planning Australia: An Overview of Urban and Regional Planning* New York: Cambridge University Press.

Tiesdell, S. and Allmendinger, P. (2005). Planning Tools and Markets: Towards an Extended Conceptualisation. In: Adams, D., Watkins, C. and White, M. (Eds.) *Planning, Public Policy and Property Markets.* Oxford: Black Well Publishing Ltd.

Torgerson, D. (1986). Between Knowledge and Politics: Three Faces of Policies Analysis. *Policy Sciences*, 19(1), 33–59.

Totten, V.Y., Panacek, E.A. and Price, D. (1999). Basics of Research (Part 14) Survey Research Methodology: Designing the Survey Instrument. *Air Medical Journal*, 18, 1, 26–34.

Tudzi, E.P. (1996). *Environmental Effects of Neighbourhood Economic Activities on Low Class Residential Areas: A Case of Anloga in Kumasi.* Unpublished BSc. Thesis, University of Science and Technology, Kumasi-Ghana.

Tullock, G. (1967). The Welfare Costs of Tariffs, Monopolies, and Theft. *Western Economics Journal*, 5, 224–232.

Turocy, P.S. (2002). Survey Research in Athletic Training: The Scientific Method and Development and Implementation. *Athletic Training Educational Journal*, 37(suppl. 4), 174–179.

UN. (2017). *Drivers of Migration and Urbanization in Africa: Key Trends and Issues.* New York: UN, Population Division.

UN. (2019). About the Sustainable Development Goals. [Online], Available at: https://www.un.org/sustainabledevelopment/sustainable-development-goals/ [Accessed August 10, 2019].

UN-DESA. (2018). World Urbanization Prospects 2018. New York: UN-DESA.

UNCHS. (1996). *An Urbanising World: Global Report on Human Settlements.* Oxford: Oxford University Press.

UN-Habitat. (1999). *Reassessment of Urban Planning and Development Regulations in African Cities.* Nairobi: UN-Habitat.

UN-Habitat. (2005). *Local Economic Development Series on Promoting Local Economic Development through Strategic Planning.* Volume 1-5. Nairobi: UN-Habitat.

UN-Habitat. (2008). *State of the World's Cities 2008/2009. Harmonious Cities.* London: Earthscan.

UN-Habitat. (2009). *Planning Sustainable Cities: Policy Directions, Global Report on Human Settlements.* London: Earthscan.

UN-Habitat. (2013). Equity in Urban Development Law. [Online], Available at: http://mirror.unhabitat.org/downloads/docs/12661_1_595444.pdf [Accessed January 4, 2016].

UN-Habitat. (2014). *The State of African Cities 2014: Re-Imagining Sustainable Urban Transitions*. London: Earthscan.

UN-Habitat. (2020). *Urban Impact*. Nairobi: UN-Habitat.

United States General Accounting Office (GOA). (2004). Report to the Subcommittee on African Affairs, Committee on Foreign Relations, US Senate, Foreign Assistance, USA Anticorruption Programmes in Sub-Saharan Africa will Require Time and Commitment. [Online], Available at: http://www.gao.gov/cgi-bin/getrpt?GAO-04-506 [Accessed January 10, 2011].

Viegas, C.V., Saldanha, D.L, Bond, A., Ribeiro, J.L.D. and Selig, P.M. (2013). Urban Land Planning: The Role of a Master Plan in Influencing Local Temperatures. *Cities*, 35, 1–13.

Vreaker, R. and Nijkamp, P. (2006). Methods for Evaluating Development Scenarios: Application to Thailand. In: Alexander, E.R. (Ed.) *Evaluation in Planning: Evolution and Prospects, Contributions in Honour of Nathaniel Lichfield*. London: Ashgate Publishing Ltd.

Walras, L. (1877). *Elements of Pure Economics*. London: Allen & Unwin.

Wang, P.C.M. (1997). Economic Impact Assessment of Recreation Services and the Use of Multipliers: A Comparative Examination. *Journal of Park and Recreation Administration*, 15(2), 32–43.

Watanabe, S. (1980). Planning History in Japan. *Urban History*, 7, 63–75.

Watson, V. (2002). The Usefulness of Normative Planning Theories in the Context of Sub – Saharan Africa. *Planning Theory*, 1(1), 27-52.

Watson, V. (2009a). The Planned City Sweeps the Poor Away...: Urban Planning and 21st Century Urbanisation. *Progress in Planning*, 72, 151–193.

Watson, V. (2009b). Seeing from the South: Refocusing Urban Planning on the Globe's Central Urban Issues. *Urban Studies*, 46(11), 2259–2275.

Watson, V. (2014). African Urban Fantasies: Dreams or Nightmares? *Environment and Urhanszation*, 26(1): 215–231.

Watson, V. (2016). Urban Planning and the Future of African Cities. *GIM International*. [Online], Available at: https://www.gim-international.com/content/article/urban-planning-and-the-future-of-african-cities [Accessed July 11, 2020].

Webster, C.J. (1998). Public Choice, Pigouvian and Coasian Planning Theory. *Urban Studies*, 35(1), 53–75.

Webster, C.J. and Lai, L.W.C. (2003). *Property Rights, Planning and Markets: Managing Spontaneous Cities*. Cheltenham: Edward Elgar.

Wekwete, K.H. (1995). Planning Law in Sub-Saharan Africa – A Focus on the Experience in Southern and Eastern Africa. *Habitat International*, 19(1), 13–28.

Wenders, J.T. (1987). On Perfect Rent Dissipation. *The American Economic Review*, 77(3), 456–459.

Wijen, W., Wesemann, P. and de Blaeij, A. (2009). Valuation of Road Safety Effects in Cost-Benefit Analysis. *Evaluation and Program Planning*, 32, 326–331.

Winter, S.C. and May, P.J. (2001). Motivation for Compliance of Environmental Regulations. *Journal of Policy Analysis and Management*, 20(4), 675–698.

Wilks, I. (1959). *Akwamu (1650–1750) Rise and Fall of a West African Empire*. Legon: Institute of African Studies, University of Ghana.

Williamson, O.E. (1994). Transaction Cost Economics and Organisational Theory. In: Smelser, N.J. and Swedberg, R. (Eds.) *The Handbook of Economic Sociology*. New York: Russell Sage Foundation.

Winter, G. (2000). A Comparative Discussion of the Notion of Validity in Qualitative and Quantitative Research. *The Qualitative Report*, 4(3&4). [Online], Available at: www.nova.edu/ssss/QR/QR4-3/winter.html [Accessed March 10, 2012].

Wolcott, H.F. (1992). Posturing in Qualitative Inquiry. In: Le Compte, L.D., Millroy, W.L. and Preissle, J. (Eds.) *The Handbook of Qualitative Research in Education*. New York: Academic Press.

World Bank. (2009). *World Development Report: Reshaping Economic Geography*. Washington, DC: The World Bank.

World Bank, (2011). *Africa's Development Indicators 2011*. Washington, DC: The World Bank.

World Bank. (2012). Ghana at a Glance. [Online], Available at: http://devdata.worldbank.org/AAG/gha_aag.pdf [Accessed May 10, 2012].

World Bank. (2015). *Rising through Cities in Ghana. Ghana Urbanisation Review Overview Report*. Washington, DC: The World Bank Group.

World Bank. (2016). *World Development Indicators*. Washington, DC: The World Bank Group.

World Bank. (2020). The Economic Impacts of COVID-19 and World Bank Support to Africa Roundtable. [Online], Available at: https://www.worldbank.org/en/events/2020/06/13/the-economic-impacts-of-covid-19-and-world-bank-support-to-africa-roundtable [Accessed September 4, 2020].

World Commission on Environment and Development. (1987). *Our Common Future*. Oxford: Oxford University Press.

World Health Organisation (WHO). (2020). New WHO Estimates: Up to 190,000 People Could Die of COVID-19 in Africa If Not Controlled. [Online], Available at: https://www.afro.who.int/news/new-who-estimates-190-000-people-could-die-covid-19-africa-if-not-controlled [Accessed July 15, 2020].

Yngstrom, I. (2002). Women, Wives and Land Rights in Africa: Situating Gender Beyond the Household in the Debate over Land Policy and Changing Tenure Systems. *Oxford Development Studies*, 30(1), 21–40.

Yoon, S. (2004). Welfare Losses due to Monopoly: Korea's Case. *Journal of Policy Modelling*, 26, 945–957.

Zhang, L., Yao, K. and Crossley, G. (2020). Hobbled by Coronavirus, China's First-quarter GDP shrinks for first time on record, Reuters. [Online], Available at: https://www.reuters.com/article/us-china-economy-gdp/hobbled-by-coronavirus-chinas-first-quarter-gdp-shrinks-for-first-time-on-record-idUSKBN21Z08Q. [Accessed June 1, 2020].

Zhu, N., Zhang, D., Wang, W., Li, X., Yang, B., Song, J.,et al. (2020). A Novel Coronavirus from Patients with Pneumonia in China, 2019. *The New England Journal of Medicine*, 382(8), 727–733.

Index

Note: **Bold** page numbers refer to tables; *italic* page numbers refer to figures and page numbers followed by "n" denote endnotes.

For Product Safety Concerns and Information please contact our EU representative GPSR@taylorandfrancis.com
Taylor & Francis Verlag GmbH, Kaufingerstraße 24, 80331 München, Germany

www.ingramcontent.com/pod-product-compliance
Lightning Source LLC
LaVergne TN
LVHW011132300926
849160LV00008B/622
* 9 7 8 0 3 6 7 5 6 5 8 8 6 *